Digital Politics and Cultural Contemporary India

The relationship between information and the nation-state is typically portrayed as a face-off involving repressive state power and democratic flows: Twitter and the Arab Spring, Google in China, WikiLeaks and the U.S. State Department. Less attention has been paid to those scenarios where states have regarded information and its diffusion as productive for modernity and globalization. It is the central argument of this book that the contemporary nation-state, especially in the global South, is far from hostile to the current informational milieu and in fact makes crucial use of it in order to develop adequate modes of governance, communication, and sociality in a networked world. This book focuses on India—an emerging country that has recently witnessed a "software miracle"—to highlight the critical role informatics has historically played in the national imagination and to demonstrate how the state, private capital, and civic society have drawn upon and engaged the precepts and protocols of the information age to fashion an "info-nation."

Biswarup Sen is Assistant Professor in the School of Journalism and Communication at the University of Oregon, Eugene, Oregon, United States.

Routledge Advances in Internationalizing Media Studies

Edited by Daya Thussu, University of Westminster

Digital Politics and Culture in Contemporary India
The Making of an Info-Nation

Biswarup Sen

Routledge
Taylor & Francis Group

LONDON AND NEW YORK

First published 2016
by Routledge

2 Park Square, Milton Park, Abingdon, Oxfordshire OX14 4RN
711 Third Avenue, New York, NY 10017

Routledge is an imprint of the Taylor & Francis Group, an informa business

First issued in paperback 2017

Library of Congress Cataloging-in-Publication Data

Names: Sen, Biswarup, author.
Title: Digital politics and culture in contemporary India: the making of an
info-nation / by Biswarup Sen.
Description: New York, NY: Routledge, 2016. | Series: Routledge advances in
internationalizing media studies; 16 | Includes bibliographical references.
Identifiers: LCCN 2015035521 |
Subjects: LCSH: Information society—India. | Information technology—
Political aspects—India. | Information technology—Social aspects—India. |
Technology and state—India.
Classification: LCC HN690.Z9 I5665 2016 | DDC 303.48/330954—dc23
LC record available at http://lccn.loc.gov/2015035521

ISBN: 978-1-138-95492-2 (hbk)
ISBN: 978-1-138-57576-9 (pbk)

Typeset in Sabon
by codeMantra

For my mother

Contents

Acknowledgments

This book reflects many years of thinking about the new media within the context of postcolonial societies. My greatest intellectual debt is to my former teacher and thesis advisor, James Carey. Jim's seminal formulations about a cultural approach to communications have inspired and influenced my thinking from my graduate student years to the present day. Sadly, Jim is not around any longer, and I can only hope that these pages can serve to honor his memory. I am also heavily indebted to Manuel Castells's magisterial corpus of work on informationalism and network societies. This book takes as a premise Castells's provocative suggestion that information and communication have emerged as the most fundamental dimension of human activity. My own attempt here has been to trace the development of an "info-nation" within the context of a postcolonial society, and much of my analysis has been strongly influenced by David Scott's brilliant and productive notion of postcolonial governmentality. The book also incorporates the insights of three prominent South Asian scholars. From Ashis Nandy I take the view that cultures adopt abstractions in their own peculiar way; Dipesh Chakrabarty's finely nuanced essays on the nature of Indian modernity have served as a model for my own inquiries into the digital present; from Partha Chatterjee's work I draw the lesson that an analysis of social structures must be a necessary part of every effort to understand cultural formations.

The book had its genesis at a conference on Indian television that I organized at the Indian Institute of Advanced Study, Shimla, in the summer of 2009. Though the papers that were presented there dealt ostensibly with a "legacy medium," the discussions as a whole pointed to television's rapid convergence with the new media. I want to thank all the participants, especially Shanti Kumar, Purnima Mankekar, Abhijit Roy, and Daya Thussu for stressing how information had emerged as a crucial thematic for media studies. Though Arvind Rajagopal could not attend the conference, he graciously wrote an Afterword for the volume that was published in its wake. Rajagopal's incisive work on media, modernity, and the public sphere has greatly influenced my arguments in this monograph. I must also acknowledge the pioneering work done in the field of South Asian new media studies by Radhika Gajjala, Ashish Rajadhyaksha, and Ravi Sundaram, as well as the seminal research of scholars such Payal Arora, Bidisha Chaudhuri, Anandam Kavoori, Jyoti Saraswati, Pratap Sharma, and Pradip Thomas, among others.

I have, over the years, profited from long and fruitful intellectual engagements with several individuals. Jack Bratich was once my student, but happily he now instructs me in the latest developments in "theory" and in media studies. I am delighted to have Colin Koopman as a colleague at the University of Oregon. Colin is a keen philosopher of new media and has been extremely generous in sharing ideas and resources with me and other like-minded colleagues. Sujata Moorti's sharp insights on the state of Indian media in the age of globalization have always energized my own take on these matters. I am lucky to have her as both a dear friend and a stimulating colleague. Tom Streeter and I went to graduate school together and have stayed close all this time. Tom's marvelous work on the cultural meanings of computer technology in recent American history was a great model and inspiration for my own efforts.

I am also grateful for the rich work done a by group of outstanding scholars that includes Radha Hegde, Robin Jeffrey, Jyotsna Kapur, Rashmi Luthra, William Mazzarela, Nalin Mehta, Peter Manuels, Manju Pendakur, and Aswin Punathambekar. I hope that my work will contribute in some measure to furthering their collective effort to make South Asian media studies an exciting field in which to work. I have also profited immensely from my exchanges with a number of scholars in my discipline: Jon Crane, Michael Curtin, Charles Michael Elavsky, Chiara Ferrari, Harsha Gangadharbatla, Ivy Glennon, Lawrence Grossberg, Dana Heller, Joli Jensen, Chuck Kleinhans, Julia Lesage, John Nerone, Tasha Oren, Jeff Pooley, Lana Rakow, Sharon Sharaf, Angharad Valdivia and Chuck Whitney to name only a few. Closer to home, Janet Wasko's energizing mentorship and intellectual vigor have enriched me at every step while Gabriela Martinez's gift of sage collegiality has always proved beneficial in negotiating the academic environment.

I need to note several institutions that played a role in the making of this book. Thanks are first due to the Centre for Internet & Society, Bengaluru, for hosting me for a week in January 2012 and allowing me access to the library and seminar proceedings and other facilities. I applaud the Centre for the pathbreaking work its fellows have been conducting in the area of South Asian new media studies. In particular, I must thank Nishant Shah and Sunil Abraham for being so generous with their time and providing me with a thorough grasp of the issues surrounding digital technology in the Indian context and to Lawrence Liang for giving me a comprehensive tutorial on the legal ramifications of digital technology in India.

Portions of the book were presented to audiences at the Indian Institute of Advanced Study, Shimla; the Department of Film Studies, Jadavpur University; The American Center, Kolkata; the Flow conference at the University of Texas, Austin; and The International Communication Association Conference, Seattle. I am grateful to my hosts for affording me the opportunity to present my research and to my fellow panelists as well as audience members for the stimulating inputs I received in response to these talks.

This book would not have been possible without generous assistance from a variety of sources at the University of Oregon. I would like to thank the Dean's Office of the School of Journalism and Communication for awarding me two research grants that helped me travel to India and gather research materials for the book. I would like to express my gratitude to former Dean Tim Gleason and current Interim Dean Julie Newton for the unstinting support they gave to this project. I am also very grateful to Leslie Steeves, Senior Associate Dean for Academic Affairs, for providing me with valuable research assistance during the time I was writing this manuscript. My heartfelt thanks to my three graduate student assistants—Farah Azhar, Patrick Jones, and Laura Strait—for the meticulous work they did on my behalf.

Thanks are also due to Doug Blandy, Senior Vice Provost for Academic Affairs; Jeff Hanes, Director Center for Asian and Pacific Studies; Dennis Galvan, Vice Provost International Affairs; Paul Peppis, Director UO Humanities Center; and Wayne Morse Center for Law and Politics for their generous support in funding the "New Media and Democracy: Global Perspectives" conference that I organized on the University of Oregon campus in April 2015. The papers presented in that conference offered stimulating perspectives on issues of new media, culture, and politics, and I must express my sincere gratitude to all the conference panelists for providing me with wide-ranging insights on many of the themes that are present in this book.

I have been favored with an incredible group of colleagues in the School of Journalism and Communication, University of Oregon. In particular, I must mention Tom Bivins, Carl Bybee, Chris Chavez, Pat Curtin, Ed Madison, Tiffany Gallicano, Deb Merskin, John Mitchell, Deb Morrison, John Russial, Kim Sheehan, and Gretchen Soderlund for all the support and critical inputs they have provided over the years. My involvement in the New Media and Culture Certificate Program at the University of Oregon has given me the opportunity to share research and exchange ideas with an extraordinary group of people: Andrew Bonamici, Karen Estlund, Alisa Freedman, Kate Mondloch, John Russell, and Sean Sharp. Special thanks to Carol Stabile who continues to inspire and lead in the area of digital scholarship. I consider myself fortunate to be involved in this campus-wide effort to make new media studies more central to the curriculum.

My colleagues and students at the University of Oregon have created a community that makes scholarship and the exchange of ideas a real pleasure. Several of my students have shared my interests in new media theory and I know that my debt to them far exceeds what this acknowledgment can convey. In particular, I thank Ben Birkenbine, Chelsea Bullock, Sonia de la Cruz, Kelsey Cummings, Sarah Hamid, Michael Hess, Patrick Jones, Younsong Lee, Randall Livingstone, Joy Mapaye, Shehram Mokhtar, Senyo Ofori-Parku, Bryce Peake, Fatoumata Sow, Laura Strait, Teddy Workneh.

Among my colleagues, Michael Allan, Michael Aronson, Michael Hames Garcia, Daniel Hosang, Loren Kajikawa, Lamia Karim, Dong Hoon Kim, Nadia Loan, Joe Lowndes, Quinn Miller, Priscilla Ovalle, and Arafaat Valiani have provided sparkling intellectual camaraderie over the years.

Many friends have sustained my intellectual life over the years. From our New Delhi days, I count Huma Ahmad, Mahazarin Banaji, Amiya Kumar, Mohan Mahapatra, Ramdas Menon, Vivek Moorthy, S. Nagarjuna, Rajni Palriwala, Deepak Sanan, Mrinalini Sinha, Peter de Souza, E. Sridharan, J. Sriram, and Chandrasekhar Tibrewal. Their friendship has enriched me over the decades. Itty Abraham, Shera Ahmad, Kanti Bajpai, John Consigli, Lennie Feldman, Toral Gajarawala, Manisha Mirchandani, Imke Meyer, Rudrangshu Mukherji, Jenifer Presto, Heidi Schlipphacke, Aditi Nath Sarkar, and Michael Stern have shared their wisdom with me, some of which I hope has found its way into these pages.

My family has been a lifelong source of warm support for me. I thank the Sens of Rawdon Street and of Ballygunge for all they have given me. My wife Sangita Gopal is simultaneously a stern critic and tender champion of my work; her rigorous intellectual companionship throughout the process of writing this book is responsible for whatever virtues it has. Our daughter Mohini has brought astonishing joy to our lives for the past six years, and I hope that one day she will get some pleasure reading her baba's words. The book is dedicated to my mother, Jayanti Sen. A poet and a reputed journalist in her younger days, my mother instilled a love of ideas in me from my earliest years and has steadfastly followed and supported my career over the years. Thank you for everything, Ma.

Introduction

On July 1, 2015, Narendra Modi, the current prime minister of India, launched a "Digital India Week" designed to highlight the progress the country has made in the use of information technology for purposes of government. The initiative was widely publicized; according to one official, "reports have been received from 438 districts wherein in 1,238 events, more than 136,000 lakh government officials and citizens have been informed on Digital India Programme and its services" (NDTV Gadgets, 2015a). The issues highlighted by this project covered almost every imaginable aspect of governmental activity: health information, utilities, public distribution systems, land records, mobile apps for civic amenities, and services for farmers, social welfare, pension schemes, electoral procedures, online courts, policing, and employment exchanges. Designated as a "party, politics, and ideology-neutral" initiative, Digital India Week turned out to be a very successful fund-raising campaign as well. Responding to the government's call for financial backing, the country's top industrial houses pledged to invest more than $90 billion in such crucial areas as mobile telephony, fast Internet access, and broadband networks that would potentially create 1.8 million jobs in the coming years (NDTV Gadgets, 2015b).

These seven days encapsulated a much larger project—Digital India—that, according to the Department of Electronics and Information Technology's mission statement, seeks to "transform India into a digitally empowered society and knowledge economy" (DeitY, 2015). Such a goal has three core components: the creation of a *Digital Infrastructure*, including such functionalities as "cradle-to-grave digital identity" and access to a "safe and secure cyberspace;" *Governance & Services on Demand* including real-time services on online and mobile platforms and seamless digital integration throughout departments or jurisdictions; and *Digital Empowerment of Citizens* by universal digital literacy and universally accessible digital resources (ibid.). Several projects launched by the Indian government in the past year testify to its resolve in making Digital India a reality: the Digital Locker, which eliminates the need for hard-copy versions of official documents; Twitter Samvad (News), which will allow citizens to hear about government initiatives and actions; Madad (Help), an online grievance site for Indian citizens living abroad; an SMS-based disaster alert system; e-money to facilitate electronic money-order transfers; and Pragati (Progress), an interactive platform that will monitor and review governmental programs and projects and also function as a platform for recording and redressing citizen complaints.

An initiative like Digital India, this book argues, is not simply a set of instrumental measures that makes day-to-day governance more effective and in line with the contemporary "best practices." It stands for an ambitious act of imagination that rethinks the nation through one central notion: information. The digital revolution, according to this emerging perspective, is capable of changing all dimensions of society by means of a technology based on the production, dissemination, and manipulation of information. This viewpoint, that can be condensed under the rubric of "informationalism," holds great allure for a postcolonial formation like India where questions of national identity and destiny are always at the forefront of public debate. It is therefore not surprising that the premise and promise of informationalism have been widely embraced by all segments of Indian society. We have already alluded to the state's vanguard role in imagining a digitized nation. To add two more examples that confirm this claim: the Indian government has very recently changed the name of the visa it issues to foreign travelers to "e-tourist visa" as if to imply that the physical act of travel could be translated into an immaterial process of data transfer. The creators think of the e-visa initiative as a "smart programme" (Quartz india, 2015). The desire to make things smarter by means of information technology extends to other more substantial domains as well. Thus, the government of India has allocated over $1.5 billion for the creation of 100 "smart cities"—cities that use information technology to solve urban problems—in 21 states over the next five-year period (smartcitiesindia.com, 2015). Prime Minister Narendra Modi enunciated the vision that animated this initiative in almost poetic fashion, when he declared, "Cities in the past were built on riverbanks … they are now built along highways. But in the future, they will be built based on availability of optical fiber networks and next-generation infrastructure" (Tolan, 2014).

The drive to put the nation on an informational path was not restricted to the state. Beginning in the 1980s, the "software miracle" achieved by India's IT industry changed the complexion of Indian capitalism. For the first time since Independence, India acquired a significant presence in the world market, providing a prestige good that was highly valued by international customers. The phenomenal export revenues generated by software services would lead to a change in the way Indians began to think about business. Whereas the typical commercial establishment had been a family-owned firm run by members of traditional *bania* (merchant) communities, the new information-based concerns represented an entirely new model of conducting business. The new businessman was a technocrat who was western in training and outlook, the new business houses were run as modern corporations, and the new business ethos was one that included notions of social responsibility and transparency along with the fundamental motive of profit-making. This sea change gave rise to a new type of "captain of industry," men like Narayana Murthy, Nandan Nilekani, and Azim Premji who are venerated as much for being "thought leaders" as for generating impressive sums of revenue. In short, this information-based "new business" is as instrumental as the state in changing the cultural landscape of contemporary India.

The impulse toward information that characterizes the state and capital has percolated to the level of the citizenry. Not only are social movements and activist projects increasingly centered on issues of information; even the "common man" (or woman) thinks and speaks in an informational idiom. The role that platforms like Facebook and Twitter play in building alternative versions of both the public and interpersonal spheres is well known. The popularity of social media—India currently has the world's second highest number of Facebook users after the United States—signifies an informatization of private and public selves on a large-scale basis (statista, 2015). Perhaps more pertinently, the average citizen thinks of informational technology not merely as an enabler of social connectivity but also as a tool and resource for the purposes of national growth and development. The web interface for the Digital India project put out a call asking the citizenry to identify the 10 most important initiatives that central and state governments should take to realize the prime minister's vision of Digital India. This ostensibly staid assignment drew nearly 800 detailed responses that suggested highly specific information-based actions that would benefit the nation. One Praveen Singh suggested that post offices and *panchayat ghars* (village headquarters) should be digitally linked to facilitate interaction with the public; Ajay Gupta recommended that broadband be used to deliver educational materials to schools in backward areas, while Swati Choubey simply demanded that "all persons be made computer literate" (mygov, 2015).

The processes I have just described point to a new way of thinking about the nation within the frame of contemporary postcoloniality. It is the goal of this book to outline the critical role the emergent informational milieu has played in the national imagination and demonstrate how the state, private capital, and public culture have all drawn upon the precepts and protocols of the information age in order to fashion an "info-nation." In what follows, I assess the "software miracle" of the 1990s in the context of a longer history of informatization. I then suggest that this miracle is but one aspect of the coming into being of an info-nation. By looking at how nationalism articulates with informatization, I develop the concept of the info-nation, briefly alluding to other global contexts. I conclude with concise descriptions of the scope of the book and its individual chapters.

The Software Miracle

In the closing decades of the last century, India witnessed, as a reputed journal put it, a "surprising economic miracle" (*The Economist*, 2010). Though the economy as a whole began to prosper in this period, it was the meteoric rise of the software sector that got most of the attention. The story of software in India is indeed a spectacular one. Established in the 1960s, the industry grew modestly for the next few years such that at the end of the 1980s its revenues stood at a paltry figure of $50 million (Bhatnagar, 2006, 95). From that point onwards, however, it "took off," growing at an astonishing rate of over 30% annually for the subsequent years. During the 2012–13 financial year, the software industry earned over $100 billion, with exports accounting for $75.8 billion; domestic revenue added up to $16.5 and the industry created 188,000 new jobs to bring its direct employment numbers up to 3 million. Further, the industry acquired global reach, delivering goods and services at 580 centers spread across 75 countries (NASSCOMM, 2015). Finally, in terms of market value, the three leading Indian software companies—Tata Consulting Services, Wipro, Infosys—all featured in the *Forbes* list of the top computer services companies in the world for 2013, beating out such familiar names as Facebook, Baidu, Linkedin, and AOL (*Forbes*, 2015).

While the success of India's software industry is an established fact, the meaning and significance of this "miracle" are open to interpretation and debate. The unexpected success of the software sector occurred against a background of India's abysmal economic performance in the first few decades after Independence. Thus in the period 1951–81, India grew at the notorious "Hindu rate of growth" amounting to between 3% and 4% annually[1] (Panagariya, 2008, 9). And while in 1947 India's share of world trade was 2.4%, by 1990 it had declined to merely 0.4% (Das, 2000, 63). Yet, even in this dismal environment, software exports had already touched $100 million. How could one industry succeed while others performed so poorly? Some analysts offered purely economic explanations of the software boom—comparative advantage due to low compensation paid to Indian computer workers (Heeks, 1996) or the availability of a deep pool of human capital (Saxenian, 2000). Another influential group of scholars argued that the real reason had to do with economic philosophy and policy. The software industry could "take off" because it was not shackled by the socialistic mindset that had regulated most other industries in the years until 1990. As Pramod Mahajan, the minister for information technology in the early 2000s humorously observed, India is a leader in "IT and beauty contests, the two areas the government has stayed out of"[2] (Kapur, 2002, 94). The renowned free-market economist Arvind Panagariya notes in a similar vein, "One of the best things that happened in India during the 1990s was the growth of the IT sector … it was largely free from other regulations, including the draconian labor laws … Therefore when the world markets offered growth opportunities, the IT sector was able to take advantage of them" (Panagariya, 2008, 38). As a result of this "negligence," a noted industry analyst observes, "India succeeded in software because of its entrepreneurs and because India had opened up and connected to the world economy" and prescribes that we should let "market forces decide who survives and who flourishes" (Arora, 2010).

The above line of reasoning is a product of what may be termed the "pro-liberalization school" in current Indian economic thought that argues that liberalization unleashed a potential that had been bottled up by three decades of Nehruvian "license raj." The software sector is merely the best example—a kind of jewel in the liberalized crown—of what the private sector is capable of when not impeded by governmental policies and regulations. Thus, "Prior to 1984, rigid policy restrictions ensured that there was virtually no software industry. In the second phase (1984 to 1990), the restrictions were eased and Indian firms entered the global market by providing low-cost programming services. In the third phase (1990 to 2000), pro-active promotion of the industry, along with economy-wide policy liberalization, led to rapid growth in exports" (Parthsarathy, 2004, 1).

Many have taken a less celebratory view of the software revolution. For some, the software boom is not all that it is heralded to be. First of all, argue such critics, the industry has an export bias and more pertinently is doomed to remain as a provider of low-level services. As one early observer of the industry pointed out, most software companies in India act as sub-contractors, executing assignments either on site or at offshore development centers in the country. Thus, "Low value/low skill activities have created a structure of the Indian software industry that is quite similar to the other sectors of the Indian industries characterized by its long tails. ... technological competitiveness not being the dynamics of such an industry, it is quite distant to think that the industry would ever be able to find its own high skill/high value niche, unless there is any strategic intervention in this regard" (Nath and Hazra, 2002, 742). This misgiving still persists today. Thus, in a recent interview with *Forbes*, Vishal Sikha, the newly appointed CEO of Infosys observes, "As an IT services firm, we are not supposed to innovate; we just do what others tell us to do. That thinking makes me angry and disturbed, and I am determined to change that" (Rai, 2015).

The second reservation concerning the software sector has to do with its "enclave nature." Thus, the reputed economist C. P. Chandrasekhar points out that experience from the developed industrial countries suggests that the growth of the ICT sector in terms of output and employment need not necessarily be accompanied by any equivalent diffusion of information technology into other sectors, especially manufacturing. As a result, "despite its rapid growth the information technology sector in India is small and marginal and the fall-out of its growth on the rest of the economy is limited" (2003, 82). Chandrasekhar's judgment may be borne out by current statistics: in the financial year 2012–13, for example, the IT industry had a share of only 8% of India's gross domestic product.

While the authors cited above represent the tendency to view the software revolution as far less consequential than it appears to its cheerleaders, another group of critical scholars acknowledges its significance but argues that its impact has been deleterious from the perspective of equity and social justice. Such a critique alleges that the entire computer/software industry and, by extension, the informational environment that is associated with it, are inextricably linked with the neoliberal market dynamics that have come to characterize Indian political economy consequent to the liberalization of 1991. Specifically, this means that the information sector was allowed both to privatize at a rate higher than that of most technical industries and also be supported with import and export breaks that enabled it to be successfully integrated with the global economy. Jyoti Saraswati's (2012) book-length study of power and policy in the Indian software industry is an excellent representative of such an approach. Saraswati's book provides a chronology of India's political economy with respect to the software sector and his main intent is to demonstrate how, at every stage that he describes, governmental policies were designed to serve the interests of domestic private capital as well as those of multinational corporations. As the book describes, the project seeks to "show how vested interests and elitist corruption have shaped one of the world's most dynamic sectors" and how current software policies "are an impediment ... to a broader-based, more egalitarian form of development in India" (Saraswati, 2012, book blurb). An earlier publication that also looked at the political economy of "information capitalism" in India argued very much along Saraswati's line, contending that despite the dynamism of India's software industry and the rhetorical flourishes of industry leaders, the benefits of the revolution in information and communication technologies had touched only the hundreds of thousands with the right skills and access (Parayil, 2006).

The Idea of an Info-Nation

The software revolution has typically been looked at as an economic phenomenon whose value can be calculated by means of an objective cost-benefit analysis. As we saw above, the answer to the question depends on the theoretical and political perspective from which the issue is examined: for those committed to the free market, the software sector is an inspiring model that the rest of the economy should emulate. For more critically minded scholars, software is a signifier of neoliberalism, reflecting the inexorable march toward privatization and global capitalism. I would, however, like to suggest that this "miracle" is not an autonomous economic event that can be studied in isolation but is instead part of a much larger and diffused cultural process that characterizes recent postcolonial history as a whole. It is the central argument of this book that the rise of digital technology and the new media signals the emergence of an informational milieu that has crucially influenced the main currents of politics and culture in the postcolonial era. In the book I examine four contexts that illustrate this ongoing process of informatization. A genealogy of the Indian computer industry reveals its roots in the informational philosophies of the colonial state and the nationalist movement. Moreover, the subsequent growth of the computer industry demonstrates how information mediated the relationship between the postcolonial state and capital and provided a blueprint for the liberalization of the economy that followed. It also redefines the state's conception of its own role, pushing it to relinquish its paternalistic stance toward communication and the flow of information and moving it toward a model of participatory e-governance. At the same time, civil society in India has witnessed the emergence of a new type of information-based activism exemplified by the implementation of the Right to Information Act, and the rise of an informational politics exemplified by the Anna Hazare movement and the Aam Aadmi Party. Finally, the growing popularity of reality television programming shows how an information-based aesthetics is decisively altering the forms and pleasures of popular commercial entertainment. The book as a whole looks at the various ways an informational mindset has undergirded the main currents of India's recent history and thus contributes to the idea of what I term an "info-nation."

It would be beneficial, at this juncture, to identify the background theories and assumptions that lie behind the arguments of this book. First, let me clarify what I mean by information. The term has a range of definitions, from the mathematically precise to the grandly cosmological.[3] My use of the term is much looser and relatively pedestrian. "Information" functions in the book as an umbrella concept that refers not so much to the set of technical phenomena—machines, devices, data, functionalities, objects, and platforms—normally associated with the digital age but rather to the entire universe of social, economic, and cultural phenomena emerging from or concerned with informational constructs and issues. The choice of such a capacious definition is a deliberate one, since it is my intent to trace out the larger implications of what may seem to be a purely technological development.

With this expanded scope, my use of "information" shades off into the associated notion of "informationalism." I conceive of the latter term in the sense proposed by Manuel Castells in his account of what he calls the network society.[4] "Informationalism," according to Castells, "is the technological paradigm that constitutes the material basis of early 21st century societies." Industrialism, based on the manipulation of energy, provided the ground for societies for the previous two centuries, but it has been replaced in the current era by informationalism, which

> ... is a technological paradigm based on the augmentation of the human capacity of information processing and communication made possible by the revolutions in microelectronics, software, and genetic engineering. Computers and digital communications are the most direct expressions of this revolution. Indeed, microelectronics, software, computation, telecommunications, and digital communications at large, are all components of one same and integrated system. Thus, in strict terms, the paradigm should be called "electronic informational-communicationalism."
>
> (Castells, 2009, 9)

Castells goes on to suggest that this new technological paradigm rose, some-time in the 1970s, in conjunction with a new social structure, which he terms network society.[5] In short, the various technical developments that led to the information revolution have come to constitute an entirely new mode of the social whole.

I am largely in agreement with Castells's account. It is undoubtedly true that the latter half of the twentieth century is one in which information comes to play an increasingly determinative role in all aspects of society. It needs to be stressed that Castells is not a technological determinist; he is not projecting information technology as a sort of "prime independent variable" that determines the course of all other things. Rather, the technical achievements of the digital revolution comprise one element in a matrix of factors that collectively constitutes the field that we can call "informationalism." It is this non-deterministic version of the notion of informationalism that I am employing throughout this book. That said, I want to suggest that Castells's account of informationalism is a little too restrictive and needs to be expanded. As James Beniger has pointed out in a masterful study, the origins of the information revolution go at least as far back as the late nineteenth century when "a complex of rapid changes in the technological and economic arrangements in the way information is collected, stored, processed and communicated" developed as means of effecting "societal control" (1989, 12). The use of machines designed by the Hollerith Tabulating Company (later known as IBM) in the 1890 U.S. Census is a perfect example in support of Beniger's claim. My analysis in this book is based on such a temporally stretched understanding of informationalism; for example, I argue that the impulse to create the first Indian computer in 1962 can be understood only by going back to the deep recesses of the colonial period. Castells's theory can also be accused of being ethnocentric; his identification of Silicon Valley and West Coast culture as the sole fount of the information revolution is both a little too obvious and limiting in terms of explanatory value. As I show in this book, informationalism could take hold in "backward" parts of the world—India, in this case—that may have lacked the advantage of a Stanford Industrial Park precisely because its appeal arose from a host of factors that went beyond semiconductors and algorithms.[6] In short, I am arguing that informationalism has a longer historical trajectory than Castells proposes and that it is far more global in its scope than his analysis would suggest.

This book attempts to place contemporary Indian history against a backdrop of informationalism as just defined. My project is in the spirit of Thomas Streeter's (2010) rich account of the evolution of informationalism in the American context. My own concern here is to demonstrate that information is at the heart of the postcolonial project of nation building. This mode of analysis is inspired by Benedict Anderson's (2006) seminal demonstration that print-capitalism—a manner of information processing and information distribution—was responsible for the emergence of the modern European nation-state. What print-capitalism did for the western state, informationalism does for the contemporary postcolonial nation—it promotes the emergence of very specific forms of economy, polity, and culture. Information begets the info-nation. Therefore, though this book focuses on one postcolonial nation, the argument I make, can, at least in principle, be relevant to a discussion about information and nationhood in other contexts. Such a claim elicits questions of the sort: Is the Indian case a unique one, or is it an example of one type of nation-state or even the template for all info-nations in general? Moreover, what are the other info-nations and how do they compare with the Indian example?[7]

My answer to questions like the ones above is a complex one. On the one hand, India is a special case because it is one of the few developing countries to have created an advanced software industry. To use the language of commercial media, it is an established "player" on the world stage. A thorough examination of the Indian case will indeed provide us with a model that will help us understand how informationalism impacts and will impact other developing nations. Thus the book's fundamental intent is to examine in some detail the vicissitudes of informationalism in the context of postcolonial India. It follows in the path of pioneering works of scholarship by a number of authors including Radhika Gajjala (2004), Pradip Thomas (2012), Bidisha Chaudhuri (2014), and Prashant Sharma (2014). Gajjala's work looked at the building of cyberfeminist networks by South Asian women communities and is a seminal contribution to the field of South Asian new media studies. Based on a critical political economy approach to the contemporary "digital moment" in India, Pradip Thomas's *Digital India* looks at such phenomena as mobile telephony, ICT for development, public sector software, and piracy to argue that "what makes the digital fascinating is that it is both structure and anti-structure, meaning that the 'dominant' digital in India is complemented with a multitude of subversive digitalities ..." (xvi). Whereas Thomas is more concerned with the current digital moment, this volume explores the historical and cultural aspects of informationalism and thus nicely complements Thomas's work. Bidisha Chaudhuri's *E-Governance in India* provides a fine-grained analysis of the evolution of this new mode of governance to argue that it arises within the context of a broader governance reform agenda. My own discussion of e-governance is somewhat broader in that it shows how its emergence is linked to policy developments in telecommunications and broadcasting, thus extending the scope of Chaudhuri's meticulous analysis. Similarly, I extend Pradip Sharma's fine account of the passage of the Right to Information Act by providing an account of the relationship between this law and other contemporaneous developments in Indian society like the rise of the Aam Aadmi Party or the unexpected popularity of Aamir Khan's talk show *Satyamev Jayate*. Finally, Jennifer Bussell's (2012) examination of corruption and reform in the digital age provides a richly empirical account of how digital technologies are used to facilitate citizens' access to the state. My discussion of info-activism develops the framework laid out by Pendakur and Harris (2002) by exploring how protests and social movements can counteract the interests of capital and state power.

Though this book seeks to add to the growing literature on India's "digital moment," it is at the same time an essay on information and postcoloniality in general. The main themes around which the chapters in the book are structured include information and capital, information and the state, information and activism, and information and popular culture, capturing relationships that are of crucial importance to the framework of every developing society. Consider, for example, the role of the state in encouraging the growth of an informational culture. One of the key claims in the book is that the information revolution did not originate solely from commercial interests. Rather, the Indian state played a foundational role in setting up the infrastructure that would enable private industry to achieve global success with its products.[8] Moreover, the state took equally active measures to incorporate informational techniques and technologies into its governmental practice. The role of the Indian state was not unique in this regard. As one recent text has shown, starting from the 1980s, the Korean state was deeply involved in initiating privatization, restructuring telecommunications, and implementing policies that would enable the creation of the world's most digitally connected country (Oh and Larson, 2007).[9] Again, it could be argued that the Indian state's efforts to open up the informational universe is comparable to similar initiatives in countries such as Singapore and Malaysia, which have also witnessed the creation of an extremely powerful commercial elite that acts as gatekeepers for statist interests, by serving as partners to global media companies (Atkins, 2001). Finally, there are parallels for India's information revolution in some of the most disadvantaged parts of the globe demonstrating that information as a factor of change is not restricted to advanced economies. For example, a recent study of six African countries argues that mobile phones—as of 2008, one in three Africans were mobile users—are the "new talking drums" that are transforming African society and culture (Bruijn, Nyamnjoh, and Brinkman, 2009). Again, the efficacy of e-governance initiatives in Africa is as contested as in the Indian case. My discussion of ICT projects in India shows that, once implemented, they run the risk of losing sight of their goals. Similarly, as another recent collection demonstrates, though ICT measures to reduce gender inequality are currently being made and implemented all over Africa, this is happening mostly in the absence of clear knowledge about the ways gender inequality and ICTs are impacting each other and are thus achieving very meager results (Buskens and Webb, 2009).

It must, however, be recognized that the informational turn in India occurs within the frame of a democratic political system where the relationship between citizens and state is one of mutual reciprocity. In my analysis of the rise of info-activism in India, I show how a paradoxical combination of conflict and cooperation between these activists and the government resulted in the passage of progressive measures like the Right to Information Act. Info-activism acquires very different features in the context of autocratic regimes. As Guodin Yang's (2011) pioneering study of the Internet in China demonstrates, there is a constant battle between the state and its citizens over the issue of online freedom. Yang argues that the state's efforts to constrain freedom in cyberspace have led to even more creative acts of subversion. Thus he predicts that "as civic engagement in unofficial democracy expands, the distance to an officially institutionalized democracy shortens" (226). Again, the case of Iran demonstrates how info-technologies have uses that go beyond my findings in this book. In the 2009 elections, for example, new media technologies were used extensively to spread conspiracy theories and rumors in order to create a subversive counter-public that would challenge the state's account of events (Rahimi, 2009).

To recapitulate, an examination of the information revolution generates crucial insights into India's postcolonial history. Informationalism, I argue, played a major role in modulating the Indian state's relationship to an incipient private sector; its organizing principles lay at the root of the state's communications and information policies in the years before and after liberalization; it spawned an entirely new mode of political info-activism; and it is increasingly shaping the contours of Indian popular culture. To follow these processes is to track India's evolution as an info-nation. Such a project also yields an understanding of information's role in developing societies. Although its "software miracle" makes India somewhat of a special case, the analysis provided in this book has implications for any study that wishes to understand the role played by the information revolution in developing societies. In other words, the book is grounded in the particularities of India but the general premise of the info-nation that I am developing could be applicable in many other contexts. Moreover, by exploring the unique ways in which informationalism is put to work in the postcolonial context, this work complicates the presumption that the information revolution is an exclusive product of the global North.

Lineaments of the Info-Nation

The point of departure for the first chapter and the book as a whole is the inauguration of TIFRAC, the country's first electronic mainframe, by Jawaharlal Nehru, the country's first prime minister.[10] The coming to be of this computer symbolizes the dawn of India's information age; it also serves in my account as a heuristic to tease out the underlying features of the new formation. The Nehruvian halo surrounding the moment of TIFRAC's inauguration points to a cardinal truth: while India's economic transformation by IT in the post-1990s period is typically attributed to the innovative energy of the private sector, it was in fact the Indian state that laid the foundations for this information revolution. The first computer was planned, funded, and built by the government. The decision to pursue this new technology was, I argue, not a chance occurrence but was rather a consequence of a long tradition of information-centered ratiocination that stretches back to the very beginnings of the colonial era. To understand the significance of information and information technology in the contemporary moment, we must turn, therefore, to its prehistory.

The colonial state—a structure that forever needed to legitimize what was in essence a coercive formation—called for a regime that was committed to and constituted by strategies of control and management. Consequently, "colonial governmentality" relied heavily on science and technology both as instrument for, and symbol of, its sovereign mission.[11] The nationalist movement that emerged at the end of the nineteenth century may have been an avowed foe of the colonial state but was at the same time heavily indebted to its philosophy of governance. As I argue in the first chapter, insofar as the nationalist movement operated by imagining a virtual "state-in-waiting," it was, like the colonial state it aimed to replace, highly committed to a planned economy that prioritized science and technology. The Indian state that came into being in 1947 retained the ideological orientation toward information that had been characteristic of both the colonial state and its nationalist antagonist. In trying to fashion the postcolonial future, it strongly embraced a philosophy of planning that placed technology and scientific research at the forefront of the nation-building project. Prime Minister Jawaharlal Nehru, India's first prime minister, valued the "scientific temper" above all else: in the *Discovery of India* he would write, "The scientific approach and temper are, or should be, a way of life, a process of thinking, a method of acting and associating with our fellowmen. ... The scientific temper points out the way along which man should travel" (Ramesh, 2011). Interestingly, the same man—noted physicist Homi Bhabha—was commissioned with developing *both* India's nuclear energy program and its indigenous computer industry.

An examination of the early history of the computer and information industries reveals the first component of what I term the "two arrows of postcolonial time." By going backward from the birth of India's computer industry, we trace a genealogy that takes us to the founding rationality of the colonial state, which had to take constant recourse to planned courses of action to survive as a political entity. "Planning"—an endeavor that was quintessentially informational—cast a long shadow into the postcolonial period. In spite of Mahatma Gandhi's eccentric espousal of a village-based economy, both the nationalist movement as well as the independent Indian state would strongly subscribe to the notion of a centralized economy that was defined by its visible commitment to the creation of a scientific and technological postcolony. The building of that most modern machine—the computer—was thus the realization of a social philosophy as old as colonialism itself.

The state may have built the first computer, but information technology would not remain for long under its aegis. As I show in some detail in the first chapter, no sooner had the information industry been established than it began to leak out of the public sector. In slow but sure increments, it became one of the few sites of the economy that would facilitate a silent contract between the state and private capital, foreshadowing the full-scale liberalization of the economy that ensued a few decades later. I call this the "second arrow of postcolonial time" in that it traces the dramatic encounter between the universality of capital and the particularity of the postcolonial state on the stage of informationalism. We must recall that following decolonization in the post-World War II era a number of states in Asia, Africa, and elsewhere embarked on a socialist path of development. The Preamble to the Indian Constitution, for example, declares a resolve to "constitute India into a sovereign, *socialist*, secular democratic republic" (The Constitution of India, italics mine).[12] Such a commitment meant that the nation had to steer an awkward and challenging path—symbolized aptly by the Non-Aligned Movement—between the global capitalist order of the West and the Communist alternative represented by the Soviet Union and its satellite states.[13] Given this predicament, the relation between state and capital was fraught with difficulty and in constant flux.[14]

Information technology, I argue, constituted a middle ground between the public and private sectors. The entry costs for IT meant that only the state had sufficient capital and risk-taking capacity to invest in the nascent computer industry. However, the very nature of information technology—the scale and speed of its innovations, the global reach of its products, and network effects—meant that the frame of nationalist self-sufficiency would soon need to be eschewed. I outline the successive stages of this process that forced the state to accede to the rules and protocols of the global industry and to gradually open the door to domestic private capital.[15] My periodization suggests that during the earliest phase of the info-nation (roughly 1960–80) the Indian state sometimes actively, at others tacitly, encouraged the growth of the information technology sector. But informationalism—understood as a way of governing and a mode of societal organization—was initially restricted to specific gated enclaves like the high-tech and export industries. Beginning in the 1980s, however, an informational mindset begins to be diffused more broadly into a philosophy of governance that affects the nation as a whole. As if acknowledging Manuel Castells's claim that information and communication constituted "the most fundamental dimension of human activity," the Indian state initiated a comprehensive set of measures that would redefine its stance toward its citizenry and its conception of itself. In other words, it set into motion a concerted drive to create what I term the "informational state."

The second chapter looks at three different processes through which this informational state is assembled: the revolution in telephony and broadcasting that brought about an era of "communicative modernity" (Rajagopal, 2011); the use of new technology to move toward a participatory framework of e-governance; and finally, the Aadhaar card project that seeks to generate a unique digital identification system for every Indian thus tying the very basis of citizenship to information. These initiatives were significant because they pointed to a new model of sovereignty according to which the state no longer stands above and apart from its citizens, but sees itself as positioned alongside other stakeholders in a shared communicative and informational milieu that is the foundation of the info-nation.

One of the decisive steps in the constitution of the informational state occurred through developments in the telecommunications sector in the 1980s that dismantled the information order that had been in place since Independence. The Nehruvian era had been characterized by two features typical of all "early postcolonial" societies: state ownership and control over broadcasting and a restrictive and dysfunctional system of interpersonal communication. Both radio and television functioned as organs of the state on the premise that broadcasting was too powerful an instrument to be left to private hands. It is true that a thriving free press that was frequently antagonistic toward the government flourished during this period, but this was so in the context of a society where illiteracy was still very high.[16] Cinema, too, lay outside of the governmental sphere insofar as Bombay film (later known as Bollywood) and its regional counterparts were entirely based on private sector production, distribution, and exhibition. Yet in the case of cinema, the state would make its presence felt in both direct and indirect ways. Screenings of feature films were routinely preceded by documentaries produced by the Films Division of India that employed the same didactic and pedagogical impetus that characterized state-run broadcasting.[17] Moreover, as several authors have shown, a strong censorship system ensured that entertainment would not exceed the limits of the discursive proprieties that the state had instituted for the industry (Bhowmik, 2009; Mehta, 2012). Moreover, as has been persuasively argued by many film scholars, Bombay film, in its early years, saw itself as an important participant in the nation-building process and adopted a quasi-statist mode of address that sought to bring a responsible and patriotic citizenry into existence (Chakravarty, 1993; Vasudevan, 2015).

In short, the Nehruvian state invested heavily in a public communicative space in which it would be ubiquitous. The realm of what may be called "private communication" was, in contrast, strikingly impoverished. While nineteenth-century technologies like the post and telegraphy were available for all, telephony—the quintessential modern channel for interpersonal communication—was run as a skeletal operation that primarily served the bureaucracy and a small elite. This strategy was a consequence of an ideology of asceticism concerning the consumer goods sector in general. Both consumption and interpersonal communication were seen as constitutive of a type of private individualism that conflicted with the state's notion of the ideal citizen. The paucity of telephone services, for example, had little to do with censorship; it was rather a reflection of an unconscious effort to keep private individualism at bay. It is fitting, therefore, that the restructuring of communicative space would begin with a revolution in telephony.

As I show in the second chapter of this book, the democratization of telephony, signaled by the STD (State Trunk Dialing) revolution, was a crucial phase in the creation of a technologically networked society insofar as it freed interpersonal communication from the mediation of the state. Such a condition would be more completely realized in the next decade when the privatization of cellular telephony would lead to a "mobile revolution" whose impact is still being felt today (Jeffrey and Doron, 2013).

The complete restructuring of telephonic communication would be accompanied by equally momentous change in the realm of broadcasting, which as I have stated above, had been based on the idea that the primary task of the mass media was to serve as a tool for nation building. As the mission statement for All India Radio (AIR) put it, its purpose was to "to provide information, education and entertainment, for promoting the welfare and happiness of the masses." State broadcasting—via All India Radio and Doordarshan—was "nationalist" at the levels of organization, infrastructure, and content. Policies were formulated in the capital by the Ministry of Information and Broadcasting, while officials recruited from a vast pool of career bureaucrats ran day-to-day operations. As the order of the tasks set out in AIR's mission statement indicates, entertainment had very low priority in the eyes of the ruling bureaucracy. Hence, broadcasting content was also aggressively nationalist: programming prioritized reportage of governmental accomplishments in the areas of growth and development, educational talks aimed at the young and the poor, and "light entertainment" sought to uplift listeners without diverting them from the obligations of citizenship.

This model began to be dismantled during the course of the 1980s, leading to a completely reorganized broadcasting universe by the mid-1990s. As in the instance of the telecommunications sector, these changes occurred largely as a result of governmental initiatives. When Vasant Sathe, minister of information and broadcasting (1980–82), promoted the introduction of color television in 1982, it was suggested that an underdeveloped country like India could ill afford such a luxury in the face of pressing needs elsewhere. As political scientist Peter de Souza recalls, on the occasion of a dance recital by the noted artiste Yamini Krishnamurthy, Sathe observed, "Can you imagine seeing Yaminiji in black and white?" De Souza reflected, "On that day 'culture' which had been waiting in the wings of national policy trumped 'development,'" which pithily sums up the new vision of broadcasting that the Indian state would employ from this point onward (de Souza, 2013, xi).

The new regime of mass communications instituted an era of what Arvind Rajagopal has aptly termed "communicative modernity" characterized by "the proliferation of media technology and the inter-animation of media forms across print, cinema, television, mobile telephones, and the Internet" (2011, 11). As I see it, communicative modernity arises out of several simultaneous processes: changes in technology and policy, the introduction of commercials, the growth of privatized media, and the redefinition of the audience as a group of individuals who exercise choice in a quest to be entertained. Broadcasting, especially television broadcasting, played a huge role in instituting this paradigm shift. The cultural implications of television's post-statist phase have been brilliantly analyzed by several scholars including Gupta (1998), Kumar (2006), Mankekar (1999), Mehta (2008), Rajagopal (2001), and Thussu (2007). My own take on communicative modernity in the second chapter focuses more on the kind of discourse network of which it is a part.[18] Seen in informational terms, communicative modernity has four consequences of note. First, it implies an increase in the sheer volume of interpersonal communication, thus constructing a sort of proto-network that would anticipate the coming of the Internet. Second, the increasing capitalization of the communicative industries meant that the idea of a public communicative space that was independent of the state began to emerge by the early 1990s. Third, the turn to entertainment had an "expressionist" effect in that it allowed fractional discourses to enter the public sphere or fray. What emerges from such expressions is a sociology that transcends the state's vision of unitary society—a perfect example being the rise of Hindutva that accompanied the showing of the epic serials *Ramayana* and *Mahabharat* in the late eighties in spite of the state's secular commitments. Finally, communicative modernity allowed for an alliance between consumerism and individualism that bypassed the concerns and actions of the state, the global dimension of which has been extremely well elaborated by a recent of essays (Curtin and Shah, 2010).

This redefinition of communicative space is the first step, the second chapter suggests, in the formation of an informational state. Through the process of self-devolution that I have indicated, the Indian state revisited its status as the sole proprietor and regulator of the communicative structure, gradually adopting a more participatory stance in which it represents itself as one stakeholder among many in a networked society. As I show in the remaining sections of the chapter, information plays a very significant role in this reorientation. I make my case with a detailed exploration of a widely publicized initiative in e-governance—the Aadhaar (base) card project—that weaves together these emerging conceptions of state, citizenship, information, and governance. Designed to provide every citizen of India with a unique biometric profile, the Aadhaar card was literally a new foundation for citizenship. Though the project may run to a halt following a change in government, the idea behind it continues to have strong appeal. The Aadhaar scheme as well as its proposed alternatives represents the convergence between state and capital to reassemble governance around notions of access, information, sustainability, and social justice. In other words, projects like Aadhaar reflect the push to construct a new citizen-subject who will function as a node within an emergent ecology of information.

I extend this line of thinking in the third chapter of the book to propose that changes in the domain of politics brought about by the information revolution constitute a third vector of the info-nation. Whereas the previous chapter looked at the state's role in constructing the info-nation, both with regard to its relationship to capital and its citizens, here I focus on how civil society supplements the state's efforts by instituting wholly novel ways of collective political action. Specifically, I argue that the spread of the informational milieu is giving rise to a new type of politics based on digital citizenry and "info-activism." Politics in India, at the level of practice, has usually been conceptualized in terms of categories like class, caste, religion, and more recently gender and sexuality. Thus, political parties—like the BJP and Congress or the AIADMK and Trinamool Congress—have usually been characterized in common discourse as either national/regional or secular/fundamentalist. Academic analyses of electoral politics and of other "political phenomena" like social movements, strikes, or village-level politics have also used the same sociological and anthropological categories. The politics of the info-nation is based on a number of premises marking a significant departure from these traditional assumptions. First, it treats information as an integral element of economic growth and, hence, crucial to the fight for social justice. Informational rights, from this perspective, are as important as the right to land, health services, or just wages. Second, it conceptualizes the citizen-subject as an informational subject. In other words, the proper citizen is one who not only has access to information but is also inserted into and constructed by the network society that the informational state as well as privatized media have brought into being. Finally, the realm of politics is redefined such that it is no longer restricted to electoral battles fought through the mediation of political parties, or what may be loosely termed "group activism" conducted at the local, regional, or national level. Rather, politics now becomes a matter of channeling and utilizing the network itself. In other words, the political is constituted in every instance as an informational event (following Twitter, hits on YouTube, likes on Facebook, as well as more state-generated initiatives like the right to information or transparency in governance). In the course of the third chapter, I examine the rise of digital politics by looking at three sites of info-activism: the nationwide campaign for the right to information for every citizen, the rise of a political party whose platform was based on informational issues, and a highly successful talk show that makes extensive use of digital tools and sociological data to address issues of inequity and social justice.

The fourth and final chapter of the book examines the imprint of the informational turn on the realm of commercial entertainment and popular culture to show how it embeds the "logics of globalization" into national cultural products (Kavoori, 2009). Here I focus on Indian television, particularly reality programming, as a crucial engine of informatization. I suggest that if we look at television history from an "information-theoretic" perspective we notice a progressive shift from a news-based conception of information to one that is vested in entertainment. As a result, the explosion of entertainment programming in the cable era becomes a major agent of the informatization of the medium in the new millennium. While both news and entertainment are densely informative in content, I argue that is only with the advent of reality television that the very *form* of television programming has taken an informational turn.[19] Reality television—steadily on the rise for the past two decades—is a radically new mode of storytelling that relies fundamentally on the production of information that could be construed as "real." By being home to this novel information-based cultural form, Indian television emerges as a vanguard site for cultural production.

The second and concluding section of the fourth chapter consists of an analysis of reality television as an embodiment of informational culture. I begin by briefly examining current theories of reality television to suggest that these accounts need to be supplemented with an analysis that gives due weight to reality television's informational aspect. I then go on to examine three key Indian reality shows of the past decade—*Kaun Banega Crorepati*, *Indian Idol*, and *Bigg Boss*—to demonstrate how their format "runs" on different modes of information in order to create a new aesthetic. My analysis of *Crorepati*, the Indian version of *Who Wants to Be a Millionaire*, locates the show in the context of a statist informational culture characterized by the "general knowledge" that is tested by examinations for key governmental services, as well as the culture of quizzing prevalent among high school and college students. *Crorepati*, I argue, is statist information translated into entertainment. I then analyze one season of *Indian Idol* to show how a singing contest gives rise to an info-politics based on ethnic differences. Finally, an examination of the hit show *Bigg Boss* (the Indian version of *Big Brother*) shows how particular instantiations of global formats become informational devices concerning the process of globalization. My examination of the informational features of popular reality shows in India demonstrates how information extends into the world of commercial entertainment.

The book as a whole tries to argue that though the information revolution's most recognizable markers—Silicon Valley, Google, Amazon, and Facebook, for example—are associated with the advanced societies of the West, it has also had a radical impact on countries in the global South. Indeed, given the relative ease with which information technology can be capitalized, developed, and implemented, the information revolution is perhaps of even greater significance for developing nations, allowing them to get globally connected and "catch up" with advances elsewhere. In this monograph, I focus on the specific case of India to argue that the digital revolution has affected all aspects of social formation and thus has led to the emergence of an "info-nation." The info-nation, as I conceive it, is a formation where the vectors of social action are modulated and mediated by informational logic. Information therefore constitutes a significant historical force in contemporary India as well as in other parts of the global South. By showing how the info-nation is visible in the realms of political economy, state governance, citizen activism, and popular culture, I suggest that we are poised at the dawn of an informational age that takes us to an uncharted future.

Notes

1. This figure would rise to 4.8% between 1981–88 and then jump up to 6.1% between 1988–2004.
2. Pramod Mahajan (1949–2006) served as minister for information technology in the right-leaning BJP government in power between 1999 and 2004.
3. See Shannon and Weaver (1949) for a mathematical theory of communication that defines information as a logarithmic function. Some recent physicists have proposed a grander conception positing that the entire universe is nothing but information (Deutsch and Marletto, 2014).
4. See Castells (2009) for a seminal analysis of this concept.
5. He identifies three processes that engendered this conjunction: the crisis and restructuring of industrialism and its two associated modes of production, capitalism and statism; the freedom-oriented, cultural social movements of the late 1960s and early 1970s; and the revolution in information and communication technologies.
6. Stanford Industrial Park was set up in 1951 at behest of Stanford's visionary Dean of Engineering Frederic Terman. Most commentators consider it to be the catalyst that would create the Silicon Valley boom.
7. I owe these questions to an anonymous reviewer for Routledge.
8. For a sharp discussion on the role of the Indian state in the software miracle, see Balakrishnan (2006).
9. For a fascinating account of the extent to which Korea has been "wired," see Ahonen and O'Reilly (2007).
10. Tata Institute of Fundamental Research Automatic Calculator, a name suggested by Nehru himself.
11. See David Scott's (1995) seminal essay for a superb analysis of this notion.
12. While the word "socialist" was inserted into the sentence due to an amendment enacted in 1976, the state and its leaders always conceived of India in socialistic terms. Thus for Nehru, in the words of one commentator, socialism and nationalism "were inextricably connected" (Mohan, 1975, 183).
13. The Non-Aligned Movement (NAM), founded in Belgrade in 1961, was an organization representing a group of states (of whom India was among the most prominent) that was not formally aligned to either of the two major power blocs led by the United States and the Soviet Union.
14. Though consumer goods constituted one-third of economic output in the 1960s, capital goods were almost entirely produced by the public sector (Kochanek, 1974, 91).
15. It needs to be pointed out that the advent of the information sector altered the character of domestic capital. No longer a monopoly protected by the state and, hence, not affected by the exigencies of global capital, domestic capital in the computer and software industries became firmly inserted in the global marketplace.
16. The literacy rates as recorded in the first four Census years after Independence were as follows: 18.33% (1951), 28.30% (1961), 34.45% (1971), and 43.57% (1981) (indiabudget). By 2011, the literacy rate had risen to 70.04%.
17. The Films Division of India was established in 1948. It was housed in the Ministry of Information and Broadcasting and continues to function to this day. For an informative account of its early days, see Deprez (2013).

18. The concept of discourse network was first introduced by Friedrich Kittler (1992).
19. As of 2014, there were 788 television channels on the air in India. Of these, approximately half were permitted to carry news.

References

Ahonen, Tomi T., and Jim O'Reilly. 2007. *Digital Korea: Convergence of Broadband Internet, 3G Cell Phones, Multiplayer Gaming, Digital TV, Virtual Reality, Electronic Cash, Telematics, Robotics, E-Government and the Intelligent Home.* London: Futuretext.

All India Radio. Mission. Retrieved July 9, 2015, from http://allindiaradio.gov.in/Profile/mission/Pages/default.aspx.

Anderson, Benedict. 2006. *Imagined Communities: Reflections on the Origins and Spread of Nationalism.* London: Verso.

Arora, Ashish. 2010. Why India's Software Industry Prospers. *New York Times*, November 7, 2010. Retrieved July 2, 2015, from http://www.nytimes.com/roomfordebate/2010/11/07/what-obama-can-learn-from-india/why-indias-software-industry-prospers.

Atkins, William. 2001. *The Politics of South East Asia's New Media.* New York: Routledge.

Balakrishnan, Pulapre. 2006. Benign Neglect or Strategic Intent? Contested Lineage of Indian Software Industry. *Economic and Political Weekly*, 41(36), 3865–72.

Beniger, James. 1989. *The Control Revolution: Technological and Economic Origins of the Information Society.* Cambridge: Harvard University Press.

Bhatnagar, Subhash. 2006. India's Software Industry. In Vandana Chandra (Ed.), *Technology, Adaptation, and Exports: How Some Developing Countries Got It Right* (pp. 95–126). World Bank.

Bhowmik, Someswar. 2009. *Cinema and Censorship: The Politics of Control in India.* New Delhi: Orient Blackswan.

Bruijn, Mirjam de, Francis Nyamnjoh, and Inge Brinkman (Eds.). 2009. *Mobile Phones: The New Talking Drums of Everyday Africa.* Bamenda, Cameroon: Langa RPCIG.

Buskens, Ineke, and Anne Webb (Eds.). 2009. *African Women & ICTs: Investigating Technology, Gender and Empowerment.* London: Zed Books.

Bussell, Jennifer. 2012. *Corruption and Reform in India: Public Services in the Digital Age.* Cambridge: Cambridge University Press.

Castells, M. 2009. *The Rise of the Network Society: The Information Age: Economy, Society and Culture, Vol. 1.* Hoboken, NJ: Wiley-Blackwell.

Chakravarty, Sumita S. 1993. *National Identity in Indian Popular Cinema, 1947–1987.* Austin, TX: University of Texas Press.

Chandrasekhar, C. P. The Diffusion of Information Technology. *Social Scientist*, 31(7/8), 42–85.

Chatterjee, Shoma. 2008. Women on Television: Looking back on Hum Log. *India Together*, July 5, 2008. Retrieved July 9, 2008, from http://www.indiatogether.org/2008/jul/wom-humlog.htm.

Chaudhuri, Bidisha. 2014. *E-Governance in India: Interlocking Politics, Technology and Culture.* New York: Routledge.

Constitution of India, The. Retrieved July 9, 2015, from http://india.gov.in/sites/upload_files/npi/files/coi_part_full.pdf.

Curtin, Michael, and Hemant Shah (Eds.). 2010. *Reorienting Global Communication: Indian and Chinese Media Beyond Borders*. Urbana-Champaign: University of Illinois Press.

Das, Gurcharan. 2000. *India Unbound: From Independence to the Global Information Age*. New Delhi: Penguin Books.

DeitY 2015. Digital India. Retrieved July 21, 2015, from http://deity.gov.in/sites/upload_files/dit/files/Digital%20India.pdf.

Deprez, Camille. 2013. The Films Division of India, 1948–1964: The Early Days and the Influence of the British Documentary Film Tradition. *Film History*, 25(3), 149–73.

de Souza, Peter. 2014. "Foreword." In Biswarup Sen and Abhijhit Roy (Eds.), *Channeling Cultures: Television Studies from India* (pp.) New Delhi: Oxford University Press.

Deutsch, David, and Chiara Marletto. 2014. Reconstructing Physics: The Universe Is Information. *New Scientist*. Retrieved July 4, 2015, from http://www.newscientist.com/article/mg22229700.200-reconstructing-physics-the-universe-is-information.html.

Economist, The. 2010. India's Surprising Economic Miracle. Retrieved July 2, 2015, from http://www.economist.com/node/17147648.

Forbes(2015). Forbes Global 2000: Three Indian Software Companies Are In 2013 List. Retrieved October 14, 2015, from http://www.woolor.com/thetechbook/forbes-global-2000-three-indian-software-companies-are-in-2013-list/.

Gajjala, Radhika. 2004. *Cyber Selves: Feminist Ethnographies of South Asian Women*. Lanham, MD: AltaMira Press.

Gupta, Nilanjana. 1998. *Switching channels: ideologies of television in India*. New Delhi: Oxford University Press.

Heeks, R. 1996. *India's Software Industry; State Policy, Liberalization and Industrial Development*. New Delhi: Sage.

Indiabudget. Literacy as Seen in the 2001 Census. Retrieved July 10, 2015, from. http://indiabudget.nic.in/es2001-02/chapt2002/chap106.pdf.

Jeffrey, Robin, and Assa Doron. 2013. *Cell Phone Nation: How Mobile Phones Have Revolutionized Business, Politics And Ordinary Life In India*. Gurgaon, India: Hachette India.

Kapur, Devesh. 2002. The Causes and Consequences of India's IT Boom. *India Review*, 1(2), 91–110.

Kavoori, Arindam P. 2009. *The Logics of Globalization: Case Studies in International Communication*. New York: Lexington Books.

Kittler, Friedrich. 1992. *Discourse Networks 1800/1900*. Redwood City, CA: Stanford University Press.

Kochanek, Stanley A. 1974. *Business and Politics in India*. Berkeley: University of California Press.

Kumar, Shanti. 2006. *Gandhi meets primetime: globalization and nationalism in Indian television*, Urbana: University of Illinois Press.

Mankekar, Purnima. 1999. *Screening Culture, Viewing Politics: An Ethnography of Television, Womanhood, and Nation in Postcolonial India*. Durham: Duke University Press.

Mehta, Monika. 2012. *Censorship and Sexuality in Bombay Cinema*. Austin, TX: University of Texas Press.

Mehta, Nalin. 2008. *India on television: how satellite news channels have changed the way we think and act.* New Delhi: HarperCollins.

Mohan, Jag. 1975. Jawaharlal Nehru and His Socialism. *India International Centre Quarterly*, 2(3), 183–92.

mygov. 2015. 10 Initiatives for Digital India. Retrieved July 21, 2015, from https://mygov.in/task/10-initiatives-digital-india/.

NASSCOM. 2015. Positive Outlook for IT-BPM industry in FY 2014. Retrieved November 15, 2014, from http://www.nasscom.in/positive-outlook-itbpm-industry-fy-2014.

Nath, Pradosh, and Amitav Hazra. 2002. Configuration of Indian Software Industry. *Economic and Political Weekly*, 37(8), 737–42.

NDTV Gadgets. 2015a. Digital India Week Received a Huge Response: Prasad. Retrieved July 21, 2015, from http://gadgets.ndtv.com/internet/news/digital-india-week-received-a-huge-response-prasad-714144.

NDTV Gadgets. 2015b. Digital India: CEOs to Invest Rs. 4,50,000 Crores. Retrieved July 21, 2015, from http://gadgets.ndtv.com/internet/news/digital-india-ceos-commit-to-invest-rs-450000-crores-710571.

Oh, Myung, and James Larson. 2013. *Digital Development in Korea: Building an Information Society.* New York: Routledge.

Panagariya, Arvind. 2008. Transforming India. In Jagdish Bhagwati and Charles W. Calomiris (Eds.), *Sustaining India's Growth Miracle* (pp. 9–50). New York: Columbia Business School Publishing.

Parthsarathy, Balaji. 2004. Globalizing Information Technology: The.

Domestic Policy Context for India's Software Production and Exports. *Iterations*, 1–38. Retrieved October 25, 2015 from www.cbi.umn.edu/iterations/parthasarathy.pdf.

Payaril, Govindan. (Ed.). 2006. *Political Economy and Information Capitalism: Digital Divide, Development Divide and Equity.* London: Palgrave Macmillan.

Pendakur, Manjunath, and Roma Harris (Eds.). 2002. *Citizenship and Participation in the Information Age.* Toronto: University of Toronto Press.

Quartz india. 2015. What's in a Name: India's E-visa Is Actually a Smart Programme. Retrieved July 21, 2015, from http://qz.com/386802/whats-in-a-name-indias-e-visa-is-actually-a-smart-programme/.

Rai, Saritha. 2015. Infosys CEO Vishal Sikha on the End of India's "IT Miracle." *Forbes/Asia.* Retrieved July 3, 2015, from http://www.forbes.com/sites/saritharai/2015/06/25/infosys-ceo-vishal-sikka-on-the-end-of-indias-it-miracle/.

Rahimi, Babak. 2009. The Politics of Informational Communication: Conspiracy Theories and Rumors in the 2009 (Post-)Electoral Public Sphere. In George Dalziel (Ed.), *Rumor and Communication in Asia in the Internet Age* (pp. 78–93). New York: Routledge.

Rajagopal, Arvind. 2011. Notes on Postcolonial Visual Culture. *Bioscope*, 2(1), 11–22.

Rajagopal, Arvind. 2001. *Politics after Television: Hindu Nationalism and the Reshaping of the Public in India.* Cambridge: Cambridge University Press.

Ramesh, Jairam. 2011. Nehru's Scientific Temper Recalled. Retrieved July 7, 2015, from https://www.google.com/#q=nehru+scientific+temper.

Saraswati, Jyoti. 2012. *Dot.compradors: Power and Policy in the Development of the Indian Software Industry.* London: Pluto Press.

Saxenian, AnnaLee. 2000. Bangalore: The Silicon Valley of India. Center for Research on Economic Development and Policy Reform, Stanford. Retrieved July 2, 2015, form http://people.ischool.berkeley.edu/~anno/Papers/bangalore_svasia.html.

Scott, David. 1995. Colonial Governmentality. *Social Text, 43*, 191–220.

Shannon, Claude E., and Warren Weaver. 1949. *The Mathematical Theory of Communication*. Urbana-Champaign: The University of Illinois Press.

Sharma, Prashant. 2014. *Democracy and Transparency in the Indian State: The Making of the Right to Information Act*. New York: Routledge.

Smartcitiesindia. 2015. Welcome to Smart Cities India 2016 exhibition and conference. Retrieved July 21, 2015, from http://www.smartcitiesindia.com.

statista. 2015. Leading Countries Based on Number of Facebook Users as of May 2014 (in millions). Retrieved July 21, 2015, from http://www.statista.com/statistics/268136/top-15-countries-based-on-number-of-facebook-users/.

Streeter, Thomas. 2010. *The Net Effect: Romanticism, Capitalism and the Internet*. New York: New York University Press.

Thomas, Pradip. 2012. *Digital India*. New Delhi: Sage.

Thussu, Daya K. 2007. *News as Entertainment: The Rise of Global Infotainment*. London: Sage.

Tolan, Casey. 2014. Cities of the Future? Indian PM Pushes Plan for 100 "Smart Cities." Retrieved June 20, 2015, from CNN.com http://www.cnn.com/2014/07/18/world/asia/india-modi-smart-cities/.

Vasudevan, Ravi. 2015. *The Melodramatic Public*. New Delhi: Permanent Black.

Yang, Guodin. 2011. *The Power of the Internet in China: Citizen Activism Online*. New York: Columbia University Press.

1 The Computer in Postcolonial History

India's information age can be said to have begun in January 1962, when Prime Minister Jawaharlal Nehru inaugurated the TIFRAC, an indigenously manufactured first-generation mainframe computer that was meant to boost the nation's scientific capabilities (*Deccan Herald*, 2010). Named after the prestigious research institution in which it was housed, the Tata Institute of Fundamental Research Automatic Calculator (TIFRAC), which had been many years in the making, would remain in operation for a mere two years. Its impact upon Indian society, however, was incalculable insofar as it announced the dawning of a new era that sought to make the country realize itself as an info-nation.[1] This chapter intends to explore the full import of this historic moment by analyzing the crucial role information has played in the constitution and functioning of the Indian state and polity in both the colonial and postcolonial periods in the country's history. I undertake this broad exercise by tracing what I term the "two arrows of postcolonial time." TIFRAC's roots, I argue, go back to the ideology of information developed in the colonial period, which was to be highly determinative of the ways in which independent India would structure policies and programs in the area of science and information technology. At the same time, TIFRAC and the software industry it spawned were a portent of things to come, for they laid out a template for the relationship between the forces of capital and the Indian state that would emerge in subsequent decades. "TIFRAC" is thus shorthand for the large and complex manner in which information—understood both as technology and social process—has modulated the trajectory of both colonial and postcolonial time. The double history of the TIFRAC therefore enables us to outline the genealogy of the concept of the info-nation, as well as to trace its role in constituting the lineaments of an emergent power in the making.[2]

Information and the Colonial State

In the autumn of 1858, a young British civil servant named William Herschel, serving at the time in the north Bengal district of Maldah, entered into a contract for the supply of road-making material with a local businessman called Rajyadhar Konai. As Konai was preparing to sign the contractual document in the traditional way—at the upper right-hand corner—Herschel who had come to "distrust ... all evidence tendered in Court" and had come to "despair of any good coming from orders and decisions based on such slippery facts" decided on a sudden impulse to ask the contractor to stamp the contract with a print of his right hand (Sengoopta, 2003, 57). Thus was born the idea of the *fingerprint*, an impression that recorded an individual in the form of unvarying ridge-pattern data taken from the finger. Subsequently appointed magistrate and collector of the Hooghly District, Herschel implemented the practice of fingerprinting in court proceedings, in the district jail, and in the Deeds Registration department. In spite of Herschel's enthusiasm for this novel informational procedure, the colonial government remained indifferent to its possibilities and fingerprinting may have died with Herschel's return to England. It did not, however, due the efforts of another British civil servant named Edward Henry. Following a posting to Bengal, Henry became inspector general of the Bengal police in 1891 and almost immediately began to "informatize" the department. His first initiative was to make anthropometry—the systematic measurement of the physical properties of the human body—a routine procedure in all police work. Becoming aware of Herschel's pioneering work, Henry added fingerprinting to the list of measurements that all criminals had to undergo. Soon it became apparent that it was only the latter method that yielded valid information. In 1897, Henry announced a system of fingerprint classification that was such that "the greatest sceptic would be at once convinced of identity on being shown the original and duplicate impressions" (Sengoopta, 2003, 139). The Bengal system of fingerprinting soon spread all over British India and then back "home" in England as well as in the rest of the English-speaking world.

The introduction of fingerprinting as a standard mode of bureaucratic governance points to the crucial role that was played by information in the constitution of the colonial state. As numerous scholars have demonstrated, the entire colonial period was marked by a series of efforts at generating information that would produce a comprehensive "knowledge" of the territory and its peoples. The annals of colonialism are dotted with such epistemological projects: histories of the conquered nation written by such notable authors as Alexander Dow, James Mill, and James Tod; surveys of the land conducted by geographers like James Rennall, Colin Mckenzie, and Frances Buchanan; the recovery and recodification of native language, literature, law, and lore compiled by Orientalists like Thomas Munro, William Jones, and N. B. Halhed. What lay behind this unbounded thirst for information? In the words of one distinguished commentator, such enterprises were undertaken in order "to enable the British to classify, categorize, and bound the vast social world that was India so it could be controlled" (Cohn, 1996, 4–5).

Such an observation stems from a distinctive historiography regarding colonialism. If traditional Marxist scholarship analyzed colonialism as a unique mode of production that arises in "the last stage of capitalism,"[3] Michel Foucault's distinctive account of modernity allows us to read colonialism not only in economic terms, but also as a mode of governance that imposes knowledge, precepts, and rules upon a subject population in order to make the colonial project viable. In a well-known essay, anthropologist David Scott has argued that we attend to the "*political rationalities* of colonial power" that "characterize those ways in which colonial power is organized as an activity designed to produce effects of rule" (1995, 193). Following Foucault's observation that "Maybe what is really important for our modernity—that is for our present—is not so much the statization [*etatisation*] of society, as the "governmentalization" of the state" (2001, 220), Scott rethinks colonialism in terms of a "colonial governmentality" that sets up the very terms and logic of societal discourse "so as to produce not so much extractive-effects on colonial bodies as governing-effects on colonial conduct" (1995, 204).

The notion of colonial governmentality is a particularly apt one. If governmentality was the defining feature of the modern European state, it had an even stronger salience in the colonial context. Imposed by military methods on an alien population, and dedicated to crude extraction and unfair imperial trade, the colonial state could scarcely turn to notions of sovereignty and the natural order as the basis for its rule. Its hold and legitimacy could therefore only be established by reorganizing its human territory by means of the conceptual apparatus and strategic tactics that were, at the same time, instituting contemporary western modernity. In other words, the constitutive logic of the colonial state implied that it was "governmental" from the very moment of its inception. Consequently, the Indian colonial state, first as Company Bahadur and then as British Raj, could sustain itself and evolve by expanding the scope of this governmentality. One can map this endeavor, as Scott suggests, by looking at the targets of colonial power—where it was applied and the means and instrumentalities deployed—as well as the field of its operation—the zone it constructs for its functionality (1995, 193). It is my claim that information, understood in its broadest sense, constituted a critical zone for the operation of British colonial governmentality. That is, the exercise of colonial governmentality depended crucially on a ceaseless process of information gathering, information processing, and information distribution. There is by now a vast literature that critically examines this process as it unfolded in domains like historiography, social statistics, mapping, legal studies, literary studies, and aesthetics that ably demonstrate the thesis that such endeavors created a "discourse" that provided the cognitive underpinning for colonialism as a political and economic phenomenon.[4] My focus here is on two specific aspects of colonial governmentality—*science* and *planning*—that would have far-reaching consequences for the direction in which postcolonial India would evolve. Not only would these guiding notions come to play an important role in the policy-making of the colonial state, but also they were subsequently "bequeathed" to nationalist discourse, adopted eagerly by the Indian elite, and thus provided a foundation for the developmental logic of the postcolonial state. For the entire period beginning with Independence till the end of the millennium, planning—the state's attempt at nudging history—was instrumental in determining the fundamental direction that Indian society was to take. In other words, modern India can quite justifiably be seen as synonymous with a "planned society."[5] Additionally, planning as a philosophy of governance was strongly entwined with a scientific vision of human life. The talismans of the Nehruvian era—physics and nuclear reactors, engineering and hydro-electric power, agricultural sciences and the green revolution—tell us that from the state's perspective the pursuit of science and technology was the only guaranteed means of achieving modernity. In the eyes of the postcolonial state, therefore, *planning* and *scientific thinking* constituted the central pillars of a rational mode of governance. Thus, the "miracle story" of India's software revolution cannot be properly told without first demonstrating how the postcolonial state's deep commitment to informational science and technology had its origins in the logic of colonial governmentality.

Science in its modern western form was an integral part of the East India Company's dominion in India. Lord Wellesley, governor-general of India from 1798 to 1805, opined that "to facilitate and promote … general science" was a task "imposed on the British government of India in its present exalted position" (Arnold, 2000, 22). This "general science" was not restricted to glorious intellectual achievements like those of Newtonian physics; it had an equally important material aspect that would be imprinted on the colonial landscape. In other words, general science manifested itself through magnificent public works.[6] Thus, the first railway lines had been set up in 1853 and by 1919 India had the fourth-largest railway system in the world with nearly 35,000 miles of track. There was a similar growth in irrigation projects, and by 1900 nearly one-fifth of the total cultivated land in British India was served by some sort of irrigation works (Tomlinson, 1993, 55, 86). These efforts to enhance the productive apparatus of the state were accompanied by similar investments in scientific institutions and practices: the Bengal Medical Services (founded 1763), the Asiatic Society of Bengal (f. 1784), the Agricultural and Horticultural Society of India (f. 1820), the Medical and Physical Society (f. 1823), *Gleanings in Science* (f. 1829), *The Journal of Natural History* (f. 1840), the Geological Survey of India (f. 1851), Telegraph Services (f. 1851), the Tropical School of Medicine (f. 1921), and the Indian School of Mines (f. 1926). Science then was a means of advertising the prowess of western reason. In his popular book on modern Indian history, Percival Spear describes how in the post-Mutiny period the British vigorously pursued material projects while avoiding interference in the social system. As Spear put it, "These public works provided the means for the growth of western influence … the Indian people were left to make what they liked of it" (Spear, 1965, 152).

The "Indian people" would treat science as a privileged mode of inquiry whose use-value was not compromised by its deployment in the furtherance of colonial hegemony.[7] Even during the heyday of Empire, the supposed "objects" of governmentality seemed eager for its benefits. Thus, at its third annual session held in 1887, the Indian National Congress asked that the government "be moved to elaborate a system of technical education ... encourage indigenous manufacturers ... and to employ more extensively than at present the skill and talents of the people of the country" (Sinha, 1991, 162). The enthusiasm for western science long predated this resolution, as the following examples illustrate: in 1817 leading Bengali intellectuals established the Hindu College of Calcutta with the intention of providing instruction in European literature and science; in 1823 the great reformer Rammohun Roy appealed to the governor-general asking for English education that would provide "a more liberal enlightened system of instruction embracing mathematics, natural philosophy ... and other useful sciences" (Dasgupta, 2011, xli); under the leadership of Master Ram Chandra, the faculty at Delhi College began translating scientific works into Urdu; in 1862 Sir Syed Ahmed Khan established the Aligarh Scientific Society to translate current works into Urdu; Maulana Imdad Ali founded the Bihar Scientific Society in 1868; under the initiative of Mahendra Lal Sircar, the Indian Association for the Cultivation of Science (IACS) was established in 1876 to provide Indians with "an institution like the Royal Institute of London" in order "for economic betterment but also for their regeneration" (Basu, 1991, 132); leaders of the Swadeshi movement started an engineering college in Jadavpur, Calcutta, in 1907, and in 1909 the Indian Institute of Science was founded in Bangalore.

This wholehearted embrace of science by social reformers and nationalists constitutes what I term a "transfer of governmentality."[8] For even as the Indian intelligentsia strove to construct a movement that would demand a sharing of power and ultimately sovereignty, it turned to science as a means of establishing the credentials of the nationalist project. The fusion of science and nationalism had two aspects. On the one hand, there was an attempt to demonstrate the scientific basis of Indian, especially Hindu, civilization exemplified by titles like B. N. Seal's *The Positive Sciences of the Ancient Hindus* (1915) and Benoy Kumar Sarkar's *Hindu Achievements in the Exact Sciences* (1918). Most influential in this regard was P. C. Ray's *History of Hindu Chemistry* (1902). Observing that "it is generally taken for granted that Hindus are a dreamy, metaphysical people," Ray—the country's preeminent chemist at the time—argued that ancient India was in fact the cradle of the mathematical sciences. Hence, he hoped his text "will have the effect of stimulating my countrymen to strive to regain their old position in the intellectual hierarchy of nations" (Chakrabarti, 2004, 221).

The recuperation of the nation's scientific past was accompanied by a concerted attempt to *do* science. The turn of the century saw science education blossom in various colleges and universities across the country. Consider the case of Calcutta (now Kolkata), clearly the leader in this regard. As we saw, the Indian Society for the Cultivation of Science was founded in 1876. Presidency College (as the Hindu College came to be known after 1855) became a leader in original scientific research, boasting the reputed physicist Jagadish Chandra Bose and the chemist Prafulla Chandra Ray on its faculty. Bose, in the words of the prominent postcolonial theorist Dipesh Chakrabarty, was one of the few contemporary intellectuals who attempted "to develop dialogues between science and religion," in order to connect antiquity and modernity (2002, 25).

Postgraduate studies in the sciences began in 1914 when the vice-chancellor at the time, Asutosh Mukherjee, laid the foundation for the University College of Science. P. C. Ray was the first chaired professor at the Science College; he would subsequently be joined in 1917 by C. V. Raman, India's first Nobel laureate in the sciences (Ghosh, 1994, 52–56). The college faculty also included another famous physicist, Meghnad Saha, a figure who would play a crucial role in the history of Indian planning. The fervent enthusiasm for science was not restricted to professional scientists like P. C. Ray and amateur enthusiasts like Mahendra Lal Sircar. The eminent jurist Rashbehary Ghosh donated large sums of money toward the establishment of the Science College; philosophers like Akshay Kumar Dutt promoted Baconian natural philosophy; literary figures like the novelist Bankim Chattopadhya dabbled with positivism; the Parsi industrialist Jamshedji Tata was instrumental in setting up the Indian Institute of Science; a religious icon like Swami Vivekananda extolled the discoveries science had made, while Swadeshi leaders like Pandit Madan Mohan Malaviya—founder of the Benares Hindu University—became a great champion of science education (Dasgupta, 2011).

To recapitulate the argument so far, colonial governmentality consisted not only of the imposition of cognitive maps and grids on native territories and practices; it also involved a more material strategy that involved the imposition of science (and technology) on a widespread basis. Unlike other manifestations of colonial power, science—read as a universal mode of inquiry that produced value-free information—was seen by Indians as independent of the colonizer and therefore an ideal instrument for the pursuit of nationalist modernity. Science, then, came to operate as a crucial third term between nationalism and governmentality. Nationalism in the colonial period, I want to suggest, was both an actual and a virtual process. It was enacted through a series of events, maneuvers, and strategies that arose from the taut dialectic between rulers and the ruled, this history—that of the freedom struggle—is the *actual* history of nationalism. At the same time, nationalism was a *virtual* exercise that had to imagine a nation that would come to fruition at the moment of independence. Virtual nationalism dwelt in the realm of the potential and expressed itself through a series of blueprints, projections, resolves, and resolutions that calculated and calibrated what was yet to be. *Planning*, understood as "informed

futurity," that is, an activity that imagines the future on the basis of information regarding the present, was the manifest form of virtual nationalism
as I just defined it. Not surprisingly, then, planning played a big role in the
nationalist movement and was to play an even more significant role in the
destiny of postcolonial India.

Planning

The years immediately before 1947 saw a succession of "plans" that were
blueprints for developing the independent nation that was already visible on the horizon. The Resolution of Fundamental Rights and Economic
Programme passed at the Karachi Congress held in 1931 is perhaps the very
first document of this sort. Though not technically a "plan," the sentiments
expressed in the resolution certainly assumed state planning as the fundamental component of the future economy. Thus, it declared that in the age
of Swaraj, "the State shall provide free and compulsory education … safe-
guard the interests of industrial workers … protect indigenous industries"
and "shall own or control key industries and services, mineral resources, railways, waterways, shipping and other means of public transport" (National
Planning Committee, 1988, 31–33). The specificity of these demands should
not obscure the more general principle at work here, one that is quite clear in
the 1937 Congress Working Committee's recommendation for "the appointment of a Committee of Experts to consider urgent and vital problems the
solution of which is necessary to any scheme of national reconstruction
and *social planning*" (National Planning Committee, 39, italics mine). The
Karachi Resolution presaged a flood of similar publications. In 1934 the
noted economist Sir M. M. Visvesvarya published his *Planned Economy for
India*, followed in 1935 by N. S. Subba Rao's *Some Aspects of Economic
Planning*. At the behest of its president, Netaji Subhas Chandra Bose, the
Congress Party constituted a National Planning Committee under the chairmanship of Jawaharlal Nehru. The committee, formed in 1938, would release
several reports in the next few years, many authored by Nehru himself. In
1944 a group of industrialists that included two of India's most famous business leaders—J. R. D. Tata and G. D. Birla—released "The 'Bombay' Plan
for India's Economic Development." The same year also saw the publication
of a "People's Plan" authored by the radical humanist and ex-communist
M. N. Roy on behalf of the Indian Federation of Labour. In 1945, the government of India issued two documents—the "Second Report on Reconstruction Planning" and the "Industrial Policy Statement," both of which outlined
a vision for postwar India. Finally, a "Gandhian Plan" for India (1949), written by S. N. Aggarwal, was the last such anticipatory document to come out
before planning became a reality in the early fifties with the establishment of
the Planning Commission and the launching of the First Five Year Plan.

These proposals represented very different constituencies of the emerging
nation and one would expect them to have widely divergent prescriptions

for development and growth. The People's Plan and the Gandhian Plan were quite clearly the outliers in this respect. Roy's Marxist roots were very evident in his call that "the entire land will have to nationalize thus leaving no intermediary between the cultivator of the soil and the State" (Nag, 1949). Aggarwal's proposals drew from the Mahatma's principle that "the essence of non-violence is de-centralization" (Austin, 1999, 30); consequently, the Gandhian Plan envisaged a society that grew upward from the panchayat level in which the state had few and limited functions and in which political parties had no place at all.

Such eccentric agendas do not obviate a central truth about all these plans. In his analysis of the national postcolonial state, the eminent postcolonial theorist Partha Chatterjee points out that planning appeared first and foremost as a *form* of determining state policy. Executed by "experts," planning "emerged as a crucial instrumental modality by which the state would determine the material allocation of productive resources within the nation: a modality of political power constituted outside the immediate political power itself." What this implies is that "a developmental ideology ... was a constituent part of the self-definition of the postcolonial ideology" (1993, 202–03).[9] I would supplement Chatterjee's observations by pointing out that while planning is clearly the key instrument for a "developmental ideology," it is at the same time the ground for the emergence of an informational order. Consider the following definition of planning put forward by a subcommittee of the National Planning Committee:

> What is planning? Planning under a democratic system may be defined as the technical co-ordination, by disinterested experts, of consumption, production, investment, trade and income distribution in accordance with social objectives set by bodies representative of the nation. Such planning is not only to be considered from the point of view of economics and the raising of the standard of living, but must include cultural and spiritual values and the human side of life.
>
> (National Planning Committee, 1988, 51)

Defining planning as an activity consisting of "the technical co-ordination, by disinterested experts" may be indicative of the emergent middle-class "bourgeois" ideology that would come to dominate Nehruvian India but at the same time such a vision unleashes an informational program that comes to strongly influence and characterize the nature of the postcolonial formation. In other words, the idea of planning is inconceivable without the idea of information, and at the same time the project of planning would, as I discuss in the next section, be directly responsible for India's information revolution.

Though the vision of societal construction animated all segments of the intelligentsia, the "turn to planning" could not have come about without the express agency of a few individuals. In other words, the list of factors that lay behind the institution of a planned economy included a *discursive* element characterized by governmentality, a *material* element in the shape of science and technology, and finally, a *human* element that operated as a set of connections and influences that facilitated the crystallization of the nascent developmental and informational regime. Jawaharlal Nehru, the face of Indian politics after Gandhi, was the central figure in this respect. In a note directed at his fellow-member on the National Planning Committee, he wrote:

> To realize the social objectives, the state has to plan through its rep-resentatives … This planning will deal with production, distribution, consumption, investment, trade, income, social services and the many other forms of national activity which act and react on each other. Briefly put, planning aims at the raising of the material and cultural standard of living of the people as a whole.
>
> (Gopal, 1980, 306)

Nehru's devotion to the idea of planning was partly due to his strong commitment to a socialistic model of governance and his unabashed admiration for successes of the Soviet model. As he wrote to his daughter, "Everybody talks of 'Planning' now, … the Soviets have put magic into the world" (Chakrabarty, 1992, 278). Socialism also played a big part in the ideological makeup of another key figure in this saga—Netaji Subhas Chandra Bose. In his famous Haripura Presidential Address of 1938, Bose told Congress that "I have no doubt in my mind that our chief national problems … can be effectively tackled *only along socialistic lines*" (Bose, 1962, 12). Bose's fealty to socialism guaranteed an equally strong commitment to industrialization since "the rising generation are now thinking in terms of Socialism as the basis of national reconstruction and Socialism presupposes industrialization." Such a stance implied that "when we have a national government for the whole country, one of the first things we shall have to do is to appoint a National Planning Commission for the whole country" (52–54). Bose, in his capacity as the president of the Congress Party, would act on his beliefs by setting up the National Planning Committee in 1938 and appointing Nehru, his ideological bedfellow, albeit his political rival, as its chairman.

Bose's decision to set up a planning committee grew out of his own personal ties with Meghnad Saha, a classmate of his from his college days. Saha was an internationally renowned physicist—he had been elected as Fellow of the prestigious Royal Society in 1927—but in the mid-thirties he decided to "come out of the ivory tower" and turn his attention to social and cultural problems. In 1935 he founded the journal *Science and Culture* with two main objectives: interpreting and popularizing current scientific research, and applying scientific research in order to implement a technological revolution in the country. Saha was convinced that only total planning could lead to the sort of industrialization that he envisaged, and the arguments he put forth in the pages of his journal made a great impression on Bose. Consequently, when the National Planning Committee was set up, Saha was appointed as a member of the Core Committee as well as the chairman of two subcommittees: Fuel & Power and Education (Chatterjee, 1994).

Bose, Nehru, and Saha can be considered as the founding fathers of Indian planning. What their cooperation and collaboration illustrate is the emergence of a *network* around the issue of planning. The success they found in their endeavors also illustrates the power that networks—informational entities *par excellence*—possess in influencing the social process. The flow of ideas and information among these three individuals would come to have a disproportionate influence on the nation's immediate future. Moreover, this network quite literally represented the *fusion* of science and planning. Saha was a scientist who felt that science's role was to enable national planning; Bose and Nehru were political leaders who believed that planning (and a just politics) could not be implemented without being grounded in science. In a question-answer session with Saha, Bose remarked, "We, who are practical politicians, need your help, who are scientists in the shape of ideas … What is wanted is far-reaching co-operation between Science and Politics" (Bose, 1962, 54). Nehru was no less enthusiastic about the centrality of science for human life in general while addressing the Indian Science Congress held in Calcutta in 1937:

> In later years, through devious processes, I arrived again at science, when I realized that science was not only a pleasant diversion and abstraction, but was the very texture of life. … It was science alone that could solve these problems of hunger and poverty, of insanitation and illiteracy, of superstition and deadening custom and tradition, of vast resources running to waste, of a rich country inhabited by starving people.
>
> (Gopal, 1980, 442)

Nehru would soon part ways with Bose at Gandhi's insistence, while Saha's increasing commitment to leftist politics turned him into a vocal opponent of the Nehru regime.[10] But the Bose-Nehru-Saha network would have a great impact on the subsequent nature of the Indian postcolonial state insofar as the Nehruvian attachment to science, technology, and planning was partly a function of the lines of mutual influence connecting these three eminent "dots" or nodes.

I want to conclude this discussion of the intersection of science, planning, and information science by considering the case of P. C. Mahalanobis, the principal architect of the Second Five Year Plan (1951–61) and perhaps the single most influential figure in the history of Indian economic planning. Mahalanobis was a statistician of international repute and had been responsible for the founding of the Indian Statistical Institute in 1932, as well as the reputed statistical journal *Samkhya* (f. 1933). Like Bose, Nehru, and Saha,

Mahalanobis was yet another key mid-century figure who believed in the essential unity of science and planning. For him statistics was "essentially an applied science" whose "aim is to reach a decision, on a probabilistic basis, on available evidence" (1950, 210). This applied science was therefore at the very heart of planning. In an address to the American Statistical Association, he drew attention to the governmental benefits of statistics: "It had its origin in the counting of men or cattle ... the very word statistics shows its connection with 'statecraft,'" and that being so, "It is essential, in underdeveloped countries to make statistics purposive" (1965, 45–46). And in another address, entitled "Science and National Planning," this time to the National Institute of Sciences of India, Mahalanobis invoked Meghnad Saha's seminal studies on Indian rivers to stress that the task of scientists is to "formulate the shape of things to come ... in accordance with the methods of science. The two basic problems, poverty and unemployment, mentioned by Saha still remain as acute as ever. The only way out is through rapid industrial development based on *science and planning*" (1958, 69–70, italics mine). Mahalanobis is the appropriate figure with whom to end this discussion of the colonial roots of science, planning, and the information age. Not only did Mahalanobis found the discipline of statistics in India, but also in his later role as the chief architect of the Second Five-Year Plan he was instrumental in setting the tone of India's policy-making for the next three decades. The primary objective of the plan was to raise the level of living in the country by means of "rapid industrialization with particular emphasis on the development of basic and heavy industries" (Second Five Year Plan). The bias toward technology would become evident in the push for developing industries like coal, electricity, iron and steel, and chemicals. There was early recognition on the part of Mahalanobis and others that information technology was a resource as important as any of the "heavy" industries. Thus, the Indian Statistical Institute under Mahalanobis built the country's first analog computer in the early 1950s.[11] Recognizing the need for more advanced technology, Mahalanobis formed a small computer group at the Indian Statistical Institute (ISI) and ordered a computer from the British Tabulating Machines (BTM), which was at the time marketing keypunch machines, sorters, and mechanical calculators in India. BTM agreed to sell a computer to the ISI in 1954, though without any technical support. The ISI was to install and maintain the machine using its own scientists and engineers. The ISI sent two of its scientists to England to learn the basics of this HEC-2M (Hollerith Electronic Computer Model 2M) computer. The computer arrived in Kolkata in July 1955 and it started working in August 1955 (Rajaraman, 2012). The planning of India's information age had begun.

Let me review the argument made thus far. The purpose of this chapter is to understand the key components of the modern Indian state's relationship to information and information technology. Such an inquiry cannot be properly conducted without examining certain key aspects of the colonial state whose legacies formed the foundations of post-Independence India. As

I have shown, the colonial state was heavily invested in what may be termed "informative governmentality." That is, science and planning—practices that both generated and relied on information—were at the core of colonial rule. I have suggested that the nationalist movement that began to take shape at the end of the nineteenth century appropriated the colonial state's informational bent. To expand on this claim a little more, while nationalism has been typically analyzed as an oppositional discourse or liberating practice, there is another aspect to it that needs to be emphasized in this context. Because all nationalism contains within it a shadow state that imagines itself even as it waits for the moment of independence, as a *state-in-waiting* it assimilates and appropriates the tools of governmentality present in the colonial order. As I have shown, the colonial regime was informational to the extent that it relied crucially on science and planning in order to maintain its rule. The nationalist movement also adopted this informational stance even as it launched a movement to free the country. What the nationalist movement appropriated from colonial governmentality would in turn constitute the postcolonial state's inheritance. As is commonly recognized, the Nehruvian postcolonial order was as much a continuation of the colonial regime it replaced as a rupture with it. For example, several facets of the colonial state including the army, the police, the civil service, and public utilities survived the transition in almost totally intact form. Even the founding document of the new nation—the Indian Constitution—retained several key features of the 1935 Government of India Act passed by the British colonial state. It is not surprising in this context that informationalism as developed by both colonizers and nationalists would be strongly embraced by the independent Indian state. The moment of independence therefore is both the dawn of something new as well as the actualization of a structure of technologized governance that will be highly predisposed toward the vision of an info-nation.

The Computer and the Postcolonial State

As outlined in the section above, the Indian state that came into being in 1947 was ideologically close to its colonial predecessor in terms of its strong commitment to planned growth by scientific and technological means. A series of steps it took in the early years of independence established planning as the lynchpin of the new socio-economic order: the Industrial Policy Statement of 1948 decreed that most important industries would either be owned by the state or would be subject to its regulation, a Cabinet Resolution issued in March 1950 argued that "the need for comprehensive planning based on a careful appraisal of resources and on an objective analysis of all the relevant economic factors has become imperative," the Industrial (Development and Regulation) Act of 1951 introduced the infamous "licence raj" in an effort to bring private enterprise under the purview of governmental planning, and finally the implementation of the

First Five Year Plan in 1952 firmly defined the nation as a planned economy.[12] Though planning's importance was to diminish after the "opening up" of the economy in 1991, the five-year plans continue to exist with the Twelfth Five Year Plan (2012–17) currently in place.[13]

The Indian government would use planning as a means of strongly promoting the growth of science and technology. The Government of India's Scientific Policy Resolution (1958) observed that "the dominating feature of the contemporary world is the intense cultivation of science on a large scale" and went on to declare that the government's intent was to "foster ... the cultivation of science, and of scientific research in all its aspects" so as to "secure for the people of the country all the benefits. ... of scientific knowledge." The government's commitment to scientific development was evident in the actions it took. Between 1948–49 and 1959–60, state expenditure on scientific research rose tenfold from INR 10.8 million to INR 133.7 million (Arnold, 2013, 361). A number of premier scientific and technological institutions were set up in this period: the National Physical Lab (1947), the Indian Space Research Organization (1966), the Electronics Corporation of India Ltd. (1967), the Department of Electronics (1970), the Electronics Commission (1971), the National Informatics Centre (1975), the Centre for Development of Telematics (1984), the National Centre for Software Technology (NCST, 1985), and the Centre for Development of Advanced Computing (1988).

The building of India's first computer was part of this drive toward technology epitomized by Nehru's 1955 description of the newly constructed Bhakra Nangal Dam as the "New Temple of Resurgent India" (Schneider, 2005). What would prove crucial in this endeavor is the emergence of several micro-networks involving the state and private "citizen-scientists." In other words, the advance of state-sponsored technology would not have been possible without informational networks—that is, lines of connectivity between key individuals—acting as a potent catalyst. I have already shown how such a micro-network would help in the establishment of the National Planning Committee (NPC) in the immediate pre-Independence period. After Independence another such small but equally efficacious network—comprised of the physicists Homi Bhabha and Shanti Bhatnagar, the statistician turned economist Prasanta Mahalanobis as well as the inevitable figure of Jawaharlal Nehru—would play a very significant role in determining the direction in which science and technology would advance in the next two decades. Mahalanobis and Nehru got acquainted in the 1940s when Nehru visited the Indian Statistical Institute that the former had set up in Calcutta. Very impressed with Mahalanobis's deep commitment to scientific rationality as well as his refined artistic and philosophical tastes, Nehru commissioned him to prepare a statistical commentary on the reports of the National Planning Committee (NPC). After Independence, Nehru appointed him "Honorary Statistical Advisor to the Government of India" in which capacity he drafted the plan frame of the Second Five Year Plan, a document that defined India's developmental regime for a long time to come (Sharma, 2009, 41–47; Das, 2001, 88–91).

The first, and perhaps most important member of this second network, was a brilliant theoretical physicist who had been instrumental in setting up the privately funded Tata Institute of Fundamental Research and had been appointed as its first director in 1945. Homi Bhabha's prowess as a scientist—he had been elected to the prestigious post of Fellow of the Royal Society at the age of 32—brought him to Nehru's attention. Bhabha's advocacy of an independent nuclear program for India resonated with Nehru's desire for a self-sufficient nation. Consequently, Bhabha became the director of the Atomic Energy Commission (AEC) upon its establishment in 1948. As one commentator has noted, "Bhabha … was enjoying close personal ties with the Prime Minister, a rapport made possible to a large extent by the similar aristocratic backgrounds and educational experiences of the two men" (Blanpied, 1977, 95). So strong was their "rapport" that, during 1952 and 1953, Bhabha was having tea or dinner with Nehru every two weeks (Sharma, 2009, 43). The ties between the two men were fully cemented when Bhabha was fully inducted into the state apparatus with his appointment as the secretary of the Department of Atomic Energy, a post he was to hold until his tragic death in 1966.

The last member of this privileged and impactful network—Shanti Swarup Bhatnagar—was a noted chemist with an expertise in industrial chemistry. He was responsible for the setting up of the Council of Scientific and Industrial Research (1942), and was appointed by Nehru as its chairman after independence. Like Bhabha, he too ended up in government, serving as secretary in the Ministry of Education. The career paths of Bhabha, Bhatnagar, and Mahalanobis may lead us to conclude that the network they were part of was merely an instrument of the state. And given the crucial role that Nehru played as the node of this (and similar) networks, it is easy to conclude that the early postcolonial period was one of statist science. Thus, David Arnold has proposed the concept of "Nehruvian science" as a means of understanding postcolonial science in general. Such a science, according to him, had five main characteristics: it was undertaken to effect social transformation; was conducted for the people but at the direction and discretion of the state; was an institution-building project; was a way of renegotiating India's relation with the world; and was, finally, a historiographic project that sought to rejuvenate India's long scientific tradition (Arnold, 2013). Arnold is quite accurate in this characterization of state-led science, but there are two dangers associated with his use of the term "Nehruvian science" as a stand-in for all postcolonial science. First, Arnold asks us to think of science primarily as a matter of discourse. As he writes in the abstract to his essay, "The problem posed by Nehruvian science—the conflict between (yet simultaneity of) science as both universal phenomenon and local effect—lies at the heart of current debates about what science means for the non-West" (360). While we certainly need to consider what science *meant* in the early postcolonial era, postcolonial science cannot be reduced entirely to its discursive effects. In fact even while science was conducted in the name of the nation, scientific practice at the ground level would be constantly creating new connections and assemblages that could not necessarily be either envisioned or comprehended by its programmatic discourse. At the same time, such a moniker, perhaps unwittingly, nominates the state as the *only* agent of scientific enterprise. I would like to suggest that this was not the case. The behemoth that was the Indian state did loom large over every kind of scientific institution, program, or practitioner, but its reach and control was never co-extensive with what it sought to purview. For at the level of the network, there were multiple engagements, negotiations, alliances, and ventures that had little to do with the state's vision of science.

Consider the following two cases, both involving the same individual. In his capacity as the chief architect of India's Five Year Plans, Mahalanobis sought to develop the country's capital goods sector by building steel mills so that "we shall ... use the steel to produce more machinery to produce more steel and tools; and also to produce machinery to produce consumer goods" (Das, 2001, 90). Since the Indian state's commitment to a socialist pattern of society ruled out foreign investment, the Indian government had to turn to other nations for help. The West Germans assisted with the plant in Rourkela; the British at Durgapur; the Soviets in Bhillai. When India approached the United States for help with a fourth steel plant, the political exigencies then prevailing in U.S.-India relations led to a refusal on the part of the Americans. Finally, it was the Russians who would build the plant at Bokaro. While Mahalanobis as agent of the state would fail in his attempt to link with the world's most developed industrial nation, Mahalanobis functioning as a node in a network would be much more successful. I have already described the efforts made by Mahalanobis at the Indian Statistical Institute (ISI) to develop an analog computer and to install India's first digital computer as well. What I want to highlight here is that such an initiative was possible because of his personal networks. Mahalanobis had strong connections with scientists in Birbeck College in London, and these would pay off when he persuaded BTM, a British computer company, to custom-make a machine for his own institution. In particular, Mahalanobis was well acquainted with John Desmond Bernal, a scientist whose colleague Andrew Booth was a pioneer in computer science. Through the offices of Bernal and Booth, Mahalanobis connected with British Tabulating Machine, a commercial concern that sold computers developed by Booth; BTM subsequently customized and installed its HEC machine at Mahalanobis's request in 1955, making the ISI the computational center of the country.[14]

The above example testifies to the astonishing power of networks. In contrast to the state that operates by grand design and is thus often thwarted by grand forces outside of its control, networks are small, nimble, flexible, and opportunistic and can achieve large effects by being conjoined with other adjacent networks. An acquaintance, a conversation, a deal can lead to fruitful linkages and far-reaching consequences. Such was definitely the case with the first computers to come to India. Much like Mahalanobis at ISI, Homi Bhabha had embarked on a similar project at the Tata Institute of Fundamental Research (TIFR). Unlike Mahalanobis, Bhabha wanted an indigenous computer that would help build India's nuclear program and thus increase the nation's self-sufficiency in defense matters. For this purpose he enlisted the help of Rangaswamy Narasimhan, an electrical engineer who had recently returned from the United States. Using his closeness to Nehru, Bhabha was able to launch a project for building an indigenous computer, and under Narasimhan's leadership the TIFR launched a project for building a fully indigenous computer. As mentioned at the beginning of this chapter, this computer—India's truly first informational machine operationally functional by 1960—was formally inaugurated in 1962 by Nehru, setting in play the country's digital revolution.

A consideration of the early history of the computer leads to the insight that the statist formation is more than just the state itself. Alongside the state there exist other levels of engagement and effectiveness that cannot be wholly subsumed by or reduced to the state as a political and economic entity. In particular, every formation is characterized by layers and webs of networks that operate *below* the level of the state, and whose logic of operation has little to do with its larger programmatic vision. Whereas the state is hermetic, deterministic, ideological, and static (in conception), networks are open, probabilistic, instrumental, and dynamic. In other words, networks constitute a political and social ontology that is not wholly determined by the state. Indeed networks can function in such a manner that their effects are at odds with the goals of the state. Networks like those created by Mahalanobis, Bhabha, and many others did a lot to develop ties between India and western capitalist countries at a time when the Indian state presented itself as non-aligned, socialistic, and often veering toward the Soviet camp on matters of foreign and economic policy. The "Indian people" as such never shared the state's partiality for the Soviet bloc; the patterns of the Indian diaspora from the 1950s onward reveal that migration occurred along the pathways of previous networks. The complete collapse of the socialistic model after 1991 indicates that network logic and not that of the state may have represented the "truth" about the nation.

During India's non-aligned phase—a period marked by considerable frigidity on the part of the Indian state toward the capitalist West—small personalized networks were the primary instrument by means of which a silent but important connection was maintained between contemporary manifestations of global capital and "India" understood as a receptor of global trends and tendencies. These human networks may have been very tiny (in comparison to the immense networks of the digital age) but could still have a huge impact precisely because they operated within a quasi-command economy and society. To put it trivially, any network with

"Nehru" as a node could alter the lines of the nation's development. The Indian diaspora to the West from the 1950s onward created a secondary level of networks that also facilitated a process of transactions between the West and the subcontinent. One example would be the substantial and dispersed network created by the alumni of the prestigious Indian Institute of Technology centers whose location within the cutting-edge sectors of industry in the West meant a constantly expanding conduit for the exchange of scientific and technological information between India and the West.[15] Though this diaspora has been analyzed in cultural terms (using notions such as identity, acculturation, resistance, etc.), it also needs to be seen in less humanistic terms as a conduit between global capital and the closed economy in the subcontinent.

Networks—understood as informational entities—constitute a level of determination and effectivity that lie between the structural models of traditional sociology and biographical "great men" accounts that focus on individual lives and actions. Traditional progressive theory is typically reluctant to descend to any level below the highest—hence, its preoccupation with the vicissitudes of state formation. While such a move may be satisfying at a high theoretical level, it runs the risk of occluding processes situated at a level intermediate between structure and individual. On the other hand, accounts that focus only on the individual are faced with the perennial problem of generalizing on the basis of the purely contingent. Networks are structurally determined—thus, the Indian Institute of Technology (IIT) diaspora referred to above largely arose out of the U.S. economy's need for highly skilled labor as well as of the Indian economy's inability to provide employment to graduates—but they also resemble humans in that they are contingent, individualistic, and unpredictable and are thus more capable than the state (or capital) of "irrational" connections that yield surprising consequences. Thus the networks involving Bhabha and Mahalanobis were effective at this middle level. They arose within the context of the postcolonial state's drive to implement modern technology but could succeed in their goals because of the linkages that both Bhabha and Mahalanobis had established at a micro level. It was the efficacy of this mechanism that enabled the development of computer technology in the face of a climate that was resolute in its determination to keep automation at bay.[16]

The history of information technology in India yields many more striking examples of the power of small networks. The revolution that occurred in Indian telecommunications is usually credited to Sam Pitroda. When Sam Pitroda returned to India after working for 15 years in the U.S. telecom industry, the Indian telephony used traditional technology that was "switch-centric" with telephone exchanges occupying a central role in the flow of communication. Pitroda had been trained in the application of computers to telephony and had been instrumental in designing a digital telephonic switch (DSS580) with multimicroprocessor control. Pitroda shared his ideas with scientists at TIFR and the Department of Telecommunications

(DoT) who had connections at the high governmental level. As Pitroda recalls, "Fortunately, I had an opportunity to make a presentation to the then Prime Minister Indira Gandhi, on a plan to modernize telecom institutions and infrastructures" (Pitroda, 2011, 121). This fortuitous encounter led, in 1984, to the formation of the Center for Development of Telematics (C-DOT) with the purpose of indigenizing digital switching technology to meet India's unique requirements.

To use network science terminology in a loose way, Pitroda was the "edge"—the line between two vertices or nodes—that connected American technical practice with Mrs. Gandhi, the node that mattered. And if she proved surprisingly open to a suggestion that would eventually lead to a dilution of the government's control over communications, then her son Rajiv Gandhi, in his capacity as his mother's successor, proved to be even more receptive to the lure of informational technology. Pitroda was just one member of a particularly influential network that coalesced around him. Rajiv Gandhi's extensive training and experience as an airline pilot had fostered a deep and abiding interest in technology—he was an early adapter of laptops and was reputedly the first Indian to own a Sony Walkman. As Dinesh Sharma has noted in his superb history of the Indian IT industry, Rajiv's circle was unique at the time since "this was the first time private sector executives and techies—not politicos or IAS officers—found a place in the inner circle around an Indian prime minister" (2009, 137). One consequence of this new network was the passage of a series of measures and initiatives that would have been inconceivable at an earlier time: the New Computer Policy of 1984, the setting up of a new Department of Telecommunications (DoT) in 1985, the liberalization of restrictions on the importation of electronics, the computerization of the railway reservation system and banks, and—as just mentioned above—the setting up of C-DOT under the leadership of Sam Pitroda.

Let me recap, once more, the argument made so far in this chapter. My central claim here is that information—as technology, as instrumentality, and as ideology—played a very significant role in shaping postcolonial India. The entire span of Indian postcolonial history can be conceptualized under three rubrics: "1947," "The Nehruvian era," and "Liberalization." For me, "1947" refers not merely to the moment of independence, but also more broadly to the substantive legacy bequeathed by the colonial state to its successor. As I have shown in the first section of this chapter, the computer revolution in India was made possible by a regime of planning that had its origins in colonial and nationalist governmentality. The newly formed postcolonial state was strongly committed to a planned development based on investment in science and technology. That an underdeveloped country like India would manufacture an indigenous computer as early as 1962 can only be explained by identifying the continuity between the colonial state and free India. Yet, while colonial India was in many respects a "western" formation whose governing logic was determined at the center, the Nehruvian era can be characterized as period of socialist autarky that envisioned a path of development that would be independent of the demands of the capitalist West. Such a hermetic vision may not have been open to the implementation of a modern technology that was only available by means of collaboration with the very economies of which Nehruvian autarky wanted to be independent.

Thus, an ambiguity surrounding modernity, such that desire for its substantial achievements was accompanied by a disavowal of its socio-economic foundations, provided the frame within which informationalism had to evolve. As my discussion of some the luminaries behind India's information revolution demonstrates, information in the shape of micro-networks played a key role in generating a "leakage" that ensured that the Indian state's relation to global capital was not as minimal as its leaders intended. Small personal networks, like Nehru-Mahalanobis-Bernal, as well as macro-scale networks emerging out of the Indian diaspora meant that information flowed across the "swadeshi curtain" with an intensity that was sufficient to disturb the autarkic republic. To take one highly instructive example, in 1972, at the height of the "Garibi Hatao" socialist phase under Nehru's daughter Indira Gandhi, when government policies ostensibly focused only on the needs of the very poor, the government of India introduced the Software Export Scheme, an initiative that strongly acknowledged the existence and utility of the global marketplace. Such an initiative alerts us to the role played by information, understood as a complex composed of technology, ideas, and business practice, in mediating the relationship between capital and the postcolonial state. It is the argument of this concluding section of this chapter that the information sector functioned as a vital bridge linking the Indian economy to the capitalist West. Thus, information not only destabilized the autarkic model set up at Independence, but the development of the information sector also presaged and prepared the way for the climacteric events of 1991 that inaugurated India's "liberalization."

The question regarding the relationship of the postcolonial state to capital is a contested one: for champions of the liberalization model the Nehruvian state was at best an impediment and, at worst, an enemy of capital. Thus the noted free-market economist Arvind Panagariya describes the period 1950–80 as the "Lost Decades" when India failed to bring down poverty. The reason for this failure lay in the fact that the problem was "that India progressively turned inward and replaced Adam Smith's invisible hand by the government's visible hand" (2013, 8). Similarly, Gurucharan Das, a best-selling commentator on India's recent history observes, "The mixed economy ended up in combining the worst features of socialism and capitalism—the 'controls' of socialism with the 'monopolies and lobbies' of capitalism—and we got the worst of both worlds" (2001, 98).

This "free-market" view posits that the early postcolonial period was characterized by a regrettable self-imposed divergence from the liberating energies of global capital. Not only was the economy deprived of the advantages of the global financial order, but also, as Das alleges, whatever domestic capital existed was perverted by the absence of the "invisible hand." For this perspective the liberalization of the economy in 1991 was a rupture that allowed capital to emerge from the suffocating clutches of the planned economy (and the attendant "Hindu rate of growth") and thus propel India toward a "shining" future. However, from the perspective of the Indian left, things appear to be diametrically opposite: the entire postcolonial period is read by Marxist scholars and their allies as one long progression toward an unabashed and deleterious capitalist order. Thus Prakash Karat, the ex-general secretary and one of the chief theoreticians of the Communist Party of India (Marxist), argues that the Indian bourgeoisie failed to engineer a democratic revolution and instead struck an alliance with the feudal land-lord class. In this scenario "State power was used as an instrument to accumulate capital and to serve the interests of the bourgeois-landlord classes. Thus, the economic policies of successive governments perpetuated and intensified the exploitation of the people by the bourgeois-landlord combine led by the big bourgeoisie" (Karat, 2000). Though other thinkers from the Left offer somewhat more nuanced accounts of this relationship, the overall analysis remains the same. Thus Partha Chatterjee, a leading representative of the neo-Marxist Subaltern School, observes that capitalism in India asserted itself by means of a "passive revolution" in that capital did not achieve full hegemony over civil society as in the western world and, thus, needed to construct a "synthetic hegemony" over the domains of both civil society and the pre-capitalist community. In such a situation "The reification of the 'nation' in the body of the state ... becomes a precondition for further capitalist development" (Chatterjee, 1993, 212). In other words, as in Karat's characterization, the primary function of the postcolonial state is to further the interests of capital, albeit in a partial and hesitant manner.

A close look at the development of the information sector following the installation of TIFRAC complicates the narrative concerning capital and the postcolonial state. The "left" analysis is quite correct in one respect: the Indian state quite clearly entered into a partnership with domestic capital from the moment India became independent.[17] Whatever irritations local industrialists felt because of the license raj and bureaucratic red tape, the relation between major industrial houses and the "socialist" state was in no ways antagonistic or contradictory. Indeed, it is an agreed upon fact that state protection allowed domestic capital to make undue profits at the expense of the public. The near monopolistic nature of domestic capital allowed it to save costs on advertising, customer relations, and service and facilitated price rigging because of the absence of a competitive market. At the same time, however, the Indian state's relationship with global capital was far less amicable. The commitment to a socialist path to development engendered a reflexive paranoia concerning the doings of foreign powers. Such a psychology led to a range of protectionist policies that closed the Indian market to foreign investment. Whatever foreign presence was allowed in was typically subject to intense scrutiny and suspicion. Thus the Industrial

Policy Resolution of 1948, which set the tone for the country's financial philosophy, held that foreign investment had to "be carefully regulated in the national interest" and that "as a rule, majority interest in ownership and effective control should always be in Indian hands." (India's Industrial Policies). Though the government's attitude to foreign investment softened a bit during the 1960s, by the end of the decade it had hardened again. Banks were nationalized, as were foreign-owned oil companies. The passage of the Foreign Exchange Regulations Act (FERA) in 1973—requiring that all firms dilute their foreign holdings to 40%—summed up the Indian state's highly antagonistic stance toward global capital. FERA was only a part of the new regulatory regime. Limits on foreign equity holdings were also combined with restrictions on technology imports. Fresh lists were drawn up of industries where foreign collaboration was still considered necessary; others, where only technical collaborations was permitted, with curtailed rates of royalty payment; and those where the domestic technological base was considered strong enough to obviate the need for imports of technology (see Athreye and Kapoor, 1999).

In other words, the postcolonial state's stance toward capital in general was both complex and contradictory: abetting and colluding with domestic capital, on the one hand, and hostile and intransigent to global capital on the other. The liberalization of the economy that took place in 1991 can be seen as a sweeping resolution of this contradiction. The wholesale restructuring of existing licensing policies and the removal of restrictions for foreign capital meant that henceforth India would embark on a path of complete integration with the free-market economic order. Thus, 1991 symbolically marked the death of the Nehruvian regime. The coming of the new liberalized order is often explained in terms of crisis and desperation: due to a long process of slow growth and economic setbacks, India's foreign exchange reserves stood at a mere $1.2 billion in January 1991. By June, there was only enough money to pay for three weeks of essential imports; thus, India was only weeks way from defaulting on its external balance of payment obligations. Faced with such a traumatic situation, the newly elected Congress government led by Narasimha Rao decided, under severe pressure from the IMF and World Bank, to go in for the set of reforms that constituted the phenomenon termed "liberalization."[18]

Such a narrative posits a sharp distinction between the Nehruvian and liberalized regimes, seeing the former as intransigently hostile to global capital and the latter as wholeheartedly welcoming of it. An analysis of India's information sector in the Nehruvian period complicates this tidy dichotomy. As even a cursory glance at the development of the computer industry will show, contrary to the received wisdom, the postcolonial state was establishing ties with global capital even at the height of the autarkic period. It is not happenstance that this covert, almost surreptitious, engagement took place in the manner that it did. The very nature of informational practices, I suggest, dictated that the state compromise its hardline ideology about foreign capital and overseas partners. The new informational technology was characterized by several features that would militate against the closing of economic borders: speed of transmission, scope of reach, constant upgrading of hardware and software, heightened obsolescence, and increasingly complex levels of connectivity. Thus, the decision to implement information technology, born of the Indian state's commitment to planned growth, would lead to a "handshake" between the state and its externalities that would lead to the dissolution of the autarkic model.[19] The post-TIFRAC period is marked by successive events that demonstrate how the digital domain provides a site for the postcolonial state's increasing engagement with global capital: the allowing of software export, the relaxation of import restrictions, the creation of Special Economic Zones (SEZ), the institution of body shopping, the opening of doors for foreign multinationals, and finally the wholesale integration of the software industry into the global marketplace. In short, the saga of the information sector in Nehruvian postcolonial India both enacts and predicts the large-scale changes brought about by liberalization.

In the immediate period after Independence, the history of information was in step with the general history of postcoloniality. Thus, as in heavy industries and sensitive sectors like defense and transportation, it was thought that the country also needed to be self-reliant in the emerging computer technologies in order to keep the nation on the professed path of self-reliant growth. Consequently, as one early analyst noted, India possessed "one of the world's most restrictive, cumbersome, and 'assertive' regimes regulating foreign direct investments" with regard to computer technology (Grieco, 1984, 16–17). It needs to be remembered that Homi Bhabha, the driving force behind the TIFRAC, was a committed nationalist who was also responsible for the country's atomic energy program. Bhabha's chief concern, one he shared with Nehru, was for self-reliance in crucial industries and technologies. Not surprisingly, the report issued by the Electronic Committee of India 1966 (chaired by Bhabha and known eponymously as the Bhabha Report) laid out the blueprint for the development of an indigenous electronics sector that would include computer technology along with other fields of telecommunications. The plan envisaged that:

> Starting with the existing electronic, electro-mechanical and ancillary industries, and by proper planning and coordinated growth of computer technology in the country, it is entirely feasible technically to become self-sufficient in the manufacture of computers of a wide variety of kinds within this period of ten years.
>
> (Greico, 1984, 22)

Though Bhabha's successors were less than sanguine about this promise of self-sufficiency, the steps they undertook were in keeping with the spirit of autarky to which both he and the Indian government were committed.

Bhabha died tragically in an air crash in January 1966, but his successors would persevere with the philosophy of self-reliance that he had championed. Thus, in 1970 the government established the Department of Electronics (DoE) as well as the Electronics Commission (EC) to ensure the proper implementation of the computer policies suggested by the Bhabha Report. Under the guidance of these two bodies, the Electronics Commission of India Limited (ECIL)—a commercial body that had been established in 1967 under the aegis of the Department of Atomic Energy (DAE)—came to play a crucial part in defining the role and status of computer technology in the decade to come. The ECIL was a nationalist organization par excellence, protected from both foreign and domestic competition so that it could become, in the words of one of its directors, "a national champion" in the field of computers and "to market a totally indigenous system, indigenous in design, assembly and materials" (Subramaniam, 2006, 179).

In spite of such a resolution, from its very beginning ECIL moved away from the autarkic model and adopted a "systems engineering" approach that amounted to importing components and peripherals from international manufacturers and assembling them into Indian-designed systems. The mode of manufacture was not the only arena where socialistic enterprise had to submit to the forces of capital, for it was soon compelled to share the domestic marketplace with private capital—both foreign and domestic. Though TIFRAC had been inaugurated with much fanfare, in the early sixties IBM, then the world's most dominant computer manufacturer, had held an almost monopolistic control over the Indian marketplace. Thus, in the period 1960–66 it accounted for a full three-quarters of all computer systems installed in the country, and it continued to dominate in the period 1967–72 as well holding 70% of market share.[20] After Indira Gandhi's resounding win in the general elections of 1971, the government made a sharp turn to the left and passed FERA (Foreign Exchange Regulation Act, 1973), an act aimed at severely limiting the presence of foreign capital in the country. In keeping with the wave of nationalization of key industries that she had initiated, the act stipulated that those foreign companies whose nonresident interest was more than 40% would henceforth have to seek the Reserve Bank's permission to continue operations in India. IBM had been one of the few companies with 100% foreign ownership operating in India, and it was loath to give up this distinction on the grounds that IBM was an integrated multinational company whose effectivity depended upon freedom from local control. The next few years saw several rounds of negotiations between the two parties, but no common ground could be found. As a result, IBM "withdrew" from India between January and June 1978. This departure did not mean that the computer industry was now safely in the hands of state-owned capital. Two foreign concerns—ICL (a British computer company) and Burroughs—indigenized themselves in accordance with FERA rules. ICL became the International Computers Indian Manufacture Limited (ICIM) while Burroughs started a joint venture with a major Indian industrial group and Tata-Burroughs. The withdrawal of IBM also created an opening for domestic computer manufacturers. Two companies—DCM (a division of the large Delhi Cloth and General Mills Company Limited) and HCL—stepped in very quickly to fill the void left by IBM's departure. In other words, all that IBM's departure signified was the replacement of one form of private capital by another.

The trajectory of the computer industry in the 1967–78 period can thus be seen as an ambiguous period in which the principles of Nehruvian post-coloniality were both being strengthened and diluted at the same time. On the hand, the establishment of ECIL and the passage of FERA were in keeping with the state's avowed mission to create a self-sufficient society based on socialistic principles. On the other hand, the dictates of technology and pragmatic decision-making meant that the face of the computer industry would not resemble the traditional nationalist sectors like steel or coal. The most interesting development in this regard was the setting up of export processing zones (EPZ) that would not be subject to the usual tariffs and duties levied on any sort of international trade. The first such EPZ was opened in 1965 in Kandla, a port town in the state of Gujarat. However, it is the Santa Cruz Electronics Export Processing Zone (SEEPZ), located in Andheri East, Mumbai, which is of more relevance to this present discussion. SEEPZ was set up in 1973 as single-product Export Processing Zone that would exclusively manufacture and export electronic items, with the objective "of (a) accelerating the progress of electronics manufacturing in India and (b) to take advantage of the growing electronics world market" (Special Economic Zone, 2015). Though this initiative could be seen as a cynical move to earn badly needed foreign exchange, it had a couple of implications that went far beyond petty calculation. First of all, there was the implicit recognition that India needed to enter the global marketplace and that doing so meant playing by rules that transgressed the autarkic principle. Second, it also signaled an implicit recognition that India had the potential to export a high-technology item. This must have come as welcome news, for in fiscal year 1972–73 Indian exports totaled INR 1607 crores while imports amounted to INR 1812 crores.[21] As the Indian government's budget statement observed, "By all accounts 1972–73 will be remembered as a very difficult year for the Indian economy," and emphasized "the urgent need for effective measures to further step up exports" (Government of India Budget Statement, 1973).

The SEEPZ scheme would be a small but promising way to step up the export sector. The announcement of the scheme had the effect of enticing the giant U.S. company, Burroughs, which then ranked amongst the top 10 computer companies in the world, to enter India and set up a joint venture with the fledgling Tata Consulting Services (TCS). TCS had been established in 1968 and was already exporting software to corporations in the United States, but its collaboration with Burroughs that began in 1975 was to vastly increase the scope and size of its operations. By 1979 Tata-Burroughs employed over 150 people in the software export program and was earning hard currency to the tune of $3 million. Most importantly, the collaboration with Burroughs gave India's software professionals an intimate knowledge concerning global business practices and would thus serve as a springboard for the growth of the entire software industry. In the words of one commentator, "The Indian software saga ... began in SEEPZ Mumbai" (Aggarwal, 2006, 4533).

The Export Processing Zone model gave birth to the phenomenon known, somewhat notoriously, as "bodyshopping." It was TCS that spearheaded the practice of sending software personnel to the United States, United Kingdom, and other countries to work on-site on temporary projects. Bodyshopping dominated the industry in the 1980s, as a consequence of utilizing the principle of mutual advantage. Most bodyshopped professionals were employees of Indian-owned firms, which meant that U.S. companies that hired them could use their skills without worrying about training, housing, salaries, and health benefits. At the same time Indian companies were given the chance to make lucrative profits with the government's support. Bodyshopping, however, was destined to be a short-lived phenomenon. Thus, the proportion of earnings from on-site contracts fell from 90% in 1988 to 56% in 1999 and then to 46% in 2003 (Upadhya, 2004, 5142). Bodyshopping declined because it was progressively replaced by a practice that has come to stand for the face, and current fate, of the Indian software industry. Offshoring— the implementation of IT services, Business Process Outsourcing (BPO), and Software Products and Engineering services from within India—would soon become the main engine for the remarkable growth of the Indian industry. Buoyed by the revenues generated by offshoring (also known as outsourcing), Indian software exports increased from Euro 5.93 billion in 2003–04 to Euro 20.20 billion in 2008–09, and the industry saw an astonishing growth rate of almost 25% (Malik, 2011). The decision to set up the Santa Cruz Electronic Export Zone as early as 1965 points to the vanguard role played by the information industry in mediating the relationship between the Indian state and global capital. Even as the country was intensifying its quest for autonomy through widely publicized initiatives like the FERA, it was taking hesitant and discreet measures to ensure that the economy maintained some linkages with the world outside. In other words, the adoption of contemporary modes of information technology and information management meant that the Indian state was compelled to reach out and build specific linkages with global firms and institutions in spite of its professed commitment to economic autarky. Thus, the lineaments of the info-nation were gradually put in place.

I want to end this chapter by briefly mentioning three state initiatives— the 1978 minicomputer policy, the New Computer and Software Policies of 1984 and 1986, and the decision to set up software technology parks (STPs) in 1990—that further confirm the thesis that the information sector was the site where the state "rehearsed" its turn to the free market before the liberalization of 1991. Each of these initiatives demonstrates that the state neither was a passive observer of developments in the computer/software sector nor was guilty of a "benign neglect" that allowed the industry to progress without being hampered by the obstacles of government bureaucracy.[22] In 1978, in the wake of the crisis engendered by IBM's departure from the Indian market, the government set up a committee to review the progress of electronics and computing. The committee suggested that special focus be placed on the development of minicomputers and microcomputers, given their increasing use in the business environment, but most crucially it recommended that private companies be allowed to manufacture these instruments. While the government-owned ECIL would continue to have sole rights for the manufacture of minicomputers (or super-microcomputers) and mainframes, the committee felt that small-scale entrepreneurs should be preferred for manufacturing special-purpose computers for dedicated applications such as data entry, data acquisition, accounting and invoicing, typesetting, and dedicated controllers (Rajaraman, 2012). Though the government tried hard to preserve a protected market for ECIL, these private firms were so successful that ECIL's market share went down from 52% in the period 1973–77 to only 10% in the period 1978–80. Thus two companies, HCL and DCM, captured more than 67% of the market between them, ending ECIL's short-lived reign as "national champion." As a consequence of this policy, the government "was in retreat in terms of using ECIL as the major (if not the only) indigenous supplier of systems" (Greico, 1984, 100).

The opening up of the computer industry would be accelerated by the passage of two subsequent policy enactments: the New Computer Policy (NCP) of 1984 and a policy on software export passed in 1986. In 1981, the government appointed Narasimaiah Seshagiri as director of the newly established National Informatics Centre. Seshagiri had to deal with the fact that the minicomputer policy had not yielded all the desired results—over 80 companies had been given licenses to manufacture minicomputers but only six had gone into production (Sharma, 2009, 135). Seshagiri noticed four negative factors responsible for the poor state of affairs of the nation's IT: the foreign exchange crisis, the prevailing anti-automation sentiment, lack of computer awareness and promotion measures, and the attitude of the Department of Electronics insiders, who became powermongers and refused to or delayed granting approvals for importing computers even in the most deserving cases. Under these circumstances, Seshagiri decided to work on the liberalization of the computer policy. Seshagiri characterized the 1984 NCP as "flood in, flood out"—flood the nation with imports and cause a larger flood of software exports (Subramanium, 2006, 38). The NCP eased the availability of computers in India by reducing the software import tariffs from 100% to 60%, and within a year of its implementation computer production grew by 100% while prices fell by 50%. Software exports too began to look up, amounting to approximately $30 million in 1985. Recognizing its huge potential, the government then introduced a policy on computer software export, development, and training whose objective was to "promote software exports to take a quantum jump and capture a sizable share in the international market" (Sharma, 2009, 140).

The last development of note that occurred in the computer/software industry before liberalization was the establishment of software technology parks (STP) to facilitate software exports. The idea behind STPs came from a proposal by Sharad Marathe, an engineer who had worked in the technology sector in the United States. Marathe realized that while India was very backward in terms of hardware and infrastructure and thus could never emulate other Asian countries like South Korea or Taiwan, it did possess a huge pool of highly qualified engineers and programmers. Marathe's revolutionary proposal was the creation of duty-free, privately managed technology parks that could attract investments and boost exports in the software industry. Almost at the same time, Seshagiri, in his capacity as director of computers at the Department of Electronics, wrote a report commissioned by UNESCO that proposed the institution of an informatics network "capable of utilizing satellites and service communication systems" (Sharma, 2009, 307). While a private company set up by Marathe for this purpose would fail, the idea of offshore development was picked up by Texas Instruments, the first foreign firm to establish a direct satellite link for offshore software development. While Texas Instruments was very successful in creating an efficient system for sending data to the United States via satellite, the private Indian companies that had been granted licenses to set up STPs could not replicate this success. The main hindrance was the lack of a satisfactory telecommunications infrastructure, specifically the lack of high-speed connectivity that was so crucial for the software industry. Realizing this deficiency, the government decided to set up state-sponsored STPs that could be utilized by Indian companies to attract foreign companies and to encourage small and medium domestic entrepreneurs to enter the software industry. The first STPs were established in Bangalore, Pune, and Bhubenswar in 1990 and within two decades there were as many as 47 such centers operating across the country (Vaidyanathan, 2008, 288).

As a noted economist has observed, STPs "were to radically transform the environment for software production in India and thus the Indian IT industry. The STP, by providing an exclusive state-of-the-art physical site for software production, especially access to high-speed communication channels, enabled the Indian IT industry to sidestep the infra-structure constraint that is stoically faced by the rest of India's manufacturing sector ... The rise of the offshore model reflected the rising confidence in the Indian software firm worldwide" (Balakrishnan, 2006, 3869). Such an assessment is borne out by current statistics from the software sector. Export figures for STP registered units stood at INR 2,51,498 crores in 2012–13, with 133 new units added on in a single year (STPI Annual Report, 2012–13).[23]

There is a common thread running through the establishment of Special Economic Zones, the passage of the minicomputer and New Computer policies, and the introduction of software technology parks. All these instances collectively symbolize the information sector's unique role in mediating the relationship between the postcolonial state and capitalist democracy. Information stood at the fault line between two "drives," one demanding that the country be dedicated to a "socialist path" that would make the nation autonomous with regard to the world capitalist order, and a second goal calling for the adoption of current technological goods and practices in order to steer the nation into modernity. The creation of the Santa Cruz Electronic Export Processing Zone indicated the state's willingness to participate in international trade even as it sought to protect the economy at large from the forces of global capital. In particular, the early linking of software to exports would presage the contours of India's trade patterns in the coming years. The passage of the minicomputer and new computer policies showed the state's reluctant concession that state-owned enterprises—the failure of ECIL to become the "national champion" is a notable case in point—were incapable of delivering on their promises. The state's response to this predicament meant that foreign capital could re-enter the Indian marketplace through the mechanism of joint-venture companies. Further, the 1984 and 1986 computer policies allowed domestic capital to display its vitality and thus become a viable alternative to the public sector. Finally, the establishment of software technology parks showed that the state had come to accept unbridled capitalism as a legitimate mode of economic activity within the larger framework of "socialism." The STPs—enterprises that were defined as a single-window clearance mechanism for software exports that could be wholly foreign-owned and that were exempt from normal export-import duties—represented a new model for Indian capitalism that was far more in tune with global "best practices." The entire trajectory from the SEZ to the STP can be described as one of "understanding global capital"—first, the industry understood global capital in the sense of figuring out its logic and demands, and second, it also came to a series of understandings with it in terms of discreet arrangements that ensured that the computer industry would be thoroughly integrated within the global network. It is thus no coincidence that the STPs were created just one year before the liberalization of 1991 that would turn India toward an unabashedly free-market model of governance.

As the title of this chapter suggests, an analysis of "The Computer in Postcolonial History" yields two substantial insights into the making of an info-nation. The decision to build an indigenous calculating machine was, as I have shown, the consequence of a centuries-old process that sought to link information and governance. In other words, the info-nation that is being aspired to in the new millennium was present in nascent form throughout the course of colonial and postcolonial history. While TIFRAC points us backward, it also portends the future of the postcolonial state. The push toward an info-nation is also predicated on reconstituting the balance between state and capital within the postcolonial formation. The information sector, as this chapter also demonstrates, becomes the fulcrum on which such an exercise is conducted. This chapter, then, analyzes the historical dimensions of the idea of an info-nation. The next chapter turns to the contemporary moment to show how information has an equally important function in modulating notions of citizenry and governance with the goal of creating an "informational state."

Notes

1. Such a goal has been partially realized in the realms of capital, state, and civil society. As of 2014, the Indian software industry would achieve export revenues of $87 billion, the Indian state was busy announcing plans for smart cities and a "Digital India," and the public at large was thoroughly immersed in the informational matrix due to the explosive growth of cell telephony, social media, and computer-mediated technology.

2. India's current GDP is the world's tenth largest by current prices and the third largest by purchasing power parity (Knoema, 2014). And as of February 2015, it had dethroned China as the world's fastest-growing big economy (Bellman, 2015).

3. A representative example of the latter approach is the Marxist historian Jairus Banaji's claim that "colonialism must be understood in terms of a specific mode of production, neither feudal or capitalist, though 'resembling' both at different levels" (1972). It needs to be pointed out that such formulations were driven by the need to plot the Indian formation within the grid of historical materialism in order to determine the correct political strategy for the moment.

4. See, for example, Dirks (1987) and Ludden (1993) as well as the work of the Subaltern School historians.

5. India is currently in the midst of its Twelfth Five Year Plan (2012–17). Though the current BJP government abolished the 65-year-old Planning Commission that produced these five-year plans and replaced it with a think tank NITI (National Institute for Transforming India), it remains to be seen if planning will lose its centrality in the years ahead.

6. For a fascinating account of the discursive logic behind this colonial imprinting, see Goswami (2004).

7. Partha Chatterjee has argued that the colonial state needs to be understood as being constituted by a "rule of difference" in that, however universal its abstract philosophy of governance, it was marked "by one factor that united the ruling bloc and separated it from those over whom it ruled. Marking this difference was race" (1994, 19). As far as the Indian public was concerned, such a rule of difference did not compromise the value of western science.

8. The wholesale acceptance of "western science" may have been due to the fact scientific activity was not as foreign to the region as some commentators have assumed. Thus, as Kapil Raj points out, "South Asia was not a space for the simple application of European knowledge, nor a vast site for the collection of diverse information to be processed in the metropolis … [but] was an active, if unequal, participant in an emerging world order of knowledge" (2007, 13).

9. David Ludden (1992) has argued persuasively that even the colonial state can be thought of as a "development regime" committed to the idea of state-guided progress for the entire citizenry.

10. In 1939 Bose was re-elected as president of the Congress Party but was forced to resign at Gandhi's urgings. Nehru, though ideologically close to Bose, did not come to his rival's rescue. Bose was compelled to leave the Congress and pursue an adventurous course that ended with his mysterious death in 1945. Saha enjoyed a prestigious career after Independence, using his leverage with the Central government to obtain funds for the Institute of Nuclear Physics, of which he became the director. Yet Nehru and he had strong disagreement about the nature of scientific institutions in India; these differences proved so great that Saha stood for and won a parliamentary seat as an independent member

opposed to the Congress Party and government. By the time of his death in 1956, his connections with Nehru were entirely a matter of the past.

11. In 1955, the Indian Statistical Institute imported India's first digital computer, a HEC-2M machine manufactured by the British Tabulating Machine Company. Two years earlier, researchers at the ISI had built the country's first analog computer (Sinha, 2012).

12. "Licence Raj" is the term used to describe the strict regulation of the private sector in India between 1947 and the early 1990s.

13. In his Independence Day Address on August 15, 2014, Prime Minister Narendra Modi announced that the Planning Commission would be disbanded and replaced by a more appropriate body. At the time of writing, no such body had been constituted. It remains to be seen if the five-year plans will follow the Planning Commission into retirement.

14. Mahalanobis had network connections with Soviet scientists as well, and the Russian Ural computer was installed in ISI in 1958.

15. The magnitude of this diaspora was immense—one study showed that one-third of students who graduated from IIT Bombay in the mid-seventies ended up settling abroad (Murali, 2003).

16. This inauguration seems all the more miraculous when we note that resistance to computers was very long-lived—thus, the computerization of the Indian railway ticketing system was held up for years by a recalcitrant bureaucracy and was only achieved in the 1980s (see Sharma, 2009).

17. As many have argued, the nationalist movement itself—the figure of Gandhi not excluded—was in bed with the Indian bourgeoisie from the beginning of the twentieth century.

18. For a representative version of this standard account, see Chandra et al. (2000).

19. In technical language a "handshake" refers to communication between a computer system and an external device, by which each tells the other that data is ready to be transferred and that the receiver is ready to accept it.

20. See Greico (1984) for an extended discussion. I am indebted to his text for much of the data included in the next two paragraphs.

21. A crore equals 10 million. In 1973, the official conversion rate was $1 = Rs. 6.550 (International Economics, 2015).

22. For a superb analysis of these two viewpoints, see Balakrishnan (2006).

23. The Indian software and services exports, including information technology enabled services (ITES)/BPM, are estimated at US$75.8 billion in 2012–13 (STPI Annual Report 2012–13).

References

Aggarwal, Aradhna. 2006. Special Economic Zones: Revisiting the Policy Debates. *Economic and Political Weekly*, 41(43/44), 4533–36.

Arnold, David. 2000. *Science, Technology and Medicine in Colonial India*. Cambridge: Cambridge University Press.

Arnold, David. 2013. Nehruvian Science and Postcolonial India. *Isis, 104*, 360–70.

Athreye S. and S. Kapur. 1999. Foreign Controlled Manufacturing Firms in India: Long Term Trends. *Economic and Political Weekly*, 34(48), 149–151.

Austin, Granville. 1999. *The Indian Constitution: Cornerstone of a Nation*. New Delhi: Oxford University Press.

Balakrishnan, Pulapre. 2006. Benign Neglect or Strategic Intent? Contested Lineage of Indian Software Industry. *Economic and Political Weekly*, 41(36), 3865–72.

Banaji, Jairus. 1972. For a Theory of Colonial Modes of Production. *Economic and Political Weekly*, 7(52), 2498–2502.

Basu, Aparna. 1991. The Indian Response to Scientific and Technical Education in the Colonial Era, 1820–1920. In Deepak Kumar (Ed.), *Science and Empire: Essays in Indian Context (1700–1947)* (pp. 126–38). New Delhi: Anamika Prakashan.

Bellman, Eric. 2015. India Passes China to Become Fastest-Growing Economy. *Wall Street Journal*. Retrieved March 9, 2015, from http://blogs.wsj.com/indiarealtime/2015/02/11/its-official-india-has-passed-china-to-become-the-worlds-fastest-growing-economy/.

Blanpied, William. 1977. "Pioneer Scientists in Pre-Independence India." *Physics Today*, May 1986, pp. 36–44. Retrieved October 13, 2015, from http://iucaa-rpl.weebly.com/uploads/1/7/1/7/17179300/pioneer.pdf.

Bose, Subhas Chandra. 1962. *Crossroads: Being the Works of Subhas Chandra Bose 1938–1940*. New York: Asia Publishing House.

Cabinet Resolution. 1950. Government of India's Resolution setting up the Planning Commission. Retrieved March 7, 2015, from http://planningcommission.nic.in/aboutus/history/PCresolution1950.pdf.

Chakrabarty, Bidyut. 1992. Jawaharlal Nehru and Planning, 1938–41: India at the Crossroads. *Modern Asian Studies, 26*(2), 275–87.

Chakrabarty, Dipesh. 2002. *Habitations of Modernity: Essays in the Wake of Subaltern Studies*. Chicago: University of Chicago Press.

Chakrabarti, Pratik. 2004. *Western Science in Modern India: Metropolitan Methods, Colonial Practices*. New Delhi: Permanent Black.

Chandra, Bipan, Mriduala Mukherjee, and Aditya Mukherjee. 2000. *India After Independence 1947–2000*. New Delhi: Penguin Books.

Chatterjee, Partha. 1994. Development Planning and the Indian State. In T.J. Byers (Ed), *The State and Development Planning in India* (pp. 82–103). Oxford: Oxford University Press.

Chatterjee, Partha. 1993. *The Nation and Its Fragments*. Princeton, NJ: Princeton University Press.

Chatterjee, Santimay. 1994. Meghnad Saha: The Scientist and the Institution Builder. *Indian Journal of History of Science*, 29(1), 99–110.

Cohn, Bernard. 1996. *Colonialism and Its Forms of Knowledge*. Princeton, NJ: Princeton University Press.

Das, Gurcharan. 2001. *India Unbound*. New York: Alfred E. Knopf.

Dasgupta, Uma. 2011. Introduction. In Uma Dasgupta (Ed.), *Science and Modern India: An Institutional History, 1784–1947* (pp. xl–lxxvi). Delhi: Center for Studies in Civilizations.

Deccan Herald, 2010. 2010: 50 Years of India's First Digital Computer. Retrieved July 13, 2015, from http://www.deccanherald.com/content/52627/2010-50-years-indias-first.html.

Dirks, Nicholas. 1987. *The Hollow Crown: Ethnohistory of an Indian Kingdom*. Cambridge: Cambridge University Press.

Foucault, Michel. 2001. Governmentality. In James D. Faubion (Ed.) and Robert Hurley et al. (Trans.), *Michel Foucault, Power: Essential Works of Foucault, Vol. 3* (pp. 201–22). New York: The New Press.

Ghosh, S. C. 1994. Calcutta University and Science. *Indian Journal of History of Science*, 29(1), 49–61.

Gopal, Sarvepalli (Ed.). 1980. *Jawaharlal Nehru: An Anthology*. Delhi: Oxford University Press.

Goswami, Manu. 2004. *Producing India: From Colonial Economy to National Space*. Chicago: University of Chicago Press.

Government of India Budget Statement. 1973. The Economy in 1972–73—An Overview. Retrieved May 25, 2015, from http://indiabudget.nic.in/es1972-73/1%20The%20Economy%20in%201972-73_An%20Overall%20View.pdf.

Greico, Joseph. 1984. *Between Dependency and Autonomy: India's Experience with the International Computer Industry*. Berkeley: University of California Press.

India's Industrial Policies from 1948 to 1991. Retrieved May 24, 2015, from http://ieoakerala.org/wp-content/uploads/2011/08/Industrial-Policy-of-GOI2.pdf.

International Economics. 2015. Retrieved July 14, 2015, from http://intl.econ.cuhk.edu.hk/exchange_rate_regime/index.php?cid=15.

Karat, Prakash. 2000. CPI(M) Programme: Basic Strategy Reiterated. *The Marxist*, 16(3). Retrieved May 25, 2015, from http://www.cpim.org/marxist/200003_marxist_progrm_pk.htm.

Knoema. 2014. Retrieved March 9, 2015, from http://knoema.com/nwnfkne/world-gdp-ranking-2014-data-and-charts.

Kumar, Deepak (Ed.). 1991. *Science and Empire*. New Delhi: Anamika Prakshan.

Ludden, David. 2005. Development Regimes in South Asia: History and the Governance Conundrum. *Economic and Political Weekly* 37(30), 4042–51.

Ludden, David. 1993. "Orientalist Empiricism and Transformations of Colonial Knowledge." In C.A. Breckenridge and Peter Van der Veer (Eds.), *Orientalism and The Post-Colonial Predicament* (pp. 250–278). Philadelphia: University of Pennsylvania Press.

Mahalanobis, P. C. 1950. Why Statistics? *Sankhya: The Indian Journal of Statistics*, 10(3), 195–228.

Mahalanobis, P. C. 1958. Science and National Planning. *Sankhya: The Indian Journal of Statistics*, 20(1/2), 69–106.

Mahalanobis, P. C. 1965. Statistics as a Key Technology." *The American Statistician*, 19(2), 43–46.

Malik, Payal. 2011. An Overview of the Indian Software Industry. Retrieved May 26, 2015, from http://is.jrc.ec.europa.eu/pages/ISG/PREDICT/documents/17.MALIKBrusselsOctober2011.pdf.

Murali, Kanta. 2003. The IIT Story: Issues and Concerns. *Frontline, 20*(3). Retrieved May 22, 2015, from http://www.frontline.in/static/html/fl2003/stories/20030214007506500.htm.

Nag, D. S. 1949. *A Study of Economic Plans for India*. Bombay: Hind Kitabs Limited. Retrieved February 8, 2015, from http://archive.org/stream/studyofeconomicp031271mbp/studyofeconomicp031271mbp_djvu.txt.

National Planning Committee (NPC). 1988. *Report of the National Planning Committee 1938*. New Delhi: Indian Institute of Applied Political Research.

Panagariya, Arvind. 2013. Indian Economy: Retrospect and Prospect. Australian Government Productivity Commission. Retrieved May 24, 2015, from http://www.pc.gov.au/news-media/snape-lectures/arvind-panagariya/snape-2013-panagariya.pdf.

Pitroda, Sam. 2011. Telecom Revolution and Beyond. In R. K. Shyamsunder and M. A. Pai (Eds.), *Homi Bhabha and the Computer Revolution* (pp. 119–27). New Delhi: Oxford University Press.

Raj, Kapil. 2007. *Relocating Modern Science: Circulation and the Construction of Knowledge in South Asia and Europe, 1650–1900*. New York: Palgrave Macmillan.

Rajaraman, V. 2012. History of Computing in India: 1955–2010. Supercomputer Education and Research Center. Retrieved May 30, 2015, from http://www.cbi. umn.edu/hostedpublications/pdf/Rajaraman_HistComputingIndia.pdf.

Sinha, Nikhil. 1996. The Political Economy of India's telecommunication reforms. *Telecommunications Policy*, 40(1), 23–38.

Scientific Policy Resolution. 1958. Retrieved February 20, 2014, from http://www. dst.gov.in/stsysindia/spr1958.htm.

Scott, David. 1995. Colonial Governmentality. *Social Text*, 43, 191–220.

Second Five-Year Plan. Retrieved February 16, 2015, from http://planningcommission. nic.in/plans/planrel/fiveyr/default.html.

Sengoopta, Chandak. 2003. *Imprint of the Raj: How Fingerprinting Was Born in Colonial India*. London: Macmillan.

Sharma, Dinesh C. 2009. *The Long Revolution: The Birth and Growth of India's IT Industry*. Noida: HarperCollins.

Sinha, Jagdish N. 1991. Science and the Indian National Congress. In Deepak Kumar (Ed.), *Science and Empire: Essays in Indian Context (1700–1947)* (pp. 161–81). Delhi: Anamika Prakashan.

Spear, Percival. 1965. *A History of India: Volume Two*. Baltimore, MD: Penguin Books.

Special Economic Zone. 2015. About SPEEZ. Retrieved May 25, 201, from http:// www.seepz.org/about_us.html.

STPI Annual Report (2012–13). Software Technology Parks of India. Retrieved May 30, 2015, from https://www.stpi.in/writereaddata/links/ARe.pdf.

Subramanium, Ramesh. 2006. India and Information Technology: A Historical & Critical Perspective. *Journal of Global Information Technology Management*, 9(4), 28–46.

Tomlinson, B. R. 1993. *The Economy of Modern India*. Cambridge: Cambridge University Press.

Upadhya, Carol. 2004. A New Capitalist Transnational class? Capital Flows, Business Networks and Entrepreneurs in the Indian Software Industry. *Economic and Political Weekly* 39(48), 5141–51.

Vaidyanathan, Geetha. 2008. Technology Parks in a Developing Country: The Case of India. *Journal of Technology Transfer*, 33, 288–95.

Visvesvaraya, M. 1934 *Planned Economy for India*. Bangalore: The Bangalore Press.

2 The Rise of the Informational State

The first chapter of the book was an exploration into the genealogy of the info-nation. In particular, I demonstrated how a singular event—the installation of TIFRAC, India's first digital computer in 1962—contains a long history of the relation between information and governmentality over the course of two centuries. The computer is a mirror into the colonial past and at the same time an augury of India's postcolonial future. In the first two decades after Independence the private sector had been compelled to serve as an obedient handmaiden to public enterprise, but in order to develop the country's information industries it was compelled to open up its autarkic framework to market forces and interests. This chapter picks up the story as it unfolds after this "second arrow" of postcolonial history had been set in motion, to show how the Indian state reconstitutes itself as an informational entity. It enacts fundamental changes in the domains of broadcasting and telecommunications to usher in an era of communicative modernity, utilizes the new information technology to modify its notions of citizenship and governance, and adopts a collaborative stance toward the private sector around the logic of informatics. It begins, in the wake of the computer revolution, to imagine itself as an informational state.

Informational Identity

After the 1999 Kargil War with Pakistan, a review committee headed by the noted defense expert K. Subrahmanyam recommended that villagers living in border areas be provided with an identity card to ensure greater security. The idea was strongly endorsed by the Bharatiya Janata Party (BJP) government then in power, which announced that it would soon create a "multi-purpose national identity card" to be issued first to villagers living near the border with Pakistan and then to others as well. That government would soon be voted out of power and replaced in 2004 by a less overtly nationalistic coalition led by the Congress Party, but the idea of an informational entity that would identify the citizenry of the nation did not disappear. In January 2009, the government of India established the Unique Identification Authority of India (UIDAI), an organization whose purpose was to construct an identity-related database that would eventually "account" for each and every citizen of the country. According to its mission statement, the UID project was "an initiative that would provide identification for each resident across the country and would be used primarily as the basis for efficient delivery of welfare services" (UIDAI, 2015). The brand name for this ambitious project was "AADHAR," an unique identity number, "through which the citizen can claim his/her rights and entitlements when assured of equal opportunities, as symbolised by the logo, which has the halo of the Sun on the imprint of a thumb" (Balchand, 2010).

The person instrumental in championing this initiative—Nandan Nilekani—happened to be one of the most visible faces of India's software industry. Nilekani had played a large role in founding Infosys, an information servicing company, and then turning it into the country's second largest IT firm with annual revenues of over $6.6 billion (Gartner, 2013) and a market capitalization of approximately $42 billion (OMICS, 2015). He had consequently become something of a folk hero with the Indian public, along with other software entrepreneurs like K. Narayana Murthy (co-founder and chairman of Infosys) and Azim Premji of Wipro. Given his reputation, Nilekani was the right person to convince the government that such an informational crusade was of great urgency. In describing how he got Aadhaar off the ground in face of strong opposition, Nilekani reportedly said, "I believe I've convinced the three who really matter" (Dharmakumar et al., 2013). Two of the three that "really mattered" represented the apex of the ruling party—Congress President Sonia Gandhi and her son Rahul Gandhi—while the third, Mukesh Ambani, owned Reliance, India's second largest company by market value and was reputedly the country's wealthiest individual. In making his case for Aadhaar, Nilekani marshaled arguments that appealed both to statist desires as well as to the priorities of private industry. The UID card, he contended, would be of crucial value to the Indian state given the nation's dismal recordkeeping with respect to its own citizens. Thus, of India's 1.2 billion inhabitants only 50 million had passports and 150 million had a driver's license. The Aadhaar card would remedy the problem of the uncounted and the unaccounted for, make the nation fully visible and cognizable to itself, and thus help a backward country "leapfrog for future development" (*Times of India*, 2013). At the same time, the card would benefit private industry by helping to create a smoother environment for capital. Ambani, for one, bought Nilekani's suggestion that Aadhaar could help private industry through schemes like direct transfer of bank subsidies. By enabling the common man to open bank accounts, Aadhaar would build a bridge between capital and citizenry. As Visa card's Uttam Nayak stated, "If 600 million Aadhaar holders get bank accounts India can leapfrog from a banking penetration of 24 percent to the 75 percent common in developed countries like the US. Simultaneously, we can go from 3 percent 'electronification' to 40–50 percent. That is unprecedented in the world" (Dharmakumar et al., 2013).

Nilekani's arguments proved persuasive and he was appointed as the first chairman of the Unique Identification Authority of India. By March 2014, within five years of its launch, Aadhaar succeeded in enrolling nearly half of the country's total population. As one UIDAI official boasted, "Aadhaar had become the fastest-growing app in the world. It has 600 million subscribers, which is more than the 450 million users on social messaging platform WhatsApp" (ET Bureau, 2014). This great success prompted a joint collaboration between the UIDAI and NASSCOM, an organization that both regulates and lobbies for the software industry, to launch the "Aadhaar ecosystem diffusion project" to encourage start-ups to develop an app economy around the Aadhaar platform. As Nilekani triumphantly observed, "When the US government launched Global Positioning system (GPS) it was only for military purposes … today the GPS economy has become a half-a-billion dollar economy. We are trying to do the same thing with Aadhaar that will provide a new platform for building apps" (Phadnis, 2013).

Aadhaar was not without its critics. Thus Nikhil Dey, a prominent social activist described the UDI as "the opposite of RTI [Right to Information]. We fought all these years to have government information made public; and now the government will have access to every act of every citizen and it'll be kept secret," while another activist, Usha Ramanathan, alleges that "such initiatives exemplify how the Indian state is currently collecting biometric data from citizens without a law, simply because no one is stopping them" (Dharmakumar et al., 2013). Its biggest challenge, however, has come from recent political developments. The change of government following the BJP's sweeping return to power in 2014 has meant that Aadhaar may not survive in its current form and may be replaced by a National Population Register (NPR) or be rechristened as the National Identity Number, a name suggested by a previous BJP government (Kumar, 2014).[1] Yet, whatever the final bureaucratic outcome, the *idea* behind Aadhaar continues to strongly resonate with all sides of the political spectrum. Informational identity is here to stay.

The story of Aadhaar forms a useful bridge between the previous and current chapter of this study. The first chapter examined, among other things, the state's role in enabling the information sector to take off and become the face of Indian capitalist modernity. This process was perfectly symbolized by the figure of Homi Bhabha, both brilliant physicist and statist functionary, whose initiative pried the Indian state out of its autarkic socialist shell into an alliance with IT, thus previewing the era of liberalization that was to ensue in the 1990s. Bhabha's career and achievements illustrate one of my central claims in the last chapter, namely that information had been the basis of a deep, often unadvertised, relationship between private capital and the postcolonial state. Aadhaar and its flag bearer Nandan Nilekani represent a development of this plot whose second act involves a wholesale rethinking of the country's destiny through the conceptual vocabulary of the information revolution. Nilekani's best-selling book *Imagining India* is the most visible example of such a project and he himself can be seen as a sort of Bhabha-in-reverse: if Bhabha was a dedicated nationalist whose efforts somewhat unintentionally begat the software boom, Nilekani is a private sector "whiz" who now seeks to "imagine India" as an info-nation.

Nilekani's aspirations are not those of a single individual; they represent a much larger shift in administrative and political philosophy. It is the central argument of this chapter that beginning in the 1980s the Indian state imposed a set of measures and undertook a series of initiatives that constituted an "informational turn" that reimagined the very definition of nationhood. These interventions ranged across a wide spectrum of communicative and informational domains: telecommunications policy, telephony, hardware design and manufacture, computer policies, data management and informatics, e-governance, and enumerative projects like the Aadhaar card initiative discussed above. The current chapter is thus concerned with the Indian state's relationship to itself in the wake of the information revolution and attempts to spell out the ways in which the state transforms its governing apparatus in its quest to become the sort of India that Nilekani calls us to imagine. The first part of this chapter looks at the telecommunications sector to argue that changes in policies concerning telephony and broadcasting create an environment of "communicative modernity" where the state gradually relinquishes control over the channels of communication in order to facilitate a freer and more voluminous flow of information. The expansion in communications, I suggest, prepares the ground for the informational turn that was to ensue. In what follows I examine a series of initiatives undertaken by the government in the area of computer-mediated communication—the establishment of new bureaucracies to deal with electronics and information technology, the moves to digitize government utilities and services, and the creation of knowledge networks and data centers—to argue that this whole-scale embrace of digitality signals an increasing "informatization of the state." In other words, the state begins to conceive itself not merely as a political or governmental entity but also as an informational object that works as a hub within a networked society. In the third and last portion I examine the boundaries and interfaces of this info-nation in the making: the structure and logic of e-governance, the blurring of lines between state and capital as exemplified by public-private partnerships, and the increasing ideological convergence between the state and the information sector on questions of economic development and social justice. I finally return briefly to the Aadhaar project to show how it augurs an emergent informational ecology. Information, I argue, is increasingly seen as the very substance of governance and rule.

Communicative Modernity

The nature of the Indian social formation in the period 1947–80 determined the state's stance toward communication and information. First, the Indian state was firmly committed to a socialist path of development. This meant that the state retained ownership of crucial capital-intensive sectors like oil, steel, railways, defense equipment, and so on. In particular, the state assumed control over both broadcasting and telecommunications, including telephony. For example, not only were telephone lines and exchanges under governmental control, but also the handsets themselves were manufactured by a public sector company.[2] Second, a paternalistic attitude toward the masses—derived partly from colonial antecedents and partly from still prevalent feudal hierarchies of caste, class, and status—meant that communication and information were thought of as the exclusive property of the state to be disseminated in a manner that could only be determined by officialdom. Third, the developmental bias of this period meant that attitudes toward communication and information were marked by extreme frugality. Thus Nehru—whose personal whimsy often translated into national policy—saw television as a luxury meant only for the affluent and thus did little to encourage its growth (Majumdar and Mehta, 2012). As a result television was inordinately late coming to India, and even when it was introduced in 1969, television broadcasting would be both skeletal and rudimentary for the first two decades after it started. In short, the communicative environment of India during this period was distinctly pre-modern in that it reflected the concerns and priorities of the ruling establishment and was far removed from the culture of global mass-mediated entertainment. This communicative and informational order has a long history that I will briefly recount in the next few paragraphs.

The Indian postal service was the first "modern" communicative system to be established in the subcontinent.[3] The East India Company Post opened several post offices meant mainly for commercial transactions between 1764 and 1766; Governor-General Warren Hastings made this postal infrastructure into a public utility in 1774, and the whole system was formalized by the Postal Act of 1837 that bestowed the government with the exclusive right to convey letters in the territory of the East India Company (British Postal Museum and Archive, 2015). The post remained the only means of communication till the middle of the nineteenth century when the first experimental telegraph lines were laid between Calcutta and Diamond Harbour in October 1851. This was followed by the introduction of telephony in 1882 with telephone exchanges being inaugurated in Calcutta (now Kolkata), Madras (Chennai), and Bombay (Mumbai). The twentieth century would see a series of additions to the growing list of communicative technologies: wireless telegraph (1902), the first automatic telephone exchange (1913–14), radio and the radio telegraph (1927), and radio telephone and trunk dialing (1960) (Gupta, 2011).

During both the colonial and the early postcolonial eras, all public communication—whether by post, telegraph, or telephone—occurred under the purview of the state. As the famous Indian Telegraph Act of 1885 announced quite unequivocally, "Within [India] the Central Government shall have the exclusive privilege of establishing, maintaining and working telegraphs" (Indian Telegraph Act, 1885). Thus, even though these technologies afforded point-to-point messaging between two private individuals, they were at the same time "public" in that they were conducted through channels owned and regulated by the state. The scope of the government's involvement with information and communication was necessarily enlarged with the advent of radio broadcasting. Although the very first radio broadcasts (1927) in India were made by the privately owned Indian Broadcasting Company, the venture failed and the colonial government took over the role of broadcasting with the formation of the Indian Broadcasting Service (IBS) in 1932. The IBS was renamed All India Radio (1936) and was then placed under a separate Ministry of Information and Broadcasting.[4] This arrangement would continue after Independence, with All India Radio and Doordarshan being in charge of all broadcasting in the country.[5]

In short, both interpersonal communication (by means of post, telegraph, and telephone) as well as mass communications (radio, television) were thought of as informational domains that needed to be subsumed within the state, either by state ownership of channels of distribution as in the case of the post, telegraph, or telephone, or by control over both content and channel in the case of radio and television. There were two notable exceptions to the absolute domination of the state over communications. From its inception in 1913, the products of the Bombay film industry (often referred to nowadays as Bollywood) were privately produced, distributed, and exhibited. However, the state would announce its presence even in the domain of "free celluloid." Documentary film in India—the "informational" aspect of cinema—was largely produced under the aegis of the Films Division, a governmental body established in 1948. Its products had a captive audience since the government made it mandatory for all exhibitors to screen the division's shorts before the main attraction was projected. Despite its statist nature, the Films Division has had a surprisingly long life. As the current website of the organization states, "for more than six decades, the organization has relentlessly striven to maintain a record of the social, political and cultural imaginations and realities of the country on film" and goes on to add that its archives currently contain more than 8,000 titles of documentaries, short films, and animation (Films Division, 2015).

In other words, in the case of cinema, the state was happy to let private actors do the "entertaining" while the more serious business of documenting reality was left in the safe hands of its officers. Ironically, even privately produced feature films were susceptible to statist ideology. As many scholars have pointed out, Hindi cinema in the first few decades after Independence can be broadly described as an exercise at nation building.[6] The Bombay film industry—as evidenced by such classics as *Mother India* (1957)—largely identified with the premises and goals of the Nehruvian state even as it purveyed a mode of entertainment more appealing than the bureaucratic content available on radio and television. Thus, the period 1947–80 can be thought of as one where print journalism—represented by both newspapers and magazines—was the only source of information production and distribution that was truly autonomous of the state. A comprehensive history and analysis of the relationship between this "free press" and the Indian state remains to be written.[7] As was evidenced by the events that transpired during the emergency declared by the Congress government under Indira Gandhi, this freedom was fragile and easily suspended. This vulnerability had a long lineage. Before Independence there was no constitutional or statutory provision to protect the press and even in the contemporary moment the freedom of the press is not explicitly granted but rather derived from the more general Article 19 that states, "All citizens shall have the right—to freedom of speech and expression" (Constitution of India, 2007). That said, the Indian state did allow for the growth of a relatively unfettered press, thus tacitly admitting that the production of information by agents other than itself was a necessary and desirable feature of modern society.

To sum up, in the period 1947–80, the Indian state's relationship to information was either proprietary or a reluctant condoning of "freedom." Such a top-down informational paradigm can be dubbed as "pre-modern" in the sense that it did not promote, and often actively blocked, the continuous flow of information between private entities that was characteristic of all advanced capitalist societies. This framework would begin to be gradually dismantled from the 1980s onward. As Arvind Rajagopal has observed, "With the proliferation of media technology and the inter-animation of media forms across print, cinema, television, mobile telephones, and the Internet, South Asia seems to have arrived at a communicative modernity in the space of hardly two decades, or from the first Gulf War onwards, when satellite television was launched in the region" (2011, 11). I take Rajagopal to be referring basically to the opening up of the communication system to private capital as attested to by the rapid privatization of the mass media, the exponential growth in advertising, and the consumerist revolution attendant with these developments. However, I would like to emphasize that "communicative modernity" has one more characteristic we should take note of: it functions as a cybernetic environment where a feedback loop connects the state and the privatized communication it brought into play. By means of this secondary feedback process, a capitalist ethos—as embodied in modern media practices that Rajagopal enumerates—begins to "tutor" the state into an appreciation of communication for communication's sake. If the Nehruvian state had conceived of information as a valuable resource that could only be produced, stored, and dispensed by itself, with the dawning of communicative modernity, its successor began to conceive of information in a radically different fashion. Henceforth, information becomes both a tool and field of governance with the state seeing itself as working in and through information in a manner that is neither proprietary nor exclusionary. The move toward such an "informational state" would begin in the late seventies and early eighties, and its most visible manifestations appeared in the universe of mass media outlets following the introduction of accessible and attractive hardware, the financial writ of commercials, and the irreversible shift to populist programing. I want to argue that an equally crucial shift would occur in the much more mundane and far less visible domain of telecommunications and information technology. The change here was incremental rather than revolutionary, but a series of small and specific innovations in technology and technical organization would ultimately be instrumental in ushering in an informational milieu that would increasingly become of paramount importance to matters of state.

Writing in 2001, noted communication scholars Everett Rogers and Arvind Singhal could observe that "India reputedly has the world's worst telephone service, with only 0.4 telephones per 100 residents, compared to 75 in the US, 65 in Japan and seven in Malaysia" (Singhal and Rogers, 2001, 177). To take another statistic, as late as 1998 only 2.2 per 100 Indians had a telephone compared to a world average of 14.26 (Kathuria, 2000). The situation was comically worse in earlier decades; in 1970, for example, the national waiting line for a telephone stood at 700,000 with a waiting period of 4 years (Jeffrey and Doron, 2013, 27). These woeful figures were markedly in contrast with those in the realm of mass communications. All India Radio, for example, covered only 46% of the population in 1957 but had nearly doubled its reach by 1974 (Baruah, 1983, 15). This disparity reflected the state's thinking about the place of communication in society. As I discussed above, in the early postcolonial period, the Indian government invested in only those sectors of the communication industries that were considered important for growth and development. While radio had the highest priority in this regard, telephony—as an interpersonal medium— was deemed to be unworthy of such support. The picture has changed dramatically in the last two decades—as of February 2015 the number of cell phone users in India was close to a billion with 76 telephones per 100 citizens (compared to 103 for the US and 97 for the world) (TRAI, 2015). This amazing numerical growth, I want to argue, was made possible by a series of measures initiated long ago as the Indian state took its first hesitant steps toward communicative and informational modernity.

The tale of a simple switch is worth recounting here. For decades, the Indian telephone system functioned by means of an obsolete switching technology in which "the control circuitry was hardwired with very limited call-processing capacity … [such that] … It used to get bogged down as soon as the number of call attempts reached beyond its capability" (Pitroda and Pitke, 2011, 132). The solution would lie in going digital, and Sam Pitroda— whose contributions I have touched upon in the previous chapter—suggested the creation of an indigenous switching system to the authorities. But governmental attitudes regarding communications had to shift before such a project could be initiated. Fortunately for Pitroda, the winds of change were in his favor. Till that time, modern telecommunications was housed in the hoary Department of Posts and Telegraph. Telecommunications did not enjoy a privileged position in this set-up. A board peopled by members from a postal background controlled the department; quite astonishingly there was only *one* member representing the entire telegraph sector responsible for telegrams, telexes, and telephones (Athreya, 1996, 12). Portending things to come, this venerable body was bifurcated in 1985 into the Department of Posts and a newly created Department of Telecommunications (DoT). This act was not merely an administrative event; it also signaled a change in the state's philosophy of governance. By granting telecommunications its very own department, the government was tacitly recognizing that contemporary technologies of information flow were essential to the building of a modern state.

Indeed, a year earlier it had, at Pitroda's behest, taken another measure in this direction by setting up an organization called C-DOT (Centre for Development of Telematics).[8] Under Pitroda's leadership, C-DOT would succeed in a manner that exceeded all expectations. Its team of engineers developed a rural exchange (RAX) that used a pulse code modulation digital switch through which one could make calls anywhere in the world. This switch was potent enough to astound seasoned observers. Traveling in a remote part of Karnataka with a French friend, N. R. Narayana Murthy, the founder of Infosys, decided to test how well the RAX could perform. "We stopped at the first ISD booth at Nagarhole and my friend dialed Paris. His wife's voice came through loud and clear … I was proud of Sam, C-DOT and India" (Pitroda and Pitke, 2011, 137). C-DOT also developed comparable systems for business telephony (PBX) and telephony in populated urban areas (MAX), but perhaps most significantly, it initiated the PCO (public call office) program that introduced cheap and efficient long-distance calling to the masses. The visible symbol for this telecom revolution was the STD (subscriber trunk dialing) booth that became ubiquitous all over India from the 1990s onward. At the height of this "yellow revolution" (the phones were yellow in color) more than 60,000 telephone kiosks employing over 200,000 people were in operation, enabling callers to connect with friends, relatives, and business contacts with very little difficulty (Divya, 2011). The cultural impact of the yellow revolution cannot be overestimated. For decades long-distance dialing in India was prohibitively expensive and notoriously unreliable. The popular culture of the period is replete with representations of callers yelling "Hello, hello" into the handset with little hope of establishing a workable connection. The comical difficulty of long-distance calling was an apt symbol for the Indian state's philosophy of treating interpersonal communication with scant regard. The introduction of subscriber trunk dialing in the 1980s reflected a radical revisioning that conceded and encouraged the citizen's "right to call." The STD revolution was thus one of the pillars upon which a new conception of communicative modernity would stand.

This hardware revolution in telecommunications would be followed by equally significant changes in the realms of policy and administration. As mentioned above, until 1984 all telephony had been provided by the Department of Posts and Telegraph. Following the creation of the Department of Telecommunications (DoT) in 1985, the government set up two public service enterprises—VSNL (Videsh Sanchar Nigam Ltd) and MTNL (Metropolitan Telephone Corporation)—that would handle international telephony and local service in the two metropolitan areas of New Delhi and Mumbai. While these enterprises operated under government supervision, they were relatively autonomous, and their creation signaled the growing belief that the informational economy was best served by opening it up to private capital.[9] While domestic long-distance calling and local services continued to be operated by DoT, even that sphere was "privatized" to some extent with the setting up of another public sector concern (Bharat Sanchar Nigam Ltd. or BSNL) that would do for the rest of the country what MTNL was already doing for Delhi and Mumbai.

These hesitant moves toward liberalization and privatization would soon lead to a wholesale rethinking on the role and structure of telecommunications. This new approach is best illustrated by the report of the Telecommunications Restructuring Committee (often referred to as the Athreya committee after its chairman, Mitryunjay Athreya) that was set up in 1990 as a response to a big strike by DoT employees that threatened to disrupt the day-to-day functioning of the economy. The Athreya committee was charged with the task of examining the state of telecommunications in the country and of making recommendations for its improvemen. It came up with three major policy recommendations that etched out the path telecommunications in India was going to follow in the coming years:

- The government to retain the role as policy maker
- All telecommunications operations to be corporatized, gradually privatized and left open to competition, thereby attracting domestic and foreign private investment
- The resultant pluralistic industry to be regulated by an independent, quasi-judicial regulatory body (Athreya, 1990).

The Athreya committee's report would strongly influence the government's thinking on telecommunications and led directly to two seminal documents—the National Telecommunications Policy 1994 and National Telecommunications Policy 1999—which irrevocably changed the telecommunications landscape in the country. Some of the goals of these manifestos—that telephones should be available on demand to anyone wanting a connection and that all villages in the country be covered by the telephonic system—might have been overly ambitious but they reflected a new belief that governance and growth were not possible without a robust telecommunications system. The new economic policy adopted by the government aimed at improving India's competitiveness in the global market's rapid growth of exports. Another element of the new economic policy was to attract foreign direct investment and stimulate domestic investment. Telecommunication services of world-class quality were necessary for the success of this policy. It was, therefore, necessary to give the highest priority to the development of telecommunications services in the country (National Telecommunications Policy, 1994).

In other words, communication and the flow of information were seen as necessary pre-conditions for economic growth. The embrace of the notion of an informational state is very apparent in the latest National Telecommunications Policy that was issued in 2012. Pointing out that the last decade has been characterized by unprecedented increase in the penetration of telecommunications—thus telephone connections at the end of February 2012 were 943 million as compared to 41 million at the end of December 2001—and that India is one of the fastest growing telecom markets in the world, the document announces that "availability of affordable and effective communications for the citizens" is at the core of its mission and that "the vision is to transform the country into *an empowered and inclusive knowledge-based society, using telecommunications as a platform*" (National Telecom Policy, 2012, italics mine).

There were two key implications of this change in policy. First, the domain of telecommunications, once solely under government control, began to be rapidly opened up to private capital. Prior to 1990 private companies had been allowed to operate in only a few areas: end-use equipment (telephone sets) for individual customers, EPBAX (Electronic Private Automatic Branch Exchange) used in business establishments, and switches. Also, as we have seen, small-scale private operators were allowed to run public call offices where any customer could walk in and make STD calls. Following the Athreya report, the government initiated the liberalization of what was referred to as "value-added services"—electronic mail, voice mail, information services, videoconferencing, and paging. Most significantly, the government licensed two competing cellular companies in the four major metropolitan cities of Delhi, Chennai, Kolkata, and Mumbai. The 1994 TCP opened up the rest of the country to private cellular services and also allowed private companies to provide fixed basic telephony (Sinha, 1996, 30). An auction to grant cellular telephony licenses was first held in 1995, and although this process had a bumpy start, the New Telecom Policy of 1999 would rationalize its operation.[10] The reforms of 1994 and 1999 paved the way for the explosive growth in the cellular industry, spawned telecommunications giants like Bharati, Reliance, and Vodafone, and created what one set of authors has termed a "cell-phone nation" (Jeffrey and Robin, 2013).

Second, the shift in telecom policy during the course of the nineties led to the establishment of a regulatory body for telecommunications in India. As we recall, the Athreya committee had recommended the setting up of an independent, quasi-judicial organization that would oversee a pluralistic industry that consisted both of public and private sector players. The Ministry of Communications set up a working group to consider this proposal and in July 1996 the government introduced a bill to set up the Telecom Regulatory Authority of India (TRAI). The rationale behind the organization as seen from the government's point of view is succinctly put forward on the organization's own website: "The entry of private service providers brought with it the inevitable need for independent regulation ... TRAI's mission is to create and nurture conditions for growth of telecommunications in the country in a manner and at a pace which will enable India to play a leading role in emerging information society" (TRAI, 2014).

There is one important conclusion to be drawn from the decision to establish such a regulatory body. By creating TRAI, the government acknowledged that the contribution of the private sector was absolutely essential if India was to become a modern society. As the 1994 National Telecommunications Policy somewhat ruefully declared about the goals it had set out, "Clearly this is beyond the capacity of Government spending and internal generation of resources. Private investment and association of the private sector would be needed in a big way to bridge the resource gap" (TRP, 1994). Yet, because such a concession probably went against the Indian Constitution's resolve "to constitute India into a sovereign, socialist, secular, democratic republic," the state felt the need to regulate the activity of the telecom market. Thus TRAI has continued to reflect a statist bias both in terms of composition and effective authority. As Vardharajan (2012) has pointed out, TRAI is heavily dependent on deputationists who constitute at least 50% of its workforce. Since these deputationists are governmental employees usually working for BSNL or MTNL, such an employee pattern severely restricts the organization's capacity to act independently of the government. Thus, "though the TRAI has been constituted as an autonomous and independent regulator, the lack of policymaking and licensing powers confines its role to only that of recommender most of the time" (Vardharajan, 2012, 33). In other words, in spite of its reformatory zeal, the state continues to cling to vestiges of statism.

The history of Indian telecommunications from the 1980s onward illustrates the turn toward the constitution of an informational state. As I have argued, the telecom revolution accompanied the profound changes that were happening in the world of Indian broadcasting. If the latter developments allowed voices other than those of the government (soap operas, religious epics, advertisers) to speak to the public, the changes in telecom policies and practices—the turnaround in hardware production initiated by Sam Pitroda and his colleagues at C-DOT, the devolution of governmental authority through the formation of corporatized entities like VSNL and MTNL, and the opening of the cellular market to private capital—allowed the same public to communicate among itself with far greater ease than before. Taken together, these two processes led to the establishment of a communicative modernity characterized by a multiplicity of platforms, registers, and discourses. It was the Indian state that *allowed* such a scenario to develop. In the section that follows I examine how this "thawing" would be accompanied by a proactive stance toward information as such. By developing the nation's information systems and by integrating information-based practices into its developmental and governing strategies, the state sought to redefine itself as an informational entity.

Information and the State

The process that helped to consolidate the informatization of the contemporary state and lay the foundations for a software industry that would signify India's place in the world capitalist order is best traced by looking at the creation and evolution of specific governmental departments and institutions that collectively contributed to the changes in the way information begins to be utilized by the postcolonial Indian state. The originating moment in this regard was the setting up of an Electronics Committee in August 1963. The impulse for this initiative came from the disastrous 1962 war with China, after which the government realized the urgent need for an indigenous electronics industry. The resolution setting up this committee acknowledged this in stating that "electronics is the nervous system of the new technology ... It is vital for atomic energy, communication and defence" (Sharma, 2009, 49). Coming after the inauguration of the TIFRAC, the committee (also known as the Bhabha Committee after its chairman) was extremely aware of the central role computers had assumed and in its 1966 report (written under the chairmanship of Vikram Sarabhai, Bhabha's successor) it exhorted greater use of computers as tools "in the development of a new outlook and a new scientific culture" (National Informatic Center, 2015). The immediate impact of the two Electronics Committees, as well as that of the National Conference on Electronics held at TIFR Mumbai, was at the governmental level. The arguments offered by scientists in these forums were instrumental in the creation of a separate Department of Electronics (DoE) in June 1970 followed by the establishment of an Electronics Commission in 1971. Electronics had previously been housed under the Department of Defense Supplies (DODS). The creation of the DoE meant that electronics (including computers) was no longer thought to be a matter of military technology but rather as a tool for all areas of society to utilize. At the same time, the Electronics Commission, under the leadership of MGK Menon, was to set the tone for the information revolution to follow. As one analyst observes, the commission's policies determined the future history of IT in India: "One of the crucial decisions of the Commission was to channelize the country's resources and energies into creating intellectual capital and knowledge base, rather than large-scale hardware production. Almost every single institution from the National Informatics Center ... the iconic Computer Maintenance Company ... to Wipro, can trace their roots to that single decision of MGK Menon" (Swaminathan, 2014).

The establishment of the DoE and the Electronics Commission is a milestone on the road to the information age. However, it must be pointed out that the idea of an informational state was still at a very nascent stage. The state's conception of information in 1970 (the year DoE was created) was in tandem with its notion of communication. As I have discussed above, in this period mass communication was prioritized over interpersonal communication with the state maintaining exclusive control over what it saw as a valuable resource. The same proprietary logic applied to information as well. The Bhabha committee, we recall, driven as it was by the concerns of the Atomic Energy Commission, envisaged computers as a tool that was necessary to build a robust and self-reliant state. Hence, its vision of an indigenous industry that would produce "national champions" serving the country's computational needs was carried over into the DoE. Though the immediate period following the creation of the DoE was still characterized by a Nehruvian stance toward information—the case study of ECIL in the previous chapter is a good example—the ensuing years witnessed a swift erosion of this perspective. In other words, no sooner had information and information technologies been apprehended for statist purposes than the inherent properties of informational systems began to dissolve such an appropriation.

The story of the Computer Maintenance Corporation (CMC) is a case in point. The company was established in 1975 under the name Computer Management Corporation Private Limited. It was initially owned entirely by the government of India and then later converted to a public limited company in 1977. The company had very little business until IBM decided to pull out of India in May 1978. At that point, the CMC took over the task of maintaining IBM installations at over 800 locations in the country. In other words, CMC was initially conceived of as a servicing company that tended to a valuable national resource—informational hardware. Very soon the company began to diversify into other aspects of the informational economy. Thus, a news item in a popular news magazine stated that "the public sector Computer Maintenance Corporation (CMC) has set its sights on the overseas software market, and has submitted to the Government a proposal to generate annual software exports worth Rs. 200 crore" (*India Today*, 1986).

By 1995 maintenance would provide only 50% of CMC's revenues. The move out of hardware maintenance came with the CMC's involvement with the UNDP-funded project Interact whose goal was to "promote technical education and develop technical know-how in emerging application areas such as meteorological image processing, real-time data acquisition, and railway freight management" (Ramamritham, 1995). The last area of collaboration with UNDP was to prove extremely significant. CMC took the lead in persuading the railways that a computerized passenger reservation system was long overdue. As Dinesh Sharma recounts, the task was a Herculean one since it involved codifying a rulebook that went back 150 years. The engineers at CMC were up for the challenge—they wrote 1,400 programs in 6 weeks—and in just one year India had a fully computerized reservation system (Sharma, 2009, 155). CMC would also be responsible for creating India's first automated stock exchange when it successfully automated the Bombay Stock Exchange, which was the largest exchange in the country (Ramaswamy, 2004). In moving from computer hardware maintenance to creating computerized systems for the railways and the stock exchange, CMC had shifted its focus from information devices to information applications. What these applications demonstrated was that information technology could be utilized not just for scientific and military tasks but for administrative and commercial ends as well.

Finally, CMC was also responsible for initiating one of India's first networks. The idea of networking was first introduced to the country by the Computer Society of India that set up several demonstrations of this new technology in the late 1970s, but till the early 1980s the only major users were large public sector organizations and a few government departments. CMC held a series of seminars between 1982 and 1986 promoting the idea of networks and, following a feasibility study, it got the government's approval for installing the INDONET network, which was made operational in March 1986 with the goal of creating the infrastructure for a network and promoting a "network culture" within the country (Rau and Rao, 1993). INDONET offered electronic mail and file transfer services, software packages and databases, specialized turnkey packages tailored to particular customers and platforms for software development, and was not only useful for CMC's internal needs but also attracted private customers including the footwear giant Bata, the Welcom Group Chain of hotels, and the Reserve Bank of India. Thus, an organization created to maintain mainframes manufactured by a multinational ended by creating applications and data networks. CMC's progression illustrates the changes in the state's understanding of information: initially information was just data upon which calculations were performed for scientific research; then information became the basis of applications having a wide range of economic benefits, and finally, we arrive at a "general-purpose" definition of information that sees it as the very basis of social conduct.

INDONET was not the only network available to Indian users. In a 1994 study commissioned by the World Bank, Nagy Hanna provides a useful snapshot of the state of informatics in India in the early 1990s. Though Nagy (1994) comments that "the setup for data communications in India is rudimentary" and that "services suffer from overloading, poor performance and high cost," his survey shows that in spite of financial and logistical hurdles India still had *eleven* operational networks in this period – INDONET, NICNET, and ERNET being three of the most prominent ones in the list.[11] Nagy's list demonstrates that the emergence of INDONET was by no means an isolated event. The Electronics Commission under the leadership of MGK Menon collaborated with the United Nations Development Programme (UNDP) to formulate a strategy for regional computing centers that could serve as hubs for manpower development and spur the growth of informatics in local economies. Each of the computing centers set up in this manner would make crucial contributions to the informatization of Indian society. The National Center for Software Development and Computing Techniques (NCSDCT) was created in 1974 and was charged primarily with software development including database and office systems, graphics, networks, and knowledge-based and real-time systems. NCSDCT was responsible for India's first e-mail system as well as for conceptualizing the railway passenger system that CMC would later implement. In 1985 the National Center for Science and Technology (NCST) was created from the remnants of NCSDCT. Under the leadership of Srinivasan Ramani, the center was responsible for India's first Internet network: ERNET. This network connected NCST with six academic and research institutions as well as the DoE and in 1986 it established the very first e-mail connection between two Indian institutions. It introduced the familiar extension ".in" for domain names in the country and also provided Indians with their very first international connection with a link to Amsterdam and then with UUNET (one of the earliest and largest Internet providers in the world) in Virginia. As Ramani recalls, "ERNET became the first Internet Service Provider (ISP) in India … The Indian academic network had come of age!" (2011, 33). ERNET, aimed primarily at academic and research institutions, would become an autonomous organization placed under the DoE (as of 2012 the Department of Electronics and Information Technology, or DeitY). It continues to function to this day as a national research network.

Another crucial institution, the National Informatics Centre (NIC), was set up in Pune in 1977 under the leadership of the noted computer scientist N. Seshagiri. According to Seshagiri, it had the "long-term objective of setting up a computer-based informatics network for decision support to the ministries/departments and the development of databases relating to India's socio-economic development. … and playing a catalytic as well as participatory role in creating information awareness, systematizing the data collection, collation, processing, and analysis in government and facilitating its online availability" (2011, 66). One of NIC's first projects was managing databases and information systems for the Asian Games held in New Delhi in 1982, thus making information technology visible to the public at large. Its most singular achievement, however, was the creation of NICNET, a satellite-based network connecting the national and state capitals and all district headquarters as well. Based on a satellite link, it was the largest data communication network in India linking more than 600 earth stations. The network's strength lay in disseminating useful information that till then had been hard to come by. As a scholar writing in the early nineties pointed out, "NICNET has over 40 informatics booths all over the country linked through satellite to its New Delhi headquarters. The computers at the booths provide seventeen information modules which include railway and airline timetables, hotel guides, university and employment guides, industrial and investment directories, hospital and medical directories, and a comprehensive statistical profile of India, census data of all villages" (Kumar, 1993, 4).

Over the years, NICNET has carried out over 3,000 projects on government informatics. These include conveying all election results to Doordarshan and the Press Information Bureau starting in 1991, linking the Supreme Court and all 18 high courts by 1997, computerizing 70% of treasuries in the country by 2000, and helping initiatives in panchyati raj. NIC would later be merged with the DoE and the Electronics and Software Export Council in 1999 to form the new Ministry of Information Technology. Sometime later the Department of Telecommunications (DoT), whose evolution was discussed in the previous section, would be merged with the IT Ministry to form an expanded Ministry of Communications and Information Technology (DeitY). This somewhat bewildering sequence of mergers and changes in nomenclature was not wholly random, for it reflected frantic efforts to keep pace with technological advances as well as evolving ideas about the role of information in good government. In what follows I want to briefly analyze the content of DeitY's website in order to provide a revealing snapshot of the main ideas behind the notion of an informational state.

The ministry's mission statement spells out the state's commitment to an information based society:

> To promote e-Governance for empowering citizens, promoting the inclusive and sustainable growth of the Electronics, IT & ITeS industries, enhancing India's role in Internet Governance, adopting a multipronged approach that includes development of human resources, promoting R&D and innovation, enhancing efficiency through digital services and ensuring a secure cyberpace.
>
> (DeitY, 2015a)

The list of organizations currently under the charge of the department includes some long-standing outfits that have been discussed above—NIC and ERNET, for example—as well as several other recent additions. These include technical bodies like NIXI (National Internet Exchange of India), a neutral meeting point for all Internet service providers in India; STQC (Standardization Testing and Quality Certification Directorate), an organization that appraises and certifies public and private organizations; the CCA (Controller of Certifying Authorities) that verifies the authenticity of digital signatures used in cyberspace transactions; STPI (Software Technology Parks of India); the ESC (Electronics and Software Export Promotion Council), a IT trade facilitation organization; the NIELIT (National Institute of Electronics &Information Technology), which is the country's premier institution for examinations and certifications; and the ICERT (Indian Computer Emergency Response Team) that is the "national nodal agency for responding to computer security incidents as and when they occur." This list of IT-based organizations illustrates the extent to which the government relies on information technology to run its "hard" daily operations. By examining the drop-down menus under the "Divisions" button, we get a sense of informationalism's "soft" side—the hopes and aspirations the state harbors about information's potential for creating a better society. The programs listed under the Divisions section all speak to the state's desire of utilizing the affordances of information technology in the cause of building a just and prosperous nation. Thus the e-learning initiative seeks to develop services and technology to "provide high value integrated learning; anytime, anyplace" by supplementing the conventional delivery of instructions in the classroom and help improve pedagogical content by means of multimedia tools; the National Digital Library aims to supplement traditional libraries by providing digital materials for instruction as well as create a mobile library with 1 million titles; IT for Masses targets disadvantaged categories: Scheduled Castes, Scheduled Tribes, gender, differently-abled, senior citizens, and disadvantaged areas of the country—like the North East or designated Backward Districts—that could benefit from digital technology, while the National Knowledge Network (NKN) can be said to be the summation of the efforts that began with ERNET and INDONET in that it seeks to interconnect all institutions of higher learning and research with a high-speed data communication network to facilitate knowledge sharing and collaborative research.[12]

The NKN's webpage further enunciates a new information-based notion of governance: "The key to successful research today demands live consultations, data sharing and resource sharing. Therefore in order to optimally utilize the potential of institutions ... it is important to connect them through a high speed broadband network" (NKN, 2015). What is unique here is the commitment to a bottom-up democratic process of information management. Thus, the project's design overview states that "NKN design philosophy is to Encourage, Enable, Enrich and Empower the user community to test and implement innovative ideas without any restriction from the network technology and its administration" (NKN, 2015). The NKN is not meant to be just an efficient technology that will enable resource sharing at a national level; it will also embody a new form of participatory democracy in action. In other words, NKN points to a new mode of governance: e-governance.

The Indian government has been embracing the idea of e-governance since the beginning of the new millennium. The vision of the National e-Governance Plan approved in 2006 and first operationalized in 2011 is to "make all Government services accessible to the common man in his locality, through common service delivery outlets, and ensure efficiency, transparency, and reliability of such services at affordable costs to realize the basic needs of the common man" (DeitY, 2015b). It is important to point out that e-governance, conceptualized in the way the Indian state did, is not merely an instrumental device to promote more efficient and cost-effective government but also a political philosophy that rethinks the very basis of the modern state. It would be useful at this point to draw a distinction between e-government and e-governance. While e-government merely connotes the adoption of electronic resources for governmental purposes, e-governance may be said to be "the use of ICT [information and communication technology] by the government, civil society and political institutions to engage citizens through dialogue and feedback to promote their greater participation in the process of governance of those institutions" (Monga, 2008, 54). The distinction between e-government and e-governance can also be described in binary fashion: electronic service delivery versus electronic consultation, electronic workflow versus electronic controllership, electronic voting versus electronic engagement, and electronic productivity versus networked social guidance (e-governance, 2015). E-governance therefore constitutes a radical *extension* of capitalist democracy by making information a field and a conduit for the political process. As I explore more fully in the next chapter, information, in this new dispensation, becomes the very substance of a politics conducted in, by, and often for information.

When and how did this shift in governing philosophy occur? The first step toward e-governance was taken when the BJP government under Atal Bihari Vajpayee established a National Taskforce of Information Technology and Software Development in 1998, with the resolve to transform India into a global IT superpower. While most of the recommendations that this committee made dealt with specific aspects of the burgeoning software industry—for example, the proposal that the country should aim at an annual export target in excess of US$50 billion for computer software and a target of US$10 billion for computer and telecom hardware by year 2008—an IT Action Plan drafted soon afterward would extend the scope of informational governance. This plan suggested that conscious efforts be made to spread the IT culture to "all walks of economic and social life of the country" and devised an Operation Knowledge campaign for universalizing IT and IT-based education in the country in a phased manner. The ultimate goal behind these endeavors was to catch up with other Asian countries—like Taiwan, Malaysia, and Singapore—that had already succeeded in harnessing digital technology for the purposes of economic growth and prosperity (Ninth Five Year Plan, 2015).

This may be an appropriate juncture to pause and briefly consider the general characteristics of e-governance. In a well-known piece, Richard Heeks has argued that e-governance offers a new way forward for developing societies where typically government "costs too much, delivers too little, and is not sufficiently responsive or accountable" (2001, 3). The power of information communication technologies (ICTs) can introduce "automation, informatization, and transformation" leading to efficiency gains in terms of costs and speed, as well as effectiveness gains, since e-governance projects work better and are more innovative. Providing a slightly different take, Sunny Marche and James McGiven write, "E-governance is a technology-mediated relationship between citizens and their governments from the perspective of potential electronic deliberation over civic communication, over policy evolution, and in democratic expressions of free will" (2003, 75). The two central categories that come into play with the introduction of e-governance are *transparency* (as both understandability and the ability to participate in an open process) and *centricity* (from organization-centricity to citizen-centricity). Since the Internet and digital technologies have changed the way governments approach their citizens, "The future simply isn't what it used to be for governments and governance everywhere," they claim (ibid., 85).

The Indian state has adopted this philosophy of governance in a whole-hearted manner. Thus a recent document brought out by the Department of Electronics and Information Technology states that

> In the early 1990s, two changes swept across the world—the focus on good governance with increasing non government participation in delivery of public services and Information Communication Technologies (ICTs) and internet—technologies that potentially could connect any and every one in real time. The concept of e-Government or e-Governance was born through the amalgamation of these two. E-Governance marked a paradigm shift in the philosophy of governance—citizen centricity instead of process-centricity and large scale public participation through ICT enablement.
>
> (DeitY, 2012)

This particular document tries to lay out the methods by which citizen engagement may be attained such that "all Government services are available to the common man in his locality." The logic of e-governance argues that "citizen participation and civic engagement are the building blocks for good governance and e-Governance is a critical component of good governance." This realization leads "to a paradigm shift in delivery of public and essential services—from human to technology based interfaces." The model of governance that emerges is an informational one based on "an interactive two-way process that encourages participation ... and flow of conversation." The way to achieve engagement is through information-sharing, consultation, joint assessment, and shared decision making and collaboration.

To rejoin the main narrative, in 2006 the ruling Congress Party approved the National e-Governance Plan and made it operational across the whole country. One of the distinctive features of the plan was the creation of a number of Mission Mode Projects that would create a citizen-centric and business-centric environment for governance. A Mission Mode Project (MMP) was defined as a single project that focused on one aspect of e-governance, the "mission mode" implying that projects have clearly defined objectives as well as measurable outcomes and service levels. A couple of examples illustrate how the philosophy of e-governance enshrined in the MMP reflects the state's attitude toward information. Take the case of acquiring a passport. Traditionally, Indian citizens had to surmount immense amounts of red tape in order to obtain a travel document. The reason for this absurd state of affairs went beyond bureaucratic inertia and was linked to the state's paranoia regarding foreign travel. Not only did journeys abroad involve the expenditure of precious foreign exchange, but also any contact with the global outside on the part of citizens was perceived as a threat to the autarkic model to which the nation was committed. In the wake of liberalization such concerns have been reduced considerably; instead identity documents and foreign travel are seen as positive factors for the emerging economy. Thus, one particular MMP—the Passport Seva Project—promises to deliver passport services "to the citizens in a comfortable environment with accessibility and reliability" and to deliver passports within 3 days for cases not requiring police verification (DeitY, 2015c). If the Indian state had been notoriously tardy in the case of passports, it was guilty of an equally infamous silence on the matter of land records. In what was a primarily agricultural society, land was both a precious asset as well as the occasion for disputes of all kinds. The opacity surrounding land records did much to maintain feudal arrangements surrounding arable land and agricultural labor. The Land Records MMP has been launched to remedy this long-standing ill; its specific mission is to digitize all data relating to land ownership, to provide legal sanctity to computerized Records-of-Rights, set up computer centers at Tehsils (an administrative division denoting a sub-district) in order to keep records current, and to create a web portal that will enable every citizen to access this database (DeitY, 2015d).

Since its inauguration, the e-governance program has had a wide imprint. In a recent review Nikita Yadav and V. B. Singh (2012) provide a comprehensive list of e-governance projects currently being executed nationwide that I reproduce below in abbreviated form:

> Transportation: Vahan and Sarathi—a backend application that helps speed up work flow in the transport department of the Tamil Nadu government
>
> Online payment: FRIENDS a project to enable Kerala citizens to make online payments of electricity and water bills, as well as revenue taxes
>
> Information and PR: LokMitra, a Himachal Pradesh government initiative that offers information about vacancies, tenders, market rates etc
>
> Municipal Services: E-Panjeeyan, started by the Assam government to deal with computerization of municipal documents
>
> Roads and Traffic: CFST (Citizens Friendly Services of Transport Department) a project of the Andhra Pradesh government to keep check on pollution control, road safety and road signs.
>
> SEEDNET started in Chattisgarh by the ministry of Agriculture
>
> Prajavani: started by AP government it is a web-based on line monitoring of public grievances

Chetana: a disaster management system started in Bihar to deal with natural disasters

Bhoomi: the first e-governance land records management system implemented by the Karnataka government.

E-Gram Viswa Gram Project: connecting thousands of gram panchyats and citizen common service centres in Gujarat.

This list illustrates the wide range and precise specificity of e-governance projects both at the central and state levels. But while the number of such projects is impressive, it is too early to make judgments about their success. In the paper cited above, Richard Heeks had warned that "most e-governance initiatives that are begun currently fail ... two main types of e-governance failure can be identified ... there is the *total failure* of an initiative never implemented ... Alternatively there is the *partial failure* of an initiative in which major goals are unattained or in which there are significant undesirable outcomes" (2001, 16).

The Gyandoot project is an excellent case in point. Gyandoot (Messenger of Knowledge), a unique low-cost and self-sustainable e-governance project, was started in January 2000 in Dhar district of central Indian state of Madhya Pradesh. The project was designed to extend the benefits of information technology to people in rural areas by directly linking the government and villagers through information kiosks. The scheme set up several telecenters situated in different locations across several districts; these telecenters were then connected through dial-up access to a central server placed at the office of Zila Panchayat at District Collectorate. Gradually, Gyandoot spread to all 13 blocks. The idea behind Gyandoot was an innovative one and the project was awarded the Stockholm Challenge IT Award in 2000 for public service and democracy. But its success was short-lived. As one United Nations study concluded, "Despite being initially successful Gyandoot could not keep pace with the rising aspiration level of people ... People were of the opinion that excessive media publicity had done more harm to the project ... and the ultimate result was non-fulfillment" (United Nations Public Administration Network, 2009). Again, the case of the Community Information Center (CIC) project launched with much fanfare and a big budget in the northeastern states and Assam tells a similar story regarding the fallibility of e-governance efforts. Though the project established over 600 information centers across the whole region, it has been plagued with a host of problems from the moment of its inception. Thus, according to an independent researcher who conducted fieldwork at its various branches, "There exists a sense of helplessness and isolation among advocates of the project in the face of the response or lack thereof from the state government. ... There is lack of user's awareness, ease of interface, motivation of the staff" (Gupta, 2010, 56).

These operational failures of e-governance notwithstanding, the commitment to informatization continues unabated. As I have tried to demonstrate in this section, along with the efforts to constitute a space of communicative modernity, the Indian state started on a self-conscious and motivated campaign to "informatize" itself. Such an effort had three aspects—investment in indigenous hardware and software related to telephony; digitization of government services and the creation of a number of information-technology-based databases and networks for public consumption; and finally a concerted move to alter modes of governing in order to create a participatory democracy based on electronic interactivity. These three factors collectively constitute a push toward an informational state and an information society.

Toward an Information Society

As we have seen, the Indian state embarked on a path of informatization from the 1980s onward. This initiative was most certainly spurred by the spectacular rise of the software industry that quickly gained the status of an economic "jewel in the crown."[13] Yet, the new theory of governance animating the state's thinking could not take hold without similar developments in civil society. If the government was in thrall of the idea that digital technology and digital democracy were the only solutions to reconciling the seemingly contradictory ends of growth and social justice, such a premise was also subscribed to by various non-governmental institutions: corporations, NGOs, civic leaders, and portions of the intelligentsia. Thus in place of the contradiction or antagonism that typically characterizes the relationship between state and civil society, we begin to see a convergence between these two domains around the idea of an info-nation. PPPs—public-private partnerships between the state and the private sector—are the perfect example of such an intersection.

The idea of a PPP is based on the notion that social programs like healthcare services, water and sanitation, and infrastructure projects have the best chance of success as joint-sector ventures. This is because, the argument goes, the private sector would provide higher-quality goods and services at lower costs while the public sector could satisfy social pressures and local needs. There are two reasons why the idea of PPPs took hold. First, the idea received general support in the wake of economic liberalization that occurred across the globe in the 1990s; second, the success of the IT industry caused the government to become aware of the asymmetric benefits of the digital revolution and thus develop a philosophy of Information and Communication Technologies in Development (ICTD) as a means for reducing social inequities. Critics of PPP allege that such good governance agendas conceal the neoliberal bias inherent in free-market approaches and that these models provide a cover for pure privatization. Others have taken a more optimistic view, and the following justification offered recently is worth quoting at some length:

> The good governance agenda implemented via PPPs is based on an idealized representation of the modern state run on business principles. We find that citizens' institutional trust in, but also disillusionment with, government creates a space for the state to renegotiate its image

by outsourcing service delivery to ICTD telecenters. These PPPs also create a space for entrepreneurs to gain the trust of citizens by strategically using the state's name and brand. In a developmental state such as India, the state can thus use service delivery through ICTD as a powerful political symbol of responsiveness and as a policy tool with which to portray a new more efficient government. Over time, and if these PPP-ICTD projects scale up, this symbolic (and partly real) responsiveness may enable Indian states to begin shedding their image of bureaucratic lethargy, and to be seen as more user-friendly by their citizens.

(Kuriyan and Ray, 2009, 1671)

The National e-Governance Plan formulated by the Ministry of Information Technology strongly encouraged the formation of PPPs in key projects like community service centers and state data centers as well as in several Mission Mode Projects that I have described earlier. In pursuance of this suggestion governmental agencies collaborated with leading private firms like IBM, TCS, CMC, and Infotech and came up with a variety of models to work these partnerships: BOO (Build, Own, and Operate), BOT (Build, Operate, and Transfer), and BOOT (Build, Own, Operate, and Transfer), joint ventures, partial privatization, and other combinations (Gupta, 2010, 54). As a result, "India, in the recent years has emerged as one of the leading PPP markets in the world as a result of several policy and institutional initiatives taken by the Central Government" (Ministry of Finance, 2015).

PPPs represent a specific type of conjunction between state and capital. While it is understandable why a state burdened with the huge task of administering to 1.2 billion citizens might be eager to "outsource" developmental initiatives, it needs to be stressed that the private sector too has a big stake in such a partnership. From the perspective of the private sector, PPPs represent a way of reducing inefficiencies in public administration and thus adding greater value to society than purely public sector concerns. As N. R. Narayana Murthy, the founder of Infosys observes, in order to make globalization work for India, "We must involve the public sector and create public-private partnerships (PPPs) to enhance the efficiency of the government. The government brings focus on the public good while the private sector brings focus on efficiency, effectiveness and accountability" (2009, 268–69). In this new age of information, state and capital are no longer in an antagonistic relation with one another as was often the case in Nehruvian India.[14] Instead, they collapse into each other across the axis of information. The corporate leader Narayana Murthy's vision of the coming age is almost identical to the government of India's:

The objective of technology is to reduce cost, reduce cycle time, simplify work, improve productivity, improve quality of implementation and enhance customer satisfaction. Who needs this more than the poor? Hence, technology is crucial in delivering basic services to the poor in India. Technology has to be embraced enthusiastically by governments at both the state and federal levels.

Technology helps democratize information ... The Internet empowers people by conquering distance and time zones and by increasing transparency. Democracies need this powerful tool to enhance interaction between governments and citizens. The Internet can act as an ombudsman for citizens ... Another important use of the Internet is in e-governance which enhances the productivity of citizens in their interaction with the government. (2009, 206)

In other words, what we see here is a convergence between the perspectives of the state and capital driven by an information-theoretic understanding of the processes and outcomes of governance. Thus information can be said to be creating a neutral zone outside of profit maximization (although informatics can, of course, lead to profits) and political administration (although the informational state is no less political). The neutrality I refer to consists of the fact that the drive both for profit and for political action is deflected and subdued by an equally strong desire to be co-present with each other within the informational matrix. Capital is forced to turn "compassionate" by the dictates of the information economy while the state is coerced into abandoning politics in favor of post-ideological governance by the pressure of its informational interface with its citizenry. Such a claim becomes more credible if we examine the vision and goals of the software industry's leading representative and spokesman. NASSCOM (National Association of Software and Services Companies), the industry association for the IT-BPM sector in India, was established in 1988 with the intention to "build a growth led and sustainable technology and business services sector in the country" (NASSCOM, 2015).

While one would assume that its primary goal is to ensure increasing profits for its 1,400 members, among NASSCOM's self-described missions is the resolve to work with government to shape policy in key areas and harness the benefits of ICT to drive inclusive and balanced growth with the overall objective of "Transform Business, Transform India." NASSCOM Foundation (Changing India Bit by Bit), an organizational offshoot of the association, was set up "with the vision to harness information and communication technologies to transform the lives of the underserved" and has four stakeholders: member companies, NGOs, social enterprises, and the government with whom it wants to build "technology for good" (NASSCOM Foundation, 2014a). The foundation seeks to set benchmarks for its members, help NGOs in the effort to build capacity for civil society, help social enterprise with ICT, and support the government with policy suggestions and IT solutions for development. According to one study (Kshetri and Dhokalia, 2007, 20–24), NASSCOM'S influence on the government can be divided into two broad categories: strengthening the rule of law and performing some of the regulative functions. Thus it partnered with the Ministry of Information Technologies to draft data-protecting and data-privacy laws to respond to privacy concerns of offshore clients and also worked with police officers, educating them about cyber security and teaching them how to recognize and persecute cybercrimes. At the same time it has also helped the government with regulation—setting up assessment and certification programs for employees and regulatory bodies like the National Skills Registry (a voluntary registry for call center workers) and the Data Security Council. The Indian government has responded to these "friendly" overtures by allowing NASSCOM to function as a powerful lobbying group that has sought to reduce income tax on profits and help develop infrastructure that would benefit the software industry. And as Jyoti Saraswati points out in his critical study on the Indian software industry, NASSCOM has come to be dominated by trans-national corporations (TNC) like IBM, Accenture, and Cap Gemini with the result that the organization's main focus shifted from one that supported the growth of Indian software firms to facilitating a business-friendly environment for attracting and maintaining IT-related Foreign Direct Investment (FDI) by global giants (2012, 70–75).

I close this discussion of the "convergence thesis" by briefly describing the NASSCOM Foundation's Rural Knowledge Network Project. The foundation first partnered with the United Nations Development Programme (UNDP) to revitalize knowledge centers—a space that provides public access to ICT for educational, personal, social, and economic development—in Orissa that had been destroyed by the catastrophic 1999 cyclone. The lesson the foundation learned from this experience was that "connectivity is critical to the success of the Knowledge Center—the basic aim of bridging the digital divide using ICTs is not served without connectivity, i.e. *horizontal and vertical transfer of knowledge cannot be realized.*" Armed with this realization, the foundation launched its Rural Knowledge Network (RKN) program in 2005 with the goal of establishing a national grid connecting over 100 knowledge centers in 65 districts over 10 states. It managed to draw several partners—including Microsoft, HP, Wipro, Qualcom, and Tata and others—into setting up knowledge centers and is now focusing on building the capacities of each of its partners to run sustainable centers offering relevant services to the community. At the moment of writing, the NASSCOM Knowledge Network (NKN) is a network of 174+ community telecenters across 13 states of India, in partnership with 30+ NGOs, providing access to information and services related to education, health, and livelihoods to marginalized communities (NASSCOM, 2014b). NASSCOM's project is an example of informational governance that is no different in substance and style from those launched by the government. As the report on RKN itself observes, knowledge centers "have … been set up by middle and large sized NGOs (M S Swaminathan Research Foundation's Knowledge Center Project; DHAN Foundation's Knowledge Center Project, gender-based projects of SEWA and Datamation Foundation), corporate (ITC's e-chaupal) and government bodies (Gyandoot, Bhoomi, eSewa and Lok Mitra, and Community Information Centers in the Northeast); and projects like TARAhaat, Dhristee and N-logue that have been set up as social enterprises" (RKN, 2006, 4).

In other words, knowledge centers as instances of informational governance exemplify a convergence between various sectors of society: government, non-profit, and for-profit. Such a convergence, I want to argue, is a necessary condition of the rise of the informational state. Whereas older forms of information could be purveyed by the state in a top-down manner—using mass media as its chief resource—the new forms of information generation and distribution call for a formation where the state positions itself *alongside* civil and commercial society to constitute a networked space of governance.[15] The Aadhaar card—discussed at the beginning of this chapter—is the perfect example of the cooperation between state, commercial society, and private citizens. The change in government following the General Elections of 2014 may cloud the future of the Aadhaar project. But whatever its fate, the informational state is not in any jeopardy. The new government is strongly committed to another initiative— The National Population Register—that, like the Aadhaar unique identity system, is an electronic database meant to aid in governance: "The Government of India has initiated the creation of this database, by collecting specific information of all usual residents in the country during the House listing and Housing Census phase of Census 2011 during April 2010 to September 2010. It is planned that the collected information of the Usual Residency (aged 5 and above) of 17 states and 2 UTs will now be digitized, and biometric data will be collected from these residents for further integration" (NPR, 2015).

The informatics of this project is outlined in a flow chart that I am reproducing in text form: House-to-house by enumerator→Scanning of NPR schedules→Data Digitization→Biometric enrollment and consolidation→LRUR (Local Register for Usual Residents) correction and validation→De-duplication by UIDAI and Issuance of Aadhaar Number →Consolidated cleansed data at ORGI→Identity/Smart Card (Proposed). In other words, with the end result in mind, whether we talk about Aadhaar or NPR, it is the same: a digital representation of the citizens of the info-nation.

This discussion stresses that the drive toward an informational state and society is unimpeded by the vicissitudes of electoral politics. Whatever the other implications of the shift from the left-of-center UPA government, which ruled from 2004–14, to the right-of-center BJP government, which is currently in power, there has been no change at all in the state's commitment to the development of what Nandan Nilekani has termed "national information utilities." NIUs—like the UDIA or the NPR—he argues "offer us a new model of governance—one that is scalable, with a single point of accountability, and where the amount of information available maintains a balance of power between the citizens and the government ... Such an elec-tronification infrastructure would reduce the knowledge asymmetries—and consequently the lopsided power dynamic—that now exists between the citizens and government ... one the opaque veils on our state are raised, the citizen will truly be in charge" (2009, 360–61).

The reason that the polity as a whole is committed to the sort of infor-mational turn that Nilekani is espousing may be an automatic consequence of a larger process of neoliberalization that grounds India's contemporary development. As Shirin Madon points out in her book-length study on e-governance in India, "India's neoliberal economic and political restruc-turing agenda has affected the direction of governance reform. In particular, the focus has been on reducing the role of government in all aspects of economic planning by broadening the role of civil society and community involvement in public affairs" (2009, 86). A more explicit account of the relationship between neoliberalism and informatics is provided by William Mazzerala's observation that "the Indian discourse of e-governance sug-gests less a historical shift between two paradigms than an ongoing attempt to bring old-fashioned centralized power into alignment with a decentral-ized consumerist-populist notion of empowerment" (2006, 480–81). This meant that government's legitimacy would depend on the zeal with which it pursued the engagements of its "customers." As one executive from Cisco India put it, the government like any other service provider should be pur-suing "citizen mindshare" (ibid., 484). Mazzarella complicates this picture in a later piece that reviews the discourses surrounding ICT4D in India.[16] Whereas some take the relevance and value of ICT4D as granted, others dis-miss it as techno-fetishism underwritten by the logic of neoliberalism. There may be a third, more productive way of looking at ICT4D. In the words of a software executive, ICT-D may be seen as facilitating a "multi-stake-holder, iterative, consultative emergent information ecosystem." In such a system, Mazzarella observes, "there could be no preconceived solutions and no quick fixes. As a matrix of stakeholders, in which no single actor's voice was louder than another's, the ecosystem generated its own challenges and opportunities, to which it was the job of attentive brokers to respond" (2009, 797).

The notion of an emergent information ecosystem is a useful one with which to summarize the main arguments of this chapter. At the moment of its inception the postcolonial state also constituted itself as a communicative state. Nehru's celebrated "tryst with destiny" broadcast announced the birth of India—an act of communication brought the nation into being. From that originating point onward, as Arvind Rajagopal has observed, "The task of media ... was understood as fulfilling the mission of education and informa-tion, in terms defined by the Indian state" (2009, 11–12). That being so, it is perfectly understandable why the Indian government would carry on the colonial tradition of not relinquishing control over the two most impactful forms of media: radio and television. It is no accident that the very first minister of information and broadcasting, Sardar Vallabhai Patel, was the second most powerful man in the cabinet serving also as deputy prime minister and home minister. The legendary influence of one of Patel's successors, B. V. Keskar, has been well documented by mass media scholars.[17] The roll call of names that followed Keskar—Indira Gandhi (later prime minister), I. K. Gujral (later prime minister), L. K. Advani (later deputy prime minister), Arun Jaitley (later finance minister), and Sushma Swaraj (later foreign minister)—demonstrate the ministry's role as a key player in the framework of independent India.

However, as I have argued over the course of this chapter, beginning in the 1980s the Indian state begins a process of transformation from a communicative to an informational state. I draw this dichotomy between communication and information somewhat hesitantly, noting that other scholars have previously proposed it as well. Thus the media activist Sean O. Siochru described the World Summit on the Information Society (first held in Geneva in 2003) "as a conjuncture or conflictual encounter between two infopolitical visions ... that of an information society organized around the principles of a neoliberal technomangerialism, driven mainly by government and corporate actors, and that of a communication society realizing the post-Third Worldist agenda of gaining a comprehensive set of material rights to communication, driven mainly by non-governmental or civil-society organizations and corresponding social movements" (Zehle, 2007, 391). Whereas Siochru poses the distinction between communication and information in political terms, my own intent in this chapter has been to read that difference from the perspective of governmental instrumentality. In the period when the postcolonial Indian state saw itself in communicative terms, it used broadcasting and other media in the statist fashion I have described at some length. When Indian communication became "modern," and information became set free from the bounds of government, the state located itself in the larger frame of the information society, refashioning itself as the informational state.

The relative importance granted to the ministries of information technology and of broadcasting provides an apt example of the point I am trying make. While the constant reorganization of the Ministry of Information Technology illustrates the government's acute attention toward IT and electronics, the Ministry of Information and Broadcasting—once a mighty department—has now been relegated to an insignificant corner of the administrative landscape.[18] Not only has it not had a Cabinet rank minister since 2012, but quite astonishingly also, both the last and the current minister (with a rank lower than that of Cabinet minister) have called for the abolition of the organization they head! Thus Prakash Javadekar, current Ministry of Information and Broadcasting (I&B) appointee under the BJP government, emphatically stated that he was philosophically or ideologically willing to work for the abolition of the I&B ministry adding that "the government should never need to exercise control, media should have its own mechanism" (dna, 2014). And days before he quit office, the I&B minister in the UPA government, Manish Tewari, questioned the relevance of his ministry saying, "In today's day and age you don't need a ministry of information and broadcasting. It belongs to another time and era, an era that is past" (Singh, 2014). These extraordinarily self-effacing "official" statements underline the transition I have been outlining in this chapter: from top-down communication to polycentric information, from broadcasting the state to the building of an info-nation.

I will offer some very tentative reasons for this fundamental paradigm change: the trajectory of the software industry, outlined in the previous chapter, that reconfigured the relationship between the state and capital; the "liberalization" of the economy in 1991 that paved the way for communicative modernity to replace state communications as the primary site of consensus formation; the rise of neoliberal philosophy that redefined the state as service provider rather than a vanguard for the people; the birth of the Internet and the World Wide Web as repositories of globally networked information; and the rise of specific digital technologies and practices that facilitated a new mode of e-governance. The net result was a fundamental change in the state's philosophy: information was no longer seen as a valuable resource that had to be produced, delivered, and policed by the state but rather as the very ground of modernity, the Subject and Mover of government, and indeed the very precondition for a successful polity to even exist.

Let me also recap the basic empirical details of this "informational turn." The move toward the informational state was made possible by a series of initiatives that began in the 1980s and would continue into the new millennium. First, the state's wholehearted support for the emerging IT industry led to an economic "miracle"—in the decade of the 1990s, for example, software exports rose from 100 million USD to 3.4 billion USD (Bhatnagar, 96, 2006). The success of the private sector not only generated badly needed foreign revenue, but it also served notice that information and its processing was a valuable commodity that was a crucial component of modern social formations. The Indian government took this lesson to heart and as a first measure it "liberalized" the telecom and broadcasting sectors. The new policies led to a huge boom in telephony—the number of phone connections doubled between 1984–91 (Jeffrey and Doron, 2013, 28)— and to a radical transformation in broadcasting philosophy that pushed Doordarshan into commercially driven entertainment programming and later "opened up the skies," thus allowing private television channels to proliferate and prosper.[19] The sum effect of these changes was to institute a climate of communicative modernity that placed information and communication at the very center of the social process and allowed a far greater degree of citizen participation. Finally, the Indian state became a lead actor in the field of information technology. It set up separate departments for telecommunications and IT at the level of central government as well as autonomous bodies like the Telecom Regulatory Authority of India (TRAI); passed new policies with the 1994 and 1994 Telecom Acts; created institutions like C-DOT and CMC that successfully increased the nation's hardware and software capabilities; and instituted networks and database centers like INDONET and the National Informatics Center that would make information processing a central part of state governance.

Taken together, these developments signal the Indian state's desire to reconstitute itself as an informational entity. Such a claim can be backed up by two very contemporary examples. The BJP government led by Narendra Modi has recently announced, as I detailed in the Introduction, a "Digital India" program that seeks to "transform India into a digitally empowered society and knowledge economy" (DeitY, 2015). The program's key goals—digital infrastructure as a utility to every citizen, governance and services on demand, and digital empowerment of citizens—all testify to the idea that henceforth the nation must necessarily be reconstituted as an "info-nation." The push for Digital India is also exemplified by the $1.2 billion project of creating 100 "smart cities" that will be outfitted with high-tech communication capabilities in order to bring about a new mode of civic life. Finally, the project of the info-nation cannot be realized solely at the behest of the state; it needs equal participation from other stakeholders in society. As this chapter shows, the views expressed by information industry leaders like Narayana Murthy and Nandan Nilekani as well as the actions undertaken by NASSCOM—the body that represents the interests of the Indian software industry—demonstrate the convergence between state and private capital around issues of digital technology and e-governance. All these factors and processes taken together signify the reconfiguration that I am designating by the notion of an informational state. The next chapter extends this mode of analysis by examining how informationalism makes its presence felt in the domain of civil society. In particular I look at three instances of what I term "info-activism"—a campaign that succeeded in establishing the right to information for every citizen, a historic political and electoral movement against corruption that was based on the premise of informational transparency, and a talk show designed around informatics that addresses issues of inequity and social justice—to demonstrate how informationalism extends beyond the bounds of the state to reconstitute the workings of Indian civil society.

Notes

1. The BJP replaced the Congress-led UPA coalition in the General Elections of May 2014. The BJP had always criticized UID on the grounds that it permitted illegal aliens to become electronically naturalized, and it sees the National Population Register as a better solution to the problem of "knowing" the country's citizens.

2. Before liberalization, all telephone sets were manufactured by the Indian Telephone Industries, established in 1948 and headquartered in Bangalore. It

enjoyed a near monopoly till the 1980s and even now is responsible for 50% of the country's telecom network (Awasthi, 2009).

3. While the Mughal Empire utilized an extensive postal system, it was not available to the entire citizenry.
4. The Ministry of Information and Broadcasting was originally known as Ministry of Information and Arts. It acquired its present name in 1946.
5. The first private television channels would come on the air in the early 1990s while the first private radio station was inaugurated as late as 2001.
6. For an excellent account of this phenomenon, see Chakravarty (1993). For a slightly different take that argues that Hindi film exposes the fractures in the nation, see Virdi (2003).
7. Jeffrey (2000) provides a stimulating analysis of India's "newspaper revolution" but his book deals with 1977 and after.
8. See Chapter 1 for an account of Pitroda's pitch to Indira Gandhi. C-DOT was aided by two government departments—DoE and DoT (Department of Electronics and Department of Telecommunications) and also drew upon the expertise of the Telecom Research Center and the TIFR (Tata Institute of Fundamental Research).
9. As a sort of self-fulfilling prophecy, VSNL would ultimately become a private sector company after being bought over by the powerful Tata group in 2009 and renamed as Tata Communications Ltd.
10. The first round of auctions did not yield any fruit because companies were forced to bid too high in order to satisfy the government's demand for both licensing fees and low consumer charges. The shortcoming in the model was corrected by NTP 1999. Companies now paid a percentage of what they earned rather than a high flat fee, they could offer any type of service they wanted, and their licenses were valid for up to 20 years.
11. The others were RABMN, I-NET, GPSS, SAILNET, OILCOMNET-OCC, SOFTNET, ICNET, and Banknet.
12. At the time of writing NKN has already connected 851 institutions and plans to ultimately connect 1,500 nodes in a comprehensive national network.
13. The exponential rise of the software sector is illustrated by the fact that between 1987 and 1990, exports rose by a factor of *ten* (Sen, 1995, 19).
14. Thus the typical Bollywood film in the early postcolonial period—*Aawara*, *Deewar*—portrayed capital and capitalists as selfish, greedy, and inimical to humanist ideals.
15. I am not suggesting that such an immanent formation is more democratic than previous ones. I am merely pointing to a topological realignment without which the informational state is hard to conceive.
16. ICT4D is the acronym for Information and Communicative Technologies for Development.
17. See my own discussion of Keskar's important role in Indian media history in Sen (2006).
18. Over the years "information" migrated out of the Ministry of Information and Broadcasting to departments like DeitY. The I&B Ministry remained as a shell that should have properly been renamed as the Ministry of Broadcasting.
19. For a succinct and lucid account of the transition from state-run to private broadcasting that occurred in the early nineties following the 1982 Asian Games, see Thussu (1999).

References

ARC. 2008. 11th Report: Promoting e-Governance. Retrieved June 19, 2015, from http://arc.gov.in/11threp/ARC_11th_report.htm.

Athreya, M. B. 1990. Indian Telecommunications Liberalization: Halting But Inexorable. Retrieved August 5, 2014, from http://w.ww.connect-world.com/~cwiml/PDFs/.../India.../India_1998_01.pdf.

Athreya, M. B. 1996. India's Telecommunications Policy: A Paradigm Shift. *Telecommunications Policy*, 20(1), 11–22.

Awasthi, I. C. 2009. Corporate Performance and Strategy: A Case of the Indian Telephone Limited Industries. Retrieved June 8, 2015, from http://abufara.com/abufara.net/images/abook_file/Corporate%20Performance%20and%20Strategy%20%20A%20Case%20of%20the%20Indian%20Telephone%20Industries%20Ltd.pdf.

Balchand, K. 2010. UID Number Gets Brand Name, Logo. *The Hindu*. April 27, 2010. Retrieved May 5, 2015, from. http://www.thehindu.com/news/national/uid-number-gets-brand-name-logo/article410397.ece?ref=relatedNews.

Baruah, U. L. 1983. *This Is All India Radio – Handbook of Radio Broadcasting in India*. New Delhi: Publications Division, Ministry of Information and Broadcasting, Government of India.

Bhatnagar, Subhash. 2006. India's Software Industry. In Vandana Chandra (Ed.), *Technology, Adaptation, and Exports: How Some Developing Countries Got It Right* (pp. 95–124). World Bank.

British Postal Museum and Archive. Postal History of India. Retrieved June 9, 2015, from http://www.postalheritage.org.uk/explore/history/india.

Chakravarty, Sumita S. 1993. *National Identity in Indian Popular Cinema, 1947–1987*. Austin, TX: University of Texas Press.

Constitution of India. 2007. Retrieved June 11, 2015, from http://lawmin.nic.in/coi/coiason29july08.pdf.

DeitY. 2012. Framework for Citizen Engagement in e-Governance. Retrieved June 19, 2015, from http://deity.gov.in/sites/upload_files/dit/files/Framework%20for%20Citizen%20Engagement%20in%20NeGP.pdf.

DeitY. 2015a. Mission. Retrieved June 14, 2015, from http://deity.gov.in/content/vision-mission.

DeitY. 2015b. National e-governance Plan. Retrieved June 14, 2015, from http://deity.gov.in/content/national-e-governance-plan.

DeitY. 2015c. Passport. Retrieved June 16, 2015, from http://deity.gov.in/content/passport-immigration-visa.

DeitY. 2015d. Land Records. Retrieved June 15, 2015, from http://deity.gov.in/content/land-records.

DeitY. 2015e. Digital India. Retrieved June 20, 2015, from http://deity.gov.in/sites/upload_files/dit/files/Digital%20India.pdf.

Dharmakumar, Rohin, Seema Singh, and N. S. Ramnath. 2013. How Nandan Nilekani Took Aadhaar Past the Tipping Point. *Forbes India*, October 8, 2013. Retrieved June 5, 2015, from http://forbesindia.com/article/big-bet/how-nandan-nilekani-took-aadhaar-past-the-tipping-point/36259/0.

Divya, A. 2011. Phone Booths: Can They Ring in a New Future? *Times of India*, January 2, 2011. Retrieved June 11, 2015, from http://timesofindia.indiatimes.com/home/stoi/deep-focus/Phone-booths-Can-they-ring-in-a-new-future/articleshow/7203320.cms.

DNA. 2014. Government Should Not Control the Media: Information and Broadcasting Minister Prakash Javadekar. dnaindia.com. June 9, 2014. Retrieved June 20, 2015, from http://www.dnaindia.com/india/report-government-should-not-control-the-media-information-and-broadcasting-minister-prakash-javadekar-1994442.

e-governance. 2015. Retrieved June 14, 2015, from http://w.ww.it.iitb.ac.in/~prathabk/egovernance/egov.html.

ET Bureau. 2014. Every Second Indian Now Has an Aadhar Number. *Economic Times*, March 11, 2014. Retrieved June 6, 2015, from. http://economictimes.indiatimes.com/news/politics-and-nation/every-second-indian-now-has-aadhaar-number/articleshow/31805325.cms.

Films Division. 2015. About Us. Retrieved June 9, 2015, from http://filmsdivision.org/about-us.html.

Gartner. 2013. Gartner Says Top Five Indian Providers Grew 13.3 Percent in 2012, Exceeding Global IT Services Industry Growth Rate of 2 Percent. Retrieved June 8, 2015, from http://www.gartner.com/newsroom/id/2496815.

Gupta, M. P. 2010. Tracking the Evolution of E-Governance in India. *International Journal of Electronic Government Research*, 6(1), 46–58.

Gupta, Sanjay. 2011. Industry Analysis Report on Telecom Industry in India. Retrieved June 9, 2015, from http://issuu.com/sanjaykumarguptaa/docs/industry-analysis-report-on-telecom-industry-in-in/9.

Heeks, Richard. 2001. Understanding E-Governance for Development. Institute for Development Policy and Management, University of Manchester. Retrieved June 23, 2014, from http://www.man.ac.uk/idpm/idpm_dp.htm#ig.

India Today. 1986. Trade Winds: Computer Maintenance Corporation Sets Its Sights on Overseas Software Market. *India Today*, November 30, 1986. Retrieved June 13, 2015, from http://indiatoday.intoday.in/story/computer-maintenance-corporation-sets-its-sights-on-overseas-software-market/1/349191.html.

Indian Telegraph Act. 1885. Retrieved June 9, 2015, from http://www.ijlt.in/pdffiles/Indian-Telegraph-Act-1885.pdf.

Jeffrey, Robin. 2000. *India's Newspaper Revolution: Capitalism, Technology and the Indian Language Press, 1977–1999*.

Jeffrey, Robin, and Asa Doron. 2013. *Cell Phone Nation: How Mobile Phones Have Revolutionized Business, Politics and Ordinary Life in India*. Gurgaon: HachetteIndia.

Kathuria, Rajat. 2000. Telecom Policy Reforms in India. *Global Business Review*, 1(2), 301–26.

Kshetri, Nil, and Nikhilesh Dholakia. 2007. Professional Associations in a Newly Emerging Sector of a Developing Economy: A Case Study of the NASSCOM Effect on the Indian Offshoring Industry. College of Business Administration, University of Rhode Island, Working Paper Series, 2007/2008 No. 3. Retrieved June 19, 2015, from http://digitalcommons.uri.edu/cgi/viewcontent.cgi?article=1008&context=cba_facpubs.

Kumar, K. J. 1993. New Information Technologies in India: Social and Cultural Implications. AMIC Conference on Communication, Technology and Development. Retrieved September 4, 2014, from http://www.researchgate.net/publication/30065485_New_information_technologies_in_India__social_and_cultural_implications.

Kumar, Manan. 2014. Narendra Modi Sarkar May Shun Aadhaar for National Population Register. *DNA*, June 6, 2014. Retrieved June 6, 2015, from http://www.

dnaindia.com/india/report-narendra-modi-sarkar-may-shun-aadhaar-for-national-population-register-1993731.

Kuriyan, Renee, and Isha Ray. 2009. Outsourcing the State? Public-Private Partnerships and Information Technologies in India. *World Development*, 37(19), 1663–73.

Madon, Shirin. 2009. *E-Governance for Development: A Focus on Rural India.* London and New York: Palgrave McMillan.

Majumdar, Boria, and Nalin Mehta. 2012. *Olympics: The India Story.* New Delhi: HarperCollins India.

Marche, Sunny, and James D. McGiven. 2003. E-Government and E-Governance: The Future Isn't What It Used to Be. *Canadian Journal of Administrative Sciences*, 20(1), 74–86.

Mazzarella, William. 2006. Internet X-Ray: E-Governance, Transparency and the Politics of Immediation in India. *Public Culture*, 18(3), 473–505.

Mazzarella, William. 2009. Beautiful Balloon: The Digital Divide and the Charisma of New Media in India. *American Ethnologist*, 37(4), 783–809.

Ministry of Finance. 2015. Public-Private Partnerships. Retrieved June 19, 2015, from http://www.pppinindia.com/overview.php.

Monga, Anil. 2008. E-Government in India: Opportunities and Challenges. *JOAAG*, 3(2), 52–61.

Murthy, NR Narayana. 2009. *A Better India, A Better World.* New Delhi: Penguin.

Nagy, Hanna. 1994. *Exploiting Information Technology for Development: A Case Study of India.* World Bank discussion papers; no. WDP 246. Washington, D.C.: The World Bank. Retrieved June 8, 2014, from http://documents.worldbank.org/curated/en/1994/07/698166/exploiting-information-technology-development-case-study-india.

NASSCOM. 2015. Vision and Mission. Retrieved June 19, 2015, from http://www.nasscom.in/vision-and-mission.

NASSCOM Foundation. 2014a. Partners. Retrieved July 14, 2014, from https://www.nasscomfoundation.org/who-we-are/partners.html.

NASSCOM Foundation. 2014b. NASSCOM Knowledge Network. Retrieved July 14, 2014, from https://www.nasscomfoundation.org/get-engaged/nasscom-knowledge-network.html#sthash.SOVid3hk.dpuf.

National Informatic Center. History. Retrieved June 14, 2015, from http://as.ori.nic.in/neworiweb/history.aspx.

National Telecommunications Policy. 1994. Retrieved October 5, 2014, from http://www.trai.gov.in/Content/telecom_policy_1994.aspx.

National Telecommunications Policy. 2012. Retrieved June 11, 2015, from http://www.trai.gov.in/WriteReadData/userfiles/file/NTP%202012.pdf.

Ninth Five Year Plan. 2015. National Task Force on IT and Software Development. Retrieved June 14, 2015, from http://planningcommission.nic.in/plans/planrel/fiveyr/9th/vol2/v2c7-5.htm.

NKN. 2015. Vision. Retrieved June 14, 2015, from http://www.nkn.in/vision.php.

NPR. 2015. About Us. Retrieved June 19, 2015, from http://ditnpr.nic.in/Aboutus.aspx.

Nilekani, Nandan. 2009. *Imagining India: The Idea of a Renewed Nation.* Penguin: New York.

OMICS. 2015. Retrieved October 13, 2015, from http://research.omicsgroup.org/index.php/Infosys.

Phadnis, Shilpa. 2013. UIDAI, NASSCOM to push Aadhaar App Development. *Times of India*, October 29, 2013. Retrieved May 4, 2014, from http://timesofindia.

indiatimes.com/business/india-business/UIDAI-Nasscom-to-push-Aadhaar-app-development/articleshow/24846616.cms.

Pitroda, Sam, and M. V. Pitke. 2011. Homi Bhabha's Role in Fostering Electronic Development. In R. K. Shyamasundar and M. A. Pai (Eds.), *Homi Bhabha and the Computer Revolution* (pp. 128–48). New Delhi: Oxford University Press.

Rajagopal, Arvind. 2009. Introduction: The Public Sphere in India: Structure and Transformation. In Arvind Rajagopal (Ed.), *The Indian Public Sphere: Readings in Media History* (pp.1–28). New Delhi: Oxford University Press.

Rajagopal, Arvind. 2011. Notes on Postcolonial Visual Culture. *Bioscope*, 2(1), 11–22.

Ramamritham, Kirthi. 1995. A Detailed Report on R&D at Indian Computer-Science Establishments. Office of Naval Research, Asian Office, November 1995. Retrieved June 14, 2014, from http://fas.org/nuke/guide/india/agency/krithi1.html#gov.

Ramani, S. 2011. R&D in Software Technology at the National Centre for Software Technology, 1960–2001. In R. K. Shyamasundar and M. A. Pai (Eds.), *Homi Bhabha and the Computer Revolution* (pp. 17–49). New Delhi: Oxford University Press.

Ramaswamy, Shobha. 2004. Sibling Synergy. Retrieved June 14, 2015, from http://tata.com/media/interviewsinside/LzJfnS7kmC0=/TLYVr3YPkMU=.

Rau, P. R., and H. Raghav Rao. 1993. INDONET: A Public Service Data Network in India. Retrieved June 15, 2015, from https://flora.insead.edu/fichiersti_wp/Inseadwp1993/93–18.pdf. Accessed 6/15/15.

RKN. 2006. NASSCOM Foundation: Rural Knowledge Network. Retrieved June 18, 2015, from https://www.nasscomfoundation.org/user-resources/manuals.html?start=5.

Saraswati, Jyoti. 2012. *Dot.compradors: Power and Policy in the Development of the Indian Software Industry*. London: Pluto Press.

Sen, Biswarup. 2006. The Sounds of Modernity: The Evolution of Bollywood Film Music. In Sangita Gopal and Sujata Moorti (Eds.), *Global Bollywood: Transnational Travels of Hindi Music* (pp. 85–104). Minneapolis: University of Minnesota Press.

Sen, Pronab. 1995. Indian Software Exports: An Assessment. *Economic and Political Weekly*, 30(7/8), 19–24.

Seshagiri, N. 2011. National Informatics Centre: Evolution and Its Impact. In R. K. Shyamasundar and M. A. Pai (Eds.), *Homi Bhabha and the Computer Revolution* (pp. 66–92). New Delhi: Oxford University Press.

Sharma, Dinesh. 2009. *The Long Revolution: The Birth and Growth of India's IT Industry*. Noida, India: HarperCollins.

Singh, D. K. 2014. Wisdom, a Bit Too Late: I&B Minister Says Don't Need I&B. *Indian Express*, May 14, 2014. Retrieved June 14, 2014, from http://indianexpress.com/article/india/india-others/wisdom-a-bit-too-late-ib-minister-says-dont-need-ib/.

Singhal, Arvind, and Everett Rogers. 2001. *India's Communication Revolution*. New Delhi: Sage.

Sinha, Nikhil. 1996. The Political Economy of India's telecommunication reforms. *Telecommunications Policy*, 40(1), 23–38.

Swaminathan, R. 2014. Is It the Dawn of an Electronic Age in India. Retrieved June 24, 2014, from http://orfonline.org/cms/sites/orfonline/modules/analysis/AnalysisDetail.html?cmaid=61301&mmacmaid=61302.

Thussu, Daya. 1999. Privatizing the airwaves: the impact of globalization on broadcasting in India. *Media, Culture & Society* 21(1), 125–131.

TRAI. 2014. History. Retrieved June 23, 2014, from http://www.trai.gov.in/Content/History.aspx.

TRAI. 2015. Highlights of Telecom Subscription Data as of February 28, 2015. Retrieved June 13, 2015, from http://www.trai.gov.in/WriteReadData/PressRealease/Document/PR-TSD-Feb-10042015.pdf.

Times of India. 2013. Aadhaar Example of Using Technology to Leapfrog: Nandan Nilekani. *Times of India.* October 16, 2013. Retrieved June 7, 2015, from http://timesofindia.indiatimes.com/india/Aadhaar-example-of-using-technology-to-leapfrog-Nandan-Nilekani/articleshow/24232069.cms.

Tolan, Casey. 2014. Cities of the Future? Indian PM Pushes Plan for 100 "Smart Cities." CNN.com. Retrieved June 20, 2015, from http://www.cnn.com/2014/07/18/world/asia/india-modi-smart-cities/.

UIDAI. UIDAI Background. Retrieved May 5, 2015, from http://uidai.gov.in/all-about-uidai/uidai-background.html.

United Nations Public Administration Network. 2009. A Critical Study on Role of Gyandoot Intranet Project in E-Governance in Madhya Pradesh. Retrieved June 18, 2015, from http://www.unpan.org/Library/MajorPublications/UNE-GovernmentSurvey/PublicEGovernanceSurveyintheNews/tabid/651/mctl/ArticleView/ModuleId/1555/articleId/18132/Default.aspx.

Vardharajan, Sridhar. 2012. *The Telecom Revolution in India: Technology, Regulation and Policy.* New Delhi: Oxford University Press.

Virdi, Jyotika. 2003. *The Cinematic Imagination: Indian Popular Films as Social History.* New Brunswick, NJ: Rutgers University Press.

Yadav, Nikita, and V. B. Singh. 2012. E-Governance: Past, Present and Future in India. *International Journal of Computer Applications,* 53(7), 36–48.

Zehle, Soenke. 2007. The Case for Communication Rights: After the World Summit on the Information Society. In Michael Feher (Ed.), *Nongovernmental Politics* (pp. 391–401). New York: Zone Books.

3   Info-Activism and Civil Society

The building of an "info-nation" requires that the social formation be restructured according to the protocols and practices of the information age. While the previous chapter outlined the policies and programs undertaken by the Indian state in its attempts to refashion itself as an informational entity, this chapter will examine the emergence of an informational perspective within the domain of civil society. My approach here is influenced by the burgeoning literature that examines how new modes of connectivity and communication—networks, databanks, and social media—have impacted all aspects of social organization and life.[1] My primary focus here is on everyday activism, as well as the politics associated with it, that has risen in the wake of the information revolution. The phenomena I examine—the campaign to establish the Right to Information Act, the India Against Corruption (IAC) movement led by the Gandhian leader Anna Hazare; the Aam Aadmi Party (AAP), a political party with strong activist roots; and *Satyamev Jayate*, a television talk show committed to advocacy—belong to civil society and are all characterized by a strong informational perspective.[2] By demonstrating the emergence of this "info-activism," that is, activism influenced by the premises and protocols of informationalism, the chapter argues that civil society is a partner to the state in conceiving the info-nation.[3]

The history of social activism in modern India is typically associated with movements such as the Narmada Bachao Andolan, the Chipko movement, Save Silent Valley, Chattisgarh Mukti Morcha, Apiko movement, and the like. In the words of a noted scholar, these and similar agitations can be described as "movements of landless, unorganized labour in rural and urban areas, adivasis, dalits, displaced people, peasants, urban poor, small entrepreneurs and unemployed youth [taking up] the issues of livelihood, opportunities, dignity and development" (Sangvai, 2007, p. 111).[4] The salience of such movements is perhaps of even greater urgency today in the context of a model of economic growth that is creating wide disparities in income and wealth. Indeed, India's income inequality has doubled in the last 20 years, making it the worst performer in this regard among all emerging countries (Times of India, 2011). Nevertheless, activism in the informational age is no longer restricted to issues of material want and deprivation. As both the economy and the state increase their deployment of informational techniques of production and governance, activism turns into "info-activism" by recognizing that the fight for social justice includes demands like the right to information, informational access for all citizens, and transparency and accountability regarding any information that pertains to matters of state. In other words, info-activism sees informational rights and informational democracy as the very foundation of a just society.[5]

In this chapter I examine three instances of info-activism in contemporary India to demonstrate how civil society participates in the info-nation. The first section of the chapter looks at how informationalism manifests itself as a grassroots social movement through an analysis of the struggle to pass the Right to Information Act (2004).[6] By positing that information was a basic right of every citizen, info-activists were issuing a revised "Bill of Rights" and seeking to redefine the very notion of citizenship. I look next at the India Against Corruption movement and the political party it gave birth to—the Aam Aadmi Party (AAP) led by Anna Hazare's one-time associate Arvind Kejriwal. In this case, info-activism finds expression in the creation of an organization that claimed to be above the fray of regular politics, as the AAP's 2014 Election Manifesto put it, "The Aam Aadmi Party is not just *another* party" (AAP, 2014). I try to evaluate the validity of this assertion by examining the history and operational logic of the India Against Corruption campaign and that of the Aam Aadmi Party. Both these movements, I suggest, are instances of a new mode of politics that is largely driven by info-activism. In the third and last section of the chapter I analyze the hugely popular talk show *Satyamev Jayate* (*Truth Alone Prevails*, hence, *Satyamev*) as an example of info-activism's presence in popular culture. Produced and hosted by the Bollywood superstar Aamir Khan, *Satyamev* features investigative reporting on issues like female feticide, domestic violence, and honor killings. The show's structured reliance on data, info-graphics, and analytics reinforces the idea that contemporary activism, even when presented as entertainment, must necessarily be informational in nature. The three cases I examine are not random instances of information-driven enterprise; rather the main actors in each case are intimately connected and can be said to constitute a network of info-activists. By tracing the impact of info-activism in the domain of citizen rights, national politics, and commercial entertainment, I seek to demonstrate its increasing viability as a social strategy and its growing visibility within all spheres of civil society.

The Right to Information

In the Hindi film classic *Mother India* (1957, dir. Mehboob Khan), the moneylender Sukhilala can ceaselessly cheat and exploit the uneducated peasants who are his clients, because only he has control over the written document that records the level of indebtedness for each individual villager. Another film from the same period, *Do Bigha Zamin* (*Two Bighas of Land*, 1953, dir. Bimal Roy), depicts a similar scenario. The protagonist Shambu goes to the landlord's accountant to pay off a debt of 65 rupees in order to save his small plot of land. The accountant informs him that his debt is not 65 but actually 235 rupees. Shambu, who has not kept good records, has no means of challenging this assertion in court and is asked by the judge to pay the inflated amount. Both films stress how exploitation is perpetrated through the written record. The landlord, in each instance, is able to fabricate what the peasants owe by blocking their access to these records. Thus Sukhilala guards his documents with the help of his henchmen, while Shambu never maintains up-to-date accounts on the debt he owes. While Shambu does not understand the importance of paperwork until it is too late, Sukhilala controls information with the help of firepower. Such exploitation, the films suggest, is enabled by the asymmetric value that each side places on information and its written documentation. The portrait of information in these two classics of Hindi cinema is an accurate depiction of its status in postcolonial India. The possession of information, both films propose, installs hierarchies of power. Such an informational regime begins to take shape within the context of colonialism, and so the attempt to understand the right to information movement must start with a historical survey.

Information in the colonial period was quite literally a "secret." A vast amount of governmental data in India was covered by the Official Secrets Act of 1923 (an almost exact duplicate of a similar act passed in Britain in 1889) whose tenor can be gauged from the following warning, "If any person for purpose prejudicial to the safety or interests of the State approaches ... or enters any prohibited place ... makes any sketch, plan, model or note ... useful to an enemy ... obtains, collects, records or publishes communicates ... any secret official code ... or other document or information ... he shall be punishable with imprisonment for a term which may extend ... to fourteen years" (Official Secrets Act, 1923). Following Independence, the act was amended twice—first in 1951 and then again 1967—and was quite astonishingly made even more stringent! So great was its hold on the Indian bureaucratic imagination that, as late as 2013, the Union Home Ministry rejected suggestions for amending it in the interest of greater transparency (Jain, 2013).

While the rhetoric of the Official Secrets Act is, to this day, simultaneously paranoid and comical, it would be a mistake to read it as merely an excess of colonial rule. Rather, it must be seen as symptomatic of the relationship between information and the state in both the colonial and postcolonial eras. Even though the colonial state was a ceaseless producer of information and different modes of knowledge, it treated this output as a resource that needed to be zealously guarded (see Cohn, 1996; Metcalf, 1997). In other words, for the colonial regime a piece of data could attain the status of "information" only by *not* being circulated among the subject population. The Official Secrets Act was but the executive embodiment of this philosophy of reticence. As in many other matters, postcoloniality recapitulated colonial thinking, and successive Indian governments would tenaciously hold on to the idea that information could be entrusted only to the hands that ruled. The notorious opacity and recalcitrance displayed toward the public by South Asian bureaucracies—embodied by the infamous "red tape"—must be seen in the context of this governing principle.[7] In passing, it is worth pointing out that the early history of Indian broadcasting, which was characterized by governmental control over both radio and television in the face of a robust free press, can only be understood in the light of such an informational doctrine.[8] The implicit assumption here was that the population at large needed to be protected from the vagaries of privately generated information, hence, the transmission of "news" through specially created government organs like All India Radio, the Films Division of India, and Doordarshan. The still present ban prohibiting private FM radio stations from carrying any news is a striking testament to the durability of this "theory" of information and communication (see Sen, 2014).

It is clear that the notion of an info-nation demands that we move from an "information-scarce" model, such as the one above, to one which is "information-driven" in the sense that information is not only made readily available but also in fact constitutes the basis of governance. The Indian state, I have argued previously, made a conscious and concerted effort to transform itself into an informational regime, yet such an initiative could not be complete unless complemented by a push for information from "below."[9] The movement to create the Right to Information Act (RTIA) is a striking example of the rise of informational thinking within civil society. Its successful passage demonstrates that the idea of information was acquiring great salience not only for the Indian state but for the "people" of the nation as well. In what follows, I give a brief historical account of the RTIA's genesis in order to bring out some crucial features of info-activism in India.[10]

An act that now holds over the entire territory of the Republic of India had its genesis in the tiny village of Devdungri in the state of Rajasthan, when three activists—Aruna Roy, Nikhil Dey, and Shankar Singh—decided to start an organization that would fight for the empowerment of the rural poor. The Mazdoor Kissan Shakti Sangathan (MKSS) was, in the words of two of its founders, committed to "using modes of struggle and constructive action for changing the lives of its primary constituents—the rural poor" (Roy and Dey, 2001, 3). The locale they had chosen was extremely "backward" being situated in an arid zone that suffered frequent droughts. Landholdings in this region were very small and not economically viable. Moreover, there were very few alternative sources of rural livelihood and, as a result, the government had to initiate a number of relief works in order to provide employment to a population in permanent distress.

This backdrop may suggest a classic scenario of rural poverty that would witness time-tested activist demands for greater wages, resources, and implementation of relief projects. Indeed, at the beginning MKSS got involved in struggles over wages and land, but its strategy would soon take an informational turn. In the course of their activities, MKSS activists discovered rampant corruption in these state-run relief programs. Specifically, local government officials were found to be making money by adding fictitious names to the "muster-roll"—the official attendance register of workers employed for relief work. When the MKSS demanded access to these rolls, it was denied on the grounds that these were classified under the Official Secrets Act! The archaic sounding "muster-roll" represented an equally archaic stance toward information: the villagers of Devdungri were being subjected to the same logic of exploitation in real life as the one Shambu and Birju had experienced on the screen in the 1950s.

Blocked by this bureaucratic firewall, MKSS came up with a very innovative strategy. Instead of using traditional tactics to secure material resources for those with grievances, the MKSS conceived of an informational instrument that would change the nature of the agitation. The idea of *Jun Sunwais* or public hearings was strikingly simple—organize a non-confrontational gathering where information regarding developmental expenditures could be openly exchanged and discussed. In other words, the struggle over resources was reconstituted as a struggle over information. The very first *Jun Sunwais* was held in December 1994 concerning public works executed in a village named Kot Kirana. As the names of people on the muster-rolls were read out:

> Outraged people came and testified that they had never gone to these work sites, that false signatures had been used and that there were names on the muster rolls of people dead and gone, and others unheard of ... The bills of roofing material, doors and windows, when read out elicited a great deal of laughter for there was no roof and only holes for doors and windows. When the laughter died down, there was consternation, anger ...
>
> (Mishra, 2003, 10–11)

This new mode of engagement had a strong ripple effect, and the hearing at Kot Kirana was followed in rapid succession by a number of similar events at Bhim, Vijaypura, Ajmer, and Thana, culminating in a mass meeting at Beawar in September 1995 that was attended by more than 2,000 poor peasants and workers from villages all over Rajasthan. The meeting was a mammoth sit-in that issued a demand centered on the right of access to governmental records, in this case the right to inspect (and, equally important, photocopy) all documents relating to developmental works executed by local *panchayat* bodies.

The publicity and momentum generated by the *Jun Sunwais* campaigns led to the formation of a national body dedicated to information rights. The National Campaign for People's Right to Information (NCPRI) was composed of activists from MKSS and other organizations, journalists, lawyers, and retired judges as well as people within the bureaucracy. The formation of the NCPRI gave the right to information movement a national profile, and its efforts along with those of the MKSS would soon bear fruit. The almost decade-old struggle for information rights that had started in Rajasthan came to a close when the state's Right to Information Act passed in January 2001, and the movement soon spread to other states with Tamil Nadu, Goa, Delhi, Maharashtra, Assam, and Madhya Pradesh passing similar acts within a two-year period. The culmination of this process came in 2005 when the government of India passed the Right to Information Act for the whole country. The fact that the government acceded so quickly to the movement's demands confirms what I have argued in the previous chapter. Even as it sought to control the dissemination of data on an almost reflexive basis, the "informational state" could no longer impede the flow of information because of the way it was committed to the building of an info-nation.

The passage of the Right to Information Act was an event of great global significance. The move toward a more open informational environment began when the United States adopted the Freedom of Information Act in 1966. This measure was a model for other countries such as Canada, Australia, and New Zealand, which all adopted similar laws by 1982, and by 2010 more than 70 nations had national laws comparable to the FOIA. However, as Alasdair Roberts has suggested, the Indian case is of special importance because, "Like the United States' FOIA, the RTIA gives Indian citizens a right to obtain information held by public authorities. However RTIA is broader in scope. While the U.S. law applies only to the national government, the RTIA applies to state and local governments as well" (2010, 925). The law has resonated strongly with the citizens for, according to one study undertaken by a coalition of civil society organizations, 2 million requests for information were filed under the RTIA in the first two and half years of its implementation. This does not imply that the act is a magical solution for the problems of governance, for the informational economy continues to suffer from bottlenecks and roadblocks. The two most notable difficulties that bedevil this measure are the barriers to the use of the law by India's rural poor and the threat to enforcement capabilities posed by the inflow of a large number of appeals to information commissioners.[11] Thus, Pankaj Shreyasakar, a member of the Central Information Commission, a government body that acts upon complaints relating to RTIA, observes that the flow of information in the country is restricted either because various public institutions do not come within the ambit of the act or because the information sought by petitioners is exempt under specific clauses of the act. And, although a large class of information is now accessible to the public, "this may be sufficient only to provide a sense of satisfaction to the information seekers but is surely not adequate to bring in systematic reforms which the complex governance space requires" (Shreyasakar, 2014, 37).

Although the RTIA clearly faces many challenges in terms of implementation and effective impact, its ultimate value may lie in what it represents as an *idea*. As the prominent right to information, activist Shekhar Singh observes:

It is not just the receiving of information that is the main attraction of the RTI Act. For a vast majority of Indians it is a new sense of *empowerment* that, for the very first time, allows them to '*demand*' information and explanation of the high and mighty, the senior government officials, whom they could till now at best observe from afar. Therefore, it is not so much the information they receive, but the fact that they have a legal right to demand it, and to receive it in a timely manner, and to have the official penalized if the information is wrongly denied or delayed, and the *flutter* that all this causes among the officials, that is the real value of the RTI Act.

> (Sarangi, 2012, 152, italics mine)

Singh's insight that a call for information leads to a "flutter" of activity is worth developing because it suggests that more than anything else the passage of RTIA constitutes an ideational revolution whose central category is that of information. This conjecture is strongly confirmed by analyzing the manner in which two of the founders of the movement—Aruna Roy and Nikhil Dey—conceptualized their mission. As noted earlier, in its earliest days the organization's main goal was to ensure minimum wages for poor peasants employed for drought relief work. "It was in fighting for minimum wages under these programmes," recall Roy and Dey, "that the MKSS first understood the significance of transparency and the right to information" (Roy and Dey, 2001, 3). Every time the workers demanded wages they were told that according to the records they had not done the work. When MKSS demanded to see the records, it was told that these records were government documents and therefore secret. Faced with this bind, "the importance of access to the government records became clear to the whole group" (ibid., 3). In other words, the organizers of MKSS received the theoretical lesson that the relationship between labor and wages (state capital in this case) was mediated by a crucial third term: *information*.

Information, then, comes to be seen by activists as constitutive of the economy not just in the glamorized sectors of software and electronics but also at the grassroots. Hence, the very nature of activism and politics had to be changed to accommodate this new vision. Traditionally, most labor movements in India had been characterized by strategies of conflict and protest—*hartals* (strikes), *gheraos* (coercive detainment), and fasts. A fight over information, rather than one over wages and material benefits, needed a new strategy and "it was in the search for a more *neutral* and *open* platform for democratic *expression* that the MKSS hit upon the idea of organizing village based public hearings called *Jan Sunwais*" (ibid., 3, italics mine). What the public hearings would institute was a new methodology of agitation and social redress based on an objective mode that was "conducted in a comfortable, informal idiom of conversation and exchange. Yet it has all the seriousness and impartiality of court proceedings" (ibid., 4).

The framing of activism as "conversation and exchange" is inherently tied to a civics of information that views its transfer and circulation as a condition for political engagement.[12] The info-activism that led to the RTIA therefore sets in motion a mode of politics that is new in the Indian context. To model a social movement on court proceedings is to embrace the notion that the elucidation of truth by means of accessing all relevant information is the fundamental axiom from which political thought and action are to be derived. The keywords of such a program—data, documents, accessibility, transparency, accountability—derive from the politics of informatics. Thus, as Roy and Dey further observe, the main purpose of the *Jun Sunwais* was to address the "yawning gap" between information and reality and provide the missing informational link that would "prove the where, the when, and the how of the misappropriation; prove the crime, and help shatter the façade created on paper" (ibid., 8). Informational objects thus become political tools. "The people, including those who had never been to school, understood the power that lay in certain documents" (ibid., 9). The state had always produced information for its own purposes, but this information was stored in the lockbox of bureaucratic orthodoxy and functioned as a sort of weapon that could intimidate and exclude the masses. The RTIA seeks to activate these vast reserves of information and thus redirect the "power that lay in certain documents" into the hands of the citizenry. It is fitting that in the process of articulating this new politics, "the 'photocopy' became a synonym for an authenticated document in the common terminology of the struggle" (ibid., 10). A photocopy after all is an informational entity par excellence. It suggests infinite replication and circulation and its formal properties make it the perfect instrument for the democratization of information.

The reaction of seasoned politicians to the right of information movement illustrates its radical nature. Thus L. K. Advani, president of the Indian People's Party (BJP) that ruled the Central government from 1999 to 2004, had himself initiated a *rath yatra* (a protest movement) that sought to root out fear, hunger, and corruption. Yet he and his party refused to legislate on the right to information. In fact, he once allegedly asked in a sarcastic vein, "Is this (RTI) an issue to have a *dharna* [agitation] on?" (ibid., 12). Although a career politician, Advani could not recognize the new type of activism and politics that was being born literally under his feet. For him, as for most of the old guard, politics was about material goods and about ideology. The BJP that he led largely stood for the interests of the business community and espoused a strident form of Hinduism, and its politics had little to do with information. The right to information movement, on the other hand, saw information as the crucial currency of a participatory democracy. As the MKSS slogan memorably put it: *Jaanne ka adhikaar, jeene ka adhikaar* (the right to know is the right to live).

The right to information is thus fundamental in two senses. It is, as the MKSS slogan announces, an ontological axiom that claims that the human subject is at the same time a *knowing* subject. To put it in familiar Cartesian language: I know, therefore I am. It is also fundamental because it posits a "just epistemology," that is, an epistemology that allows all subjects access to and understanding of all the relevant information, thus laying the groundwork for a legitimate democracy. What is striking here is that an info-activism based on such philosophical beliefs could successfully operate at the very ground zero of Indian social reality: landless and indentured labor, communities ravaged by drought and famine, subsistence farmers. The "illiteracy" of these disenfranchised populations was not, as in times past, posed as the hurdle to be overcome before they could become fully vested political subjects. The oral mode of the *"jun sunwai"* guaranteed that information could be extracted from the written document and communicated in a conversational format while the centrality of the "photocopy" ensured that doubling of the record meant that even the "unlettered" could be inserted in and participate in the information order.

However, it would be inaccurate to view such forms of info-activism as an exclusively bottom-up phenomenon. As we have already seen, the Indian state had been in the process of "informatizing" itself from the 1980s onward. In a sense, then, info-activism was following rather than leading the state in this regard. One might view the expansion of communication infrastructure, which I have explored in the previous chapter, as a necessary corollary for the installation of an information-based political ontology. More specifically, the state, even as it enjoyed and exercised the privileges of protected information, was not entirely hostile to the idea of a right to information. Ever since Independence, there were sporadic attempts on the part of the state to ameliorate the draconian aspects of the Official Secrets Act. Thus, as early as 1948, a Press Laws Enquiry Committee recommended that the act only be applicable "to matters which must remain secret in the interests of national security" (Mander and Joshi, 1999, section 6). Similar recommendations were suggested by a Working Group of the Government of India in 1977, by another governmental committee in 1989, as well as a second Working Group set up in 1997. None of these reports and recommendations had much effect on governmental policy. However, another state-sponsored group of social activists, civil servants, and lawyers that met at the National Academy of Administration in Mussoorie in 1995 would play a significant role in the eventual passing of the RTIA. The ideas that this group generated were picked up by the Press Council of India and resulted in the formulation of an initial draft of the RTIA.

If the governmental arm of the state had been inching toward informational rights even while dragging its feet, the judiciary had been strongly vocal on this issue for a quite some time. To take one example, as early as 1981, the Supreme Court (SP Gupta vs. President of India, Supp. SCC 87) opined that:

> Where a society has chosen to accept democracy as its creedal faith, it is elementary that the citizens ought to know what their government is

doing ... The people of this country have a right to know every public act, everything, that is done in a public way, by their functionaries. They are entitled to know the particulars of every public transaction in all its bearing.

(Mishra, 2003, 2)

Thirty-four years after the delivery of this judgment, the government of India would enshrine the right to know with the passage of the Right to Information Act. The official document begins by stating that this is "an Act to provide for setting out the practical regime of right to information for citizens to secure access to information under the control of public authorities" and goes on to declare that "Whereas democracy requires an informed citizenry and transparency of information ... NOW, THEREFORE, it is expedient to provide for furnishing certain information to citizens who desire to have it" (Government of India, Ministry of Law and Justice).

What we find here is an unexpected convergence between grassroots discourse and governmental ideology. In spite of the protracted struggle between activists and bureaucracy, there existed a commonality of purpose between organizations like the MKSS and a committed group of reform-minded officials and ministers. We have as an example a single individual who personifies this convergence—Harsh Mander, one of the nation's leading info-activists also spent many years as a bureaucrat in the Indian Administrative Service. What can account for this unlikely alliance? One possible answer is that the turn to information is intimately linked with the character of contemporary capitalism, and so RTIA, along with the Indian state, should be seen as agents of neoliberal governance. Thus Aradhana Sharma has argued that, "the global regime of neoliberal governmentality challenges state sovereignty and verticality by attempting to downsize governments" and that "the technocratic casting of transparent and good governance under neoliberalism lends a formalized and procedural hue to the ground-level workings of Indian RTI law (2013, 321, 309). For this line of thinking, the RTIA is ultimately a consequence of an ideology that reboots the state in a technocratic manner only to further align it with the neoliberal global order.

There is certainly enough evidence that the slogans of the RTI movement fit with the assumptions of this global fiduciary logic. Thus, the World Bank's answer to the question "What is Governance?" is replete with ideas and prescriptions that would not be out of place in any activist handbook:

> Dimensions of governance: Property rights and rule-based governance; the quality of budgetary & financial management; the efficiency of revenue mobilization; the efficiency of public expenditures; and transparency, accountability and corruption.
>
> Good governance: "Good governance is, among other things, participatory, transparent and accountable. It is also effective and equitable.

And it promotes the rule of law. Good governance ensures that political, social and economic priorities are based on broad consensus in
society and that the voices of the poorest and the most vulnerable are
heard in decision-making over the allocation of development resources."

Mechanisms for assuring good governance have three key elements:
Internal rules and restraints (for example, internal accounting and
auditing systems, independence of the judiciary and the central bank,
civil service and budgeting rules); *"Voice" and partnership* (for example, public-private deliberation councils, and service delivery surveys
to solicit client feedback); and *Competition* (for example, competitive
social service delivery, private participation in infrastructure, alternative dispute resolution mechanisms, and outright privatization of certain market-driven activities).

(World Bank, 2013)

In spite of the discursive overlap between progressive activism and the
World Bank, it is perhaps unwise to argue that they are ideologically indis-
tinguishable from each other. In her finely nuanced account of the RTI
Campaign in India, Amita Baviskar points out that, "While the Campaign uses a similar vocabulary of 'deepening democracy' through 'public
accountability' it brings very different meanings to this discourse" (2006,
21). Whereas the World Bank may militate against bureaucratic opacity to
ensure the smooth circulation of global capital, "The RTI Campaign yokes
the issue of transparency to the effective implementation of state social
security programmes for food and employment" (ibid., 21). I would concur
with Baviskar in holding that while the turn to information most certainly
occurs within the larger frame of neoliberalism, informationalism is neither
exhausted by nor reducible to such a context. There is no a priori reason why
informationalism—when thought of as a set of technologies, protocols, and
practices—should not be, at least partly, autonomous of the current phase in
capitalist development. After all, during the course of the twentieth century,
industrialism had supported both western capitalism and the communist
economies. Indeed informationalism can as easily turn against neoliberal
interests as work for them. As I have been discussing, the push for more
information and transparency comes not just from states that seek to curry
favor with neoliberal institutions like the World Bank and the International
Monetary Fund (IMF) but also from an entire spectrum of activists, governmental agencies, and public citizenry including the very poor. The lesson
here is that information does not *belong* per se to capital any more than
land or produce and is thus capable of exposing, subverting, and challenging its logic. The right to information movement is thus the most perfect
illustration of how information becomes the currency of such an activism.
What the RTIA achieves is an integration of information with the notion
of individual human rights. If such an equation is accepted as a premise,
it follows that politics will need to be reconceived of in the context of the

informational turn. In the next section of this chapter I investigate two well-publicized phenomena—the anti-corruption movement led by Anna Hazare and the emergence of the Aam Aadmi Party as a political force—to analyze how info-activism can be articulated within the sphere of collective action. By initiating a broad-based campaign against corruption and mal-practice, info-activism begins to enter the stage of national politics.

The Aam Aadmi Party: Info-Activism as Politics

In the summer of 2011, India witnessed a series of mass protests around the demand of a Lokpal (trans: ombudsman) Bill that was designed to fight rampant corruption in public life. Led by the veteran Gandhian reformer Anna Hazare, the India Against Corruption movement snowballed into what was described as a fundamental conflict between "civil society" and the state represented by both the government and by Parliament. This con-frontation led to high political theater: a series of fasts by Hazare, mass rallies in the capital New Delhi, the participation of the middle classes, and constant coverage by the media. Although the India Against Corruption movement would peter out eventually, it did succeed in its original goal when, after a protracted series of debates and revisions, the Central govern-ment passed the Lokpal and Lokayuktas Act in January 2014. Moreover, the movement would also give birth to a political party—the Aam Aadmi Party led by Arvind Kejriwal, one of Hazare's lieutenants—which would subsequently earn spectacular victories in the 2013 and 2015 elections for the Delhi Assembly.[13]

In what follows I provide an analysis that places both the India Against Corruption (IAC) movement and the Aam Aadmi Party (AAP) within the frame of the informational turn that has been the focus of this entire book. The focus on "corruption" as well as the invocation of "civil society" as the ground for the fight against injustice that characterized both IAC and AAP can be better understood, I argue, by seeing them as derived from a more general climate of info-activism that began with the right to informa-tion campaign. Whereas the RTI movement conceived of information as a matter of individual rights, what the anti-corruption movement and the AAP demonstrate is that information-based activism can become the motor for political activity as well. I develop this argument by looking closely at the career of Arvind Kejriwal, a veteran info-activist initially associated with the RTI campaign, who would later go on to create and lead the Aam Aadmi Party, an organization that, I suggest, has used the principles of info-activism to achieve its current stature. The trajectory of Kejriwal's career can thus be seen as mirroring the movement of info-activism from individual to nation-based politics, and a detailed consideration of Kejriwal's role in this trans-formation enables us to conceptualize the emergence of info-activist politics.

Arvind Kejriwal was born in the northern state of Haryana. Educated at the prestigious IIT Kharagpur, a technocratic temple of Nehruvian India, he worked for the Tata Steel Company before joining the Indian Revenue Services (IRS) in 1992. While still a government official, he created an activist group named Parivartan (trans: change) to help citizens deal with income tax related problems, unfair electricity bills, and the vagaries of the food rationing system. The organization had considerable success: it mediated grievances between citizens and the concerned government departments, and succeeded, at times, in exposing corrupt tax and utilities officials who were taking bribes (Webb, 2012, 211). In one notable case, Parivartan investigated the food distribution system in New Delhi to discover that more than 80% of the food grains meant for the poor were being siphoned off from ration shops to the black market (Deshmuskh, 2006). The populist campaign it ran in a neighborhood called Sunder Nagri would subsequently force the Delhi Public Distribution System (PDS) to change its mode of functioning and institute a framework that allowed for regular public inspections of PDS records (Webb, 2012, 212). It is clear that Parivartan was conceived of and operated as an info-activist organization. Its primary mission was to unearth "secret" information that by all rights belonged to the public. However, Parivartan did have its critics. According to one of its founding members, a Delhi colony where Parivartan had expended a lot of effort "bears no sign [today] of the change the idealistic group's efforts should have borne" (Anand, 2012). Whatever the merits of such criticism, Kejriwal earned the plaudits of the public at large. In 1996, for example, he would win the prestigious Magsaysay Award for Emergent Leadership in recognition of "his activating India's right-to-information movement at the grassroots, empowering New Delhi's poorest citizens to fight corruption by holding government accountable to the people" (Ramon Magsaysay Award Foundation, 2015).

Kejriwal quit the IRS the same year he won the Magsaysay to devote himself full time to social activism. He started the Public Cause Research Foundation, an organization that was devoted to local self-governance promotion and RTI-related campaigns "to ensure that our society becomes more inclusive and that real power rests with the common citizens of India" (Public Cause Research Foundation, 2006). The organization embarked on a range of activities: starting legal cells to help common people get relief at consumer courts as well as in the higher courts, issuing right to information awards that recognized citizens and officials who "kept the flag of RTI high," and creating local people's assemblies that would promote self-governance by acquiring control over untied funds and by having the power to appoint and dismiss local officials. The trajectory of Kejriwal's career up to this point strongly establishes his info-activist credentials. He began as a facilitator of information regarding tax laws and regulations, and with Parivartan he attempted to gather and distribute information that the poor could use to their benefit. In this period, Kejriwal had strong ties with Aruna Roy as well other leaders of the RTI campaign. As the Magsaysay citation points out he was instrumental in "activating India's right to information movement."

I would like to characterize this pre-Aam Aadmi "early Kejriwal" as representing "informationalism from below," that is, as subscribing to a perspective that sees information as one among many weapons in the fight conducted by the marginalized in the quest for expression and social justice. Such a use of information (and of information technology) in the South Asian context has been the focus of much recent research. Take, for example, Radhika Gajjala's (2014) work on cyberculture and the subaltern, Aswin Punathambekar's (2008) analysis of the use of new media platforms by cinema fans in South India to construct a public space, and Ravi Sundaram's (2011) account of the use of new media technologies by Delhi's poor.[14] Kejriwal's subsequent career, I will argue, represents a different philosophy, one that conceives of information not as one among many resources but as the very essence of contemporary democratic society. Even as he was involved with the specific aspects of the Right to Information Act, he could see its larger potential when declaring, "It will take the form of a mass movement" (Baisakh, 2006). This "late Kejriwal" represents a deeper and more pervasive brand of informationalism that goes beyond issue-oriented activism to politics itself. In the discussion that follows I offer a highly condensed account of the events that led to the passage of the Lokpal Bill and the creation of the Aam Aadmi Party in order to demonstrate how informationalism became the ground for a new type of politics.

The immediate spur for the paradigm shift in info-activism was a series of high-profile informational leaks that came to light at the close of the millennium's first decade. These included the 2G telecommunications scam of 2008, the 3G scam that followed in its wake, the Commonwealth Games scam of 2010, and the Adarsh Housing Society scam of 2011.[15] These scams came to light largely due to the efforts of what might be termed an "info-activist media" no longer content to merely report the news but committed to uncovering hidden facts through investigative techniques like sting operations.[16] The general sense of outrage and anger that these revelations caused in the public at large made the moment a propitious one for the creation of a protest group that called itself India Against Corruption. As the organization described itself, "India Against Corruption movement is an expression of collective anger of people of India against corruption" (India Against Corruption, 2012). Although grandiloquent in its vision, the organization had a very specific agenda: "We have all come together to force/request/persuade/pressurize the Government to enact the Jan Lokpal Bill. We feel that if this Bill were enacted it would create an effective deterrence against corruption" (ibid.). The Lokpal in question was to be an independent ombudsman who would entertain and investigate charges of corruption brought against high-ranking governmental figures and would possess prosecutorial powers as well. The idea for such a regulatory entity was not new; the term "Lokpal" had been coined in 1963 by a member of the Indian Parliament, and the very first Lokpal Bill was introduced in Parliament in 1968. Although it passed the Lok Sabha (lower house—loosely equivalent to the House of Commons) in 1969, it failed in the Rajya Sabha (upper house—loosely representative of the House of Lords) and then lapsed. There were several subsequent attempts in the following decades, all of which failed to be turned into law (Sharma and Shrivastava, 2012, 4).

The India Against Corruption movement was to be successful where earlier attempts had failed. How did the Lokpal Bill come into existence? In the wake of the scams described above, reformists shifted their focus from informational rights to the redress of wrongs through extra-governmental agencies. Indicative of this shift was the decision by the National Campaign for People's Right to Information (NCPRI) in September 2010 to draft a Lokpal Bill that would serve as a model for the one that eventually passed. The drafting committee responsible for this bill was headed by Kejriwal; although this group would soon disband due to internal differences, Kejriwal would go on to form a small informal team to carry on the work the committee had started. The new group included Shanti Bhushan, a former Union Law Minister who had proposed the Lokpal Bill in 1968; his son Prashant Bhushan, a Supreme Court lawyer and activist; Kiran Bedi, the policewoman turned activist; and Santosh Hegde, a former Supreme Court Justice. Kejriwal sought to expand the scope of his fledgling team beyond the circle of activists by organizing a joint anti-corruption rally near Parliament whose celebrity participants included religious figures like Baba Ramdev and Swami Agnivesh, whose politics were somewhat distant from the secular platform that Kejriwal had originally espoused. Following this successful demonstration, the group, now calling itself "India Against Corruption," sent a draft of its Lokpal Bill to Prime Minister Manmohan Singh, demanding a "total overhaul of the anti-corruption delivery system" (Jeelani, 2011).

The Indian government's refusal to respond to this letter led to a historic chain of events that pitted "civil society" against a democratically elected government and Parliament. So dramatic was this contest that *Time* magazine named it among the top 10 news stories of 2011 along with the Arab Spring and the killing of Osama Bin Laden. The human face that *Time*, as well as the Indian media, associated with the Lokpal agitation was not that of Kejriwal but of Anna Hazare, a Gandhian reformist and activist from rural Maharashtra. It's hard to imagine this diminutive, celibate octogenarian being the dynamo behind an entire popular movement. But in India, Anna Hazare cut a Gandhian pose that transfixed the world's largest democracy and put its sitting government's feet to the fire.

Hazare's repeated fasts against corruption attracted tens of thousands of supporters and paralyzed India's Parliament. While critics spy corruption within Hazare's own ranks and point to his ties to the Hindu right wing, his protest channeled the widespread exasperation and anger of India's rising middle class, frustrated with the age-old habits of graft that still dominate much of India's calcified bureaucracy (NDTV, 2011).

So dominant was Hazare's public role that during the course of 2011, India Against Corruption began to be eponymously referred to as Team

Anna. Not only did the public and the media contribute to this cult of personality, but even the critical writing on the sequence of events, which began dramatically with Hazare's fast and ended somewhat inconclusively in the winter with the passage of a Lokpal Bill in the Indian Lok Sabha, tended to focus almost exclusively on the figure of Hazare in analyzing this novel confrontation.

The emphasis placed by the media on Hazare's Gandhian background, his quixotic personality—he once suggested that the public should "slap the corrupt"—and his dramatic tactics may have obscured his deep roots in info-activism. In August 2003, for example, Hazare went on a successful "fast-unto-death" to force the Maharashtra State government to enact a local right to information measure. Hazare's commitment to the idea of informational access is evident from his comment that "once RTI becomes part of the culture, the poor will get the real taste of freedom" (Baishakh, 2006). Moreover, the overall strategy employed by the India Against Corruption campaign was not restricted to Gandhian tactics like fasting. Even at its onset the movement made itself digitally present through a Facebook page as well as websites like "I Paid a Bribe," which enabled ordinary citizens to record their own experiences of corruption (Denyer, 2011). Finally, as events titled "Seminar on Right to Information: A Potent Weapon Against Corruption" and "A Man Fights Corruption with Right to Information Act" (YouTube) testify, the public at large explicitly drew the connection between corruption and an asymmetric informational order.

India Against Corruption was therefore strongly influenced by the info-activist currents that had originated with the right to information campaign. Moreover, I argue, the movement was more indebted to Kejriwal and his brand of informational politics than has been commonly acknowledged. Though Hazare featured most prominently on national media, a closer scrutiny of the genealogy of India Against Corruption and Team Anna reveals that it was info-activism rather than Gandhian ideology that lay at the root for the anti-corruption struggle. In a sharply titled piece called "Anna Was an Afterthought in Anti-Corruption Crusade," Raman Kirpal (2011) makes the point that "If the figure of Anna Hazare has become a larger-than-life symbol of the corruption movement in India … Anna was not always the leader in waiting." Kirpal traces the story of how Team Anna began as an effort by Kejriwal to fill the vacant post of chief information officer, called for by the RTIA, with a non-governmental figure who would be immune to political pressure. In other words, the movement began as a quest for a sort of *information czar* who would be non-partisan and beyond reproach. Kejriwal's candidate for the position—the celebrity police officer Kiran Bedi—had the support of various luminaries including Hazare himself, the media mogul Subhash Chandra, Infosys chairman N. R. Narayana Murthy, and Bollywood star and producer Aamir Khan.[17] This is a list of info-activists: in the previous chapter I showed how Narayana Murthy's vision for "A Better India" offered a blueprint for an info-nation from a corporate perspective, while later in this chapter I discuss how Aamir Khan's hugely successful television talk show *Satyamev Jayate* amounts to info-activism by other means.

In other words, Kejriwal was part of an info-activist network that had begun to make its mark on the Indian political arena. When the government proved unresponsive to Bedi's candidature, Kejriwal and his team shifted their focus from RTI to corruption. This shift was not a disavowal of info-activism; it was rather tantamount to an enlargement of its goals and strategies. Tackling a huge national problem like corruption—India ranks 85th among 174 countries according to one recent report (Times of India, 2014)—would demonstrate that info-activism could go beyond the purely informational domain of the RTIA and yet impact the political process. Kejriwal needed a credible face to lead the movement and found what he was looking for in Anna Hazare. Till that point Hazare had been a reformer in the Acharya Vinobha Bhave mold; his work was restricted to rural Maharashtra, and he could hardly be described as a national figure.[18] Kejriwal calculated that such a venerable figure would be the ideal symbol for an anti-corruption movement and in recruiting Hazare reputedly told him "instead of the Gandhi of Maharashtra, we'll make you the Gandhi of India" (Jeelani, 2011). The choice of Hazare as figurehead for India Against Corruption was therefore a purely instrumental one and reflected the gap between Kejriwal's middle-class information-driven agenda and Hazare's moralistic and almost pre-modern crusade. It was thus no surprise that in spite of the historic impact that the IAC made during the course of 2011 and 2012, Hazare and Kejriwal decided to part ways. Whereas Kejriwal thought that the time was propitious for the IAC to enter electoral politics, Hazare was of the opinion that such a move would compromise the integrity of the movement. Consequently, Team Anna split into two in November 2012. Kejriwal left the organization to start the Aam Admi Party while Hazare and a few others stayed behind. The fate of these two factions has turned out to be dramatically dissimilar: while Kejriwal would lead the AAP to sensational electoral triumphs in 2013 and 2015, "Team Anna," or more correctly its rump, was to slowly sink into political oblivion.

Kejriwal's centrality to the formation and conduct of India Against Corruption, as well as his rise to prominence after the organization's dissolution, underscores the point that *both* the anti-corruption movement led nominally by Hazare and the meteoric rise of the Aam Aadmi Party must be analyzed in terms of a new mode of politics whose roots lie in info-activism. Before I provide an informationalist reading of the AAP, I want to briefly return to Team Anna and the issue of corruption. I have been trying to suggest that "corruption," ostensibly a moral category, got its heft by being integrated within an info-activist framework. In other words, corruption could become such a galvanizing concept precisely because it had been preceded by the movement for information rights and could thus be seen as an extension and enhancement of such info-activism. Whereas the Indian public had always been resigned to corrupt officials and politicians—recall that the first proposal for a Lokpal came as early as 1968—it is only in the aftermath of RTI that it embraced anti-corruption as a political weapon. RTI provided the blueprint for an info-activist methodology that could now be employed in the form of a dramatic mass agitation against corruption.

With such a framework in view we are better able to locate the critical reactions to the Hazare movement. The responses to the events of 2011 on the part of the Indian intelligentsia were roughly of two sorts. The first approach held that India Against Corruption (IAC) was nothing more than an exercise on behalf of domestic and international capital. Thus in a passionately argued piece entitled "I'd rather not be Anna" Arundhati Roy argued that Hazare's campaign demonized the government only "to call for the further withdrawal of the State from the public sphere and for a second round of reforms—more privatization, more access to public infrastructure and India's natural resources" (2011). Others pointed out that IAC was conspicuously silent on the issue of corporate corruption (Bannerjee, 2011). In other words, for a certain group of commentators, the IAC could only be analyzed by placing it within the general frame of neoliberalism. The underlying reasoning here was that to the extent Team Anna weakened the state's grip on the polity, it served the purposes of neoliberal capital to privatize every aspect of social life. A second group of critics was somewhat more measured and conceded that the IAC represented something new in Indian politics. But their conclusions questioned the political effectiveness of the movement that was variously characterized as "explicitly apolitical" (Chatterjee, 2012, 118), as a symptom that "civil society is depoliticized" (Chandhoke, 2012) or arising from "the awful decline in the legitimacy of elected politicians" (Varshney, 2011). Most in this group of authors identified the middle class as the bearer for the anti-corruption movement. The widespread decline in the quality and relevance of "politics," both in the electoral realm and in civil society, they argued, compelled the middle classes to fervently attach to a vacuous ideology of anti-corruption as a means of expressing its existence and will. Thus, even though the movement was well intentioned, its emergence pointed to a lack of real politics.[19]

Such an analysis, I suggest, can be folded in within the informational account provided earlier. What may seem at first glance to be without content and therefore "apolitical" may actually represent a turn toward info-activist politics. As one outspoken critic somewhat inadvertently notes, the anti-corruption movement wants to "render all things and people transparent, visible, accessible to its power by unleashing catastrophes like the Unique Identification Database Scheme" (Sengupta, 2011). Such an allegation has a very real basis, for as I have argued the entire movement was predicated on a logic that prioritized informational issues above all others. The push for informational democracy had been spearheaded by activists and professionals and, as several commentators have pointed out, IAC/Team Anna was in fact strongly middle class in composition and character (Sitapati, 2011; Shukla, 2013). But does the movement's strong middle-class bias mean that it was without any significance? One need not go as far as the sociologist Shiv Visvanathan in seeing it "as a magical moment and a new step in the middle-class attempt to enlarge citizenship and democratize democracy" (2012, 110). Nevertheless, the movement was not *content-free*, for it demonstrated in a dramatic manner the effects of implementing an info-activist agenda on the national stage. The IAC, as we saw, would soon give way to the Aam Aadmi Party (AAP), and in what follows I analyze the AAP's key features to more fully investigate the nature of info-activist politics.

A very brief history of the Aam Aadmi Party is due here. The party was formed in November 2012, when Kejriwal split with Hazare on the issue of participating in the electoral process. The AAP would subsequently participate in the 2013 Delhi Assembly elections and score a stunning upset by winning 28 of the 70 Assembly seats. It formed a minority government in December 2013 with the help of the Congress Party and installed Kejriwal as its chief minister. The brief tenure of this government was marked by considerable turbulence: Kejriwal and his fellow ministers turned protestors and staged several sit-ins against the Union government on the issue of control over the Delhi police; the party's Law Minister Somnath Bharti conducted a controversial midnight raid in a "red-light district" drawing accusations of vigilantism and racism; the party made constant promises about reducing electricity and water charges that were clearly not feasible. It was evident that the AAP was finding it difficult to make the transition from activism to governance and when a Jan Lokpal Bill it had sponsored failed to find any support, Kejriwal and his government abruptly resigned after a mere 49 days in power. This sudden change of heart would exact a steep price from the Indian electorate. Encouraged by its success in the Delhi elections, the AAP decided to fight the 2014 national elections on a grand scale, fielding candidates in as many as 434 constituencies. Its performance was, however, quite disappointing; it won only four seats (all of them in Punjab) and its overall appeal turned out to be very minimal—414 of its candidates ended up losing their deposits.[20] Most discouragingly for its supporters, the party failed to win a single seat in Delhi, a territory it had ruled a few months ago. Given that these elections resulted in a historic win for the Bharatiya Janata Party led by the charismatic Narendra Modi, it seemed to most observers that the AAP's brand of activist politics was a spent force. This assessment too has proved wrong, and at the time of this writing, the AAP is once more a force in Indian politics, having scored an even more comprehensive victory—winning an astonishing 67 out of 70 seats—in the recently concluded elections for the Delhi Assembly. It is still too early to come to any sort of judgment about the AAP's impact on Indian politics as a whole. It is reasonable to argue that in order to extend its support the party must go beyond issue-based politics, develop a broader vision of Indian society, and come up with a broader agenda of action in order to become a significant presence in the country's political landscape.

While its election manifesto—consisting of strong promises to end corruption, provide education and health services for all, and fight a range of evils like the "black" economy and gender and caste discrimination—may strike some as overly ambitious, the attempt to analyze the AAP as a traditional political party may itself be misguided. Within traditional theory, a political party is typically seen as being formed out of a set of social factors that include class, caste, religion, and ethnicity. Thus, in the words of two prominent political scientists, the Congress Party is "multi-regional, multi-caste and multi-religious," the BJP is "the promoter of a religion and religious culture defined by Hindu ethnicity and nationalism," the Communist parties are in effect "worker-peasant parliamentary parties," while more regional parties like the BJD in Orissa "are vehicles of the land-owning middle-peasant castes" (Sridharan and deSouza, 2006, 18–19). It is my suggestion that providing a similar characterization for the AAP obscures the nature of its intervention in Indian politics. Whereas traditional political parties try to grow beyond their natural constituencies and thus stand for the social totality, the AAP, I suggest, is better analyzed as a "partial" political party that is neither the authentic representative of particular social groups nor an aspirant to the throne of the social whole.[21] Instead, it may be more fruitful to think of it as an activist node in a network composed of other "actants" that comprise the nascent universe of info-politics: RTI, social media, corporate responsibility programs, NGOs, public-private partnerships, and the like.[22] In other words, AAP should be seen as an instance of the informational turning political, just as new media (Facebook, Twitter) are an example of the informational turning social. Such a move must be seen on its own terms: friendship in life is not the same as friendship on Facebook, similarly, AAP's mode of political activity may not be measurable yet by the yardsticks of traditional politics.

I would like to end this section by briefly examining the AAP's mode of operations in order to indicate the process by which info-activism intervenes in the political sphere. First, there is its extensive use of informational technology in order to reach and mobilize its constituency. As one observer noted after its first electoral victory, "A new political party shot into prominence in Delhi. It is not based on inherited power, wealth, community, caste or language, but on the principle of integrity. It has rapidly learnt to use social media. It follows the first Obama campaign in collecting small donations from the many, little from the rich" (Rao, 2013, 8). While the use of new media by political parties is not unique to the AAP—the BJP, for instance, made extensive use of digital technologies in its recent electoral triumph—its commitment to informational processes is deeper than most. The most striking example of this bent was the party's decision after its electoral victory in December 2013 to let the public decide whether it should form a minority government or not. In the hours leading up to the decision to assume power, Arvind Kejriwal told reporters: "A lot of public meetings are going on Sunday, including four in my own constituency New Delhi.

We will make the declaration Monday morning only after we get the opinion of the people, this is for the first time that such a thing is happening in India. Earlier, the common man's role was limited to just voting but we are going out to them and making them feel empowered ... We are the talk of the town. This is true democracy" (Colachal, 2013). What is distinctive about this episode is that an informational tool was being used not to predict an electoral outcome, but rather to determine the crucial political decision of whether to form or not to form a government. Here, clearly, the realm of the informational merged into that of the political.

The informational turn is also evident at the micro-political level of tactical practices that the party employed. In a highly illuminating account of the AAP's political practice as it pertains to party-building, Srirupa Roy describes four fundamental features of "intervention stories" that "are narratives about seemingly intractable problems encountered by the archetypical ordinary citizen, that are solved by the timely, simple, but effective intervention of an AAP party worker" (2014, 48). First, these intervention stories presented solutions as simple, ready-to-hand, and fundamentally easy; second, they relied on evidentiary practices—a smartphone photo of a potholed road, for example—to support claims of governmental wrongdoing; third, such stories were suffused by sentiments of heroic achievements; and finally they all narrated the confrontation between the powerful government and the powerless but brave people. The first two features that Roy cites are strongly informational in character. It is part of informational mantra that solutions are easily found once we have the right sort of data and procedures. And as the second feature in this list illustrates, hard data is what determines the truth about any state of affairs. It is easy to see why a positivist politics of this kind would generate the sort of affect that Roy points to; in this new world that AAP envisages, heroism may be no more than the capturing of relevant data and putting it to emancipatory use. Roy's example thus illustrates the process by which informational politics comes into being: information made available has the effect of generating affect among its consumers; that is, it makes them move into action. As Purnima Mankekar (2015) has recently argued, affect plays an increasingly important role in the articulation of Indian modernity. While Mankekar looks for traces of affect in contemporary media, I would like to suggest that the informational universe is another site that mobilizes affect to generate political energy.

The emergence and consolidation of the AAP, as well as the events of 2011–12 that led to its formation, exemplify the extension of the info-activist project into the realm of politics. If the RTI movement illustrates how information becomes constitutive of the notion of a citizen, the creation of India Against Corruption, Team Anna, and finally the Aam Aadmi Party shows how information plays a role in mobilizing collectivities for political action. As I have argued, the career of Arvind Kejriwal personifies the conceptual and substantive link between these two "emergences." The sensational impact of the Hazare movement as well as the remarkable success of the AAP in the

2013 and 2015 Delhi polls demonstrates how info-activism can successfully enlarge its scope beyond single-issue campaigns, like that for the Right to Information Act, and make demands on the polity as a whole. Whether such an enterprise can be sustainable over the long run and over the social whole is still a matter of speculation. The AAP's website reflects the conjunction of informatics and traditional political affect. While it outlines an agenda that is highly informational—changing the Delhi Electricity Regulatory Commission's laws; disqualifying a BJP MLA for providing false information, supporting the introduction of eco-friendly E-Rickshaw's—the party manifesto has to take recourse to the old Gandhian notion of "Swaraj" (just society) in order to articulate its total vision.[23] Nevertheless, the growing significance of info-activism is not a matter of dispute. My discussion so far has shown that the right to information movement placed the citizen-subject within an informational matrix and that info-activism subsequently began to mediate the realm of traditional politics. In what follows I examine how another crucial dimension of civil society—popular culture—is beginning to be influenced by information and info-activism.

Satyamev Jayate: Information as Popular Culture

The strength of an emerging social philosophy can often be accurately gauged by the extent to which it can capture the popular imagination. My intention in the concluding section of this chapter is to demonstrate info-activism's growing presence in the world of commercial entertainment and thus show its spread over the entire breadth of civil society. I argue my case through a close analysis of the talk show *Satyamev Jayate* (*Truth Alone Prevails*). I choose to focus on *Satyamev* because it is probably the first show in Indian television history to focus exclusively on issues of social justice that has garnered high ratings. In other words, *Satyamev* is an activist show that is also hugely popular. Hosted by the Bollywood superstar Aamir Khan, a longtime campaigner for progressive causes with strong connections to the RTI movement and to the Aam Aadmi Party, the show employs a whole array of informational devices and strategies in order to construct the message it wants to get across. An analysis of *Satyamev*, therefore, provides us with an excellent case study of how informationalism can operate in the world of entertainment and popular aesthetics.

   As previously noted, for the first two decades of its existence television broadcasting was synonymous with Doordarshan, the state-run broadcasting organization.[24] This meant that Indian television was much more "informative" than its counterparts insofar as it prioritized news, documentaries, and educational programming in a way that western television with its heavy bias toward entertainment did not. Moreover, information was thought of as a precious commodity that primarily "belonged" to the state. As I will show at greater length in the next chapter, with the arrival of cable television information thus became more democratized, at least on the assumption that privatization equals democratization (see Thussu, 1998; Kumar, 2006). However, it is only in recent years that television begins to get truly "informationalized" in the sense that information becomes both a milieu within which television operates and a process that structures televisual display. *Satyamev Jayate* is the perfect example of such a process.

Satyamev Jayate debuted in 2012 and has now run for three seasons. The show is hosted by the Bollywood superstar Aamir Khan, who, like many of India's big-screen stars, hailed from a "*filmi*" family—his father Tahir Hussain was a film producer, as was his uncle Nasir Hussain.[25] Khan began his acting career in 1984; his role in the tragic romance *Qayamat Se Qayamat Tak* (1988) would establish him as a popular actor, and he would then go on to star in such super-hits as *Lagaan* (2001), *Ghajini* (2008), *3 Idiots* (2009), and *Dhoom 3* (2013).[26] However, it is not Aamir Khan's significance as a film icon that is of interest here, but rather his role as an info-activist celebrity in producing and hosting a show that illustrates the informatization of popular culture. *Satyamev Jayate* is a talk show that highlights a range of social ills plaguing contemporary Indian society: female feticide, child abuse, dowry, rape, pesticide poisoning, casteism, corruption, and the criminalization of politics.[27] It operates with a classic format: an opening monologue by the host Aamir Khan, testimonies from victims, interviews with experts, and a closing plea for support and collective action to combat the social ill in question. Simulcast on seven channels including the state-run Doordarshan, the show has made a huge impact on live audiences, in the media, and in the online world. The show had a TRP (Television Rating Point) of 4.27 in its first season, a very high number in India's fiercely competitive market. Immediately after the airing of its first episode on female feticide, more than 100,000 viewers dialed in to speak with Khan. It continued its success in its second season, with nearly 80 million viewers tuning in to the season opener and its popularity with traditional audiences would be replicated in the online world. Thus, over 56,000 tweets about the show were recorded within 12 hours of the premiere launch (Satyamev Jayate Twitter Journey); it was the most searched item on Google trends in the weeks after its debut, and it currently has over 6 million "likes" on Facebook (Satyamev Jayate, 2012).

It is not a matter of chance that *Satyamev* was conceived of and created by Aamir Khan. While Khan is a legitimate Bollywood superstar, he has at the same time had strong roots in the activist community.[28] In 2006, for example, he participated in Narmada Bachao Andolan, a movement protesting the construction of large dams being built across the Narmada River led by the noted activist Medha Patkar (Sharma, 2006). He was also strongly involved with a large circle of info-activists well before he launched *Satyamev*. Thus he was a strong supporter of the RTI movement and an admirer of Kiran Bedi, one of Team Anna's key members. His involvement in info-activism is illustrated by a letter he wrote to the Indian prime minister canvassing for Bedi's appointment as chief information officer. In this letter, Khan quoted a recent study showing that only 27% of people who approach information commissions finally got the information they were seeking. "Therefore," Khan wrote, "we need a person who has demonstrated sensitivity, commitment and passion for public service. Ms Bedi qualifies on all these fronts" (vigilonline, 2015).

Khan's commitment to the goals of the anti-corruption movement are also evident from his comments to a caller who had dialed in following the first episode of *Satyamev*, in which he countered the suggestion that Hazare's ideas had fizzled out by saying that "Anna's movement could only be successful towards corruption if every individual has to ask oneself if he or she is associated with corruption or not" (dnaindia, 2012). He was equally effusive about another of the movement's leaders. Kejriwal had earlier lauded Khan's work by observing that "the kinds of films he does have a nationalistic message. For instance, see how good *Rang De Basanti* was. The film was actually about corruption" (Jeelani, 2011). And when the AAP won the Delhi elections against all expectations, Khan returned the favor: "It is a huge revolution. We had lost hope in political thinking and suddenly we have got this tidal wave that promises to be revolutionary" (oneindia, 2014).

Satyamev's "author" was therefore a dedicated info-activist. In what follows, I turn to a close analysis of one episode of *Satyamev Jayate* to demonstrate how its structure is governed by an informational logic and to look at the various ways the show is plugged into an informational matrix that combines activism, fund-raising, and marketing. The episode I look at was titled "Don't Waste Your Garbage" and first aired on March 16, 2014 (Season 2, Episode 3). The show's website provides a vivid account of the issues it addressed:

> 1,60,000 metric tonnes—that is the amount of garbage India generates every day! Most of this is wet waste, which can be used to produce fertilizer and generate electricity. Instead, huge mounds of it lie piled up in our cities and villages, posing a serious threat to public health and the environment … In this episode we bring you solutions. Some are simple ways to treat waste in our homes, so that we may reuse, recycle and revive the earth. While we must reduce our waste footprint, we must also put pressure on local authorities, especially at the municipal level, to ensure responsible waste management. We must demand that they set up effective mechanisms for the collection, segregation and treatment of solid waste.
>
> (Satyamev Jayate, 2015)

As we see above, the episode leads in with a metric—160,000 tonnes— then provides a concept—wet waste—and finally sets up the solution as a reciprocal exchange—we must reduce waste and we must demand that the public as a whole do the same. The logic can be summed up as one of "information-action." The episode's structure follows the standard format to which I have already alluded. Part I, "Dirty Business," opens with shots of garbage dumps, streets littered with garbage, and dumping grounds that are 100 feet high, shots of dangerous fires and toxic sludge that is polluting nearby water sources, and recorded interviews with farmers in a village near Bangalore that has seen outbreaks of various illnesses following the establishment of a landfill there.

This accumulation of visual and oral data is followed by a series of interviews with a number of solid waste management experts that turns this data into information by contextualizing it. Rishi Aggarwal, a Mumbai-based environmental activist, points out that there are several affordable and innovative techniques available to treat garbage but these are not being adopted by civic authorities who continue to hand out the task of waste management to private contractors. His message to the viewing public is threefold: reduce, reuse, and recycle. Then comes a success story as a Mumbai-based scientist, Dr. S. R. Maley, explains how a vast garbage dump in suburban Mumbai was transformed into a beautiful park. Part 2, "Waste Is Wealth," focuses on how garbage can be used as a resource. The guest for this segment, Dr. Sharad Kale, a scientist at Mumbai's Bhabha Atomic Research Center, explains the method by which garbage can be turned into biogas. His account is complemented by a couple of waste management specialists who talk about safe procedures for dealing with hazardous waste. The turn to experts, while a conventional authorizing move, also follows the information-action pattern outlined above. In each instance, by becoming more knowledgeable about the nature of "waste," we learn ways to convert it into "wealth." Part 3, "Invisible Environmentalists," deals with the plight of waste pickers and argues for their rights, highlighting organizations like SWaCH Plus, which works on upgrading waste pickers' skills, and *Kagad Kach Patra Kashtakari Panchayat*, a trade union of self-employed waste pickers and informal waste recyclers. This portion of the show highlights the "knowledges from below" that can be gleaned from the activities of the waste pickers who may work at the margins of a social ecology but are, in fact, crucial environmental actors whose skills can be upgraded with the help of "expert knowledges" from above. Part 4, "Frogs, Pigs, and You," veers toward the futuristic and presents the "Vellore model" that involves the use of cows, pigs, insects, and frogs as agents of waste management. While of less immediate application, this segment nonetheless connects present technologies to emergent ones while highlighting how the Vellore model is turning to non-human actors in thinking even more broadly about the ecology of waste and its management. The concluding section of the show honors pioneering waste management crusader, Dr. Almitra Patel, Convener, INTACH Waste Network, who has the distinction of bringing the issue of waste management to the attention of policy makers long before the media or the larger public became aware of it. The show ends with the catchy song "*aam ke aam*" that exhorts the listener to recognize the value of waste.

"Don't Waste Your Garbage" purveys an array of facts and techniques and anchors them in different expert regimes—scientists, garbage collectors, futurists, and pioneers—to provide an entire informational spectrum regarding waste as well as providing guidelines on how this knowledge can be operationalized. In other words, *Satyamev*'s most obvious informational feature is that it collects, processes, and presents action-oriented factual information. While waste management may be a topic especially conducive for such an exercise, the empiricist-instrumental outlook is evident in every episode of the show. In "Criminalization of Politics" (Season 2, Episode 5), for example, Khan provides detailed statistics regarding the phenomenon under consideration: of the 543 Members of Parliament elected in the 2009 general elections, as many as 30% faced criminal charges, some for serious crimes like murder, kidnapping, human trafficking, armed robbery, and rape. These figures reveal an upward trend: while the 2004 Parliament had 124 such cases, the corresponding figure for 2009 was 162. A percentage-wise break up of political parties shows that all of them are implicated. Thus, 32% of the BJP's elected members had been charged, 21% of the Congress, and quite astonishingly, 100% for the Jharkhand Mukti Morcha. As I showed in the first chapter, the field of statistics has a long and storied history in India and has been at the basis of colonial and postcolonial knowledge formation. What is worth noting here is the manner in which *Saytamev* converts data into information through sorting, structuring, and processing it, thus making it a basis for redress. Moreover, the talk show format itself makes information something to be shared and exchanged among different social actors including the audience, forming as it were a community around this information. This sort of data—presented with a variety of info-graphic aids—clearly resonates with the show's public. Lauding the eye-opening figures that "Criminalization" had provided, one viewer posted "all these datas (sic) and maps should be used in election campaigning" (Gupta, 2014). As the many responses to the show demonstrate, information can activate certain subjective processes. In other words, to become informed is to change in certain ways. Thus one viewer who watched the Season 3 episode "Accepting Alternative Sexualities" wrote to say, "I am conservative but this episode have (sic) changed my thought process, my support to LGBT" (Satyamev Jayate, 2015). Again in response to "A Ticking Time Bomb" that reported on the growing threat of tuberculosis, another viewer wrote, "I request u to plz tell dat how can I become supervisor or worker in Asha. I want to give medicines to d Patients" (sic, ibid.).

The info-activist aesthetic of *Satyamev* is not restricted to the show's format or its content. By means of its website, the show creates an informational appendix that both adds to the show and also allows it to spill over into other forums of discussion. Thus the web avatar of "Don't Waste Your Garbage" has multiple headings, each of which lets you click a button to access information related to that aired on television. Power To You button addresses households, establishments, and cities with the message that

"Whether you're a single person or a large city, make sure your waste is not wasted." From the Households button we can get six further options: composting at home, green ambassadors (young environmentally minded kids), different types of waste, recycling waste at home, quick guide to community composting, and making waste productive. And by clicking "composting at home" we can access a three-minute video featuring "social entrepreneurs" Leslie and Mayuri who make this practice a regular habit. In other words, not only does *Satyamev* transmit information by means of the show itself, but it also uses web click technology to insert audiences into an informational chain related to the topic featured on television. While such value additions and feedback loops are a feature of television's remediation by Internet technologies globally, in India where the percentage of the television audience that has web connectivity is significantly smaller, the formal and symbolic value of such "add-ons" exceeds its use value. The informational appendices function as techniques through which information can be converted into activism through a set of practices.

The show also makes use of information as a measuring device. The web feature IMPACT charts the effects of each episode that has aired to date. For instance, C. Srinivasan, the scientist who demonstrated the unexpected value of domestic animals for the purposes of waste management happily reported huge interest from the public toward his innovative methods. The calculation of "effects" through data that IMPACT computes is important for two reasons: it documents the ability of information to affect the viewer who then becomes a party interested in environmental activism. This process of measuring the work information does is also a measurement of the viewer's investment in the issue and is, therefore, one more step toward creating an activist. IMPACT also presents macro-data on Actions Taken, Votes for Change, and Public Donations. Clicking Actions Taken takes us to more info-graphics: histograms showing which regions voted the most in response to the topic, a word cloud showing the latest buzzwords, a social footprint showing the impact of the show globally (thus Waste had a high footprint in Iraq, Indonesia, Thailand, and South Africa among other places). Guest profiles give us specific information about each of the guests appearing on the show. And, finally, NGO Profiles features organizations that work in the area of waste management. The clickable "know more" at the bottom of each text box symbolizes the philosophy of *Satyamev*: it may be entertainment, but its primary purpose is to inform. As Aamir Khan once stated, "Our programmes are information and knowledge based and we are not shying away from that ... our first attempt is to gather information and in a journalistic manner, and do thorough research on every topic" (Jamkhandikar, 2012).

I have shown so far that *Satyamev* works at two informational levels: first, at the level of content, insofar as every episode depends crucially on the marshaling of a wide array of data pertinent to the issue being examined; and second, inter-medially in using its Web presence to create a large inter-linked dataset that increases the scope of the televisual content as well as presenting a link between information and action. The data generated by reactions to the airing of the show constitutes the third level of informatics associated with *Satyamev*. The huge numbers it has generated have called for big data analytics. To give a sense of the numbers involved, the show had 2.5 million views of its promo even before it first aired. The first episode (on female feticide) garnered 1.4 million responses across a range of platforms like Facebook, YouTube, Twitter, the official website, SMS, and voice call-ins (Persistent Systems, 2012). And by the end of the 13-episode first season, according to one source, there were 400 million viewers on Indian television and on YouTube, more than 8 million people contributed more than 14 million responses via Facebook and other digital platforms, and it created more than 1 billion impressions over the Web (Harris, 2012).

Anticipating this reaction, the producers hired Persistent Systems, an Indian IT consultancy firm with offices around the world, to collect and process the vast streams of data that followed in the show's wake. This was the first time in the history of Indian television that viewer responses and sentiments were tracked and analyzed on such a large scale. According to the company's publicity material, an infrastructure consisting of 50 machines, 8 servers, and a dedicated line were set up along with over 100 project analysts as well as over 1,000 crowdsourcing participants (Persistent Systems, 2012). The Persistent Big Data team developed a Content Filtering, Ranking, and Tagging System and assembled an array of automated tools to parse the data to produce "a cluster-based analysis along with trend, demographics and sentiment analysis for each message" (Ciol Bureau, 2012). As one commentator describes the process:

> As the responses begin to pour in, these are automatically tagged and scored based on factors such as sentiment and level of interest. What this means is that longer, more interesting messages will be given a higher quality score, while shorter messages that simply indicate agreement or disagreement will be ranked lower. After sorting through all of the responses, the cream of the crop is forwarded to analysts, who decide which ones should be featured on the show's website and its follow up radio show, which is aired each Friday.
>
> (Wheatley, 2012)

The data was displayed on a series of dashboards that were featured online as well as on the air. According to a vice-president for Star India, "We were very keen to understand and capture the chronology of change that is being affected through *Satyamev Jayate*" (Ciol Bureau, 2012).

The immense amount of data generated by *Satyamev* and subsequently analyzed by Persistent had an immediate impact. The show's first episode about female feticide garnered 158 million impressions online, 39 million written responses, and raised $481,470 for a charity for girls in the week before the show's second episode. During the show, Khan prompted the audience to vote whether a fast-track court should be established for doctors charged with aiding parents in female feticide; some cases had languished in the Indian court system for as long as seven years. When 99.6% of 291,313 people voted yes, Khan took the response to the prime minister of the province Rajasthan, and the court was established within a week of the show airing (Murphy, 2014). Moreover, the show's big data has become a valuable commodity. According to a senior official of Persistent, social science researchers from reputed universities have eagerly sought Facebook and Twitter comments on the show (Times of India, 2013).

It is interesting to note that the show originally found few believers. As Monika Shergill, a consultant to Star Network recalls, it was difficult for the team behind the show to make the stakeholders in the channel accept the idea. "At the end of the presentation, a couple of persons just yelled asking whether Aamir would just be giving social work *gyan* [advice] or would also be dancing to a movie song" (Times of India, 2013). In spite of its initial lack of appeal to industry insiders, *Satyamev*'s informational strategies have redefined what television entertainment means. "What social media did went far beyond anything I anticipated. It took the show and made it the people's show," Star India Network Chief Marketing Officer Gayatri Yadav observes, "So much so that I don't think that *Satyamev Jayate* is anything we own, either Star Network or Aamir Khan Productions. It's owned by the people, and they made it the people's brand. That's what the internet does, the megaphone shifts" (Murphy, 2014).

The statements that I just cited come mainly from the show's associates, boosters, and publicity agents. Though reflecting the perspectives of vested interests, they are still valuable in that they give us crucial insights into how *Satyamev* conceives of its mission. *Satyamev* sees itself as a talk show that uses information in order to mediate advocacy and activism. The show processes immense amounts of information to highlight an urgent issue and also utilizes the entire range of informational technologies and practices in ensuring that its content has the effect of encouraging activism around that issue.

What the success of *Satyamev* demonstrates is that information, in the variety of guises described above, can become part of television's entertainment complex. This suggests that information can begin to acquire an aesthetic dimension. While *Satyamev*'s vast appeal can be explained in terms of the inequities and injustices that it so vividly portrays, a significant part of its aesthetic draw lies in its ability to bring the abstract domain of charts, graphs, and surveys to life. *Satyamev* enables information to bear witness as eloquently and heart-wrenchingly as any of the victims who appear in person. This "data-speech" is the foundation for a new affective relationship between viewer and text that goes beyond traditional aesthetic categories of story, plot, drama, and so forth. At the same time *Satyamev* signals the advent of a new style of entertainment that utilizes media power in the interests of grassroots activism. In this sense, the show is on a continuum that includes the RTI, the anti-corruption movement, and AAP-brand politics.

Not only are Aamir Khan's personal ties to other activists important in this regard, but also his show itself is an example of info-activism that uses the aesthetic mode to issue calls for the democratic and socially beneficial use of information.

To sum up, this chapter has explored a third context in which the idea of an info-nation finds expression. The first chapter of this work showed that a largely unpublicized understanding between the Indian state and the computer and software industries facilitated the turn toward an informational society. The second chapter described the nascent emergence of an "informational state" by looking at changes in telecom and broadcasting regulations, at initiatives undertaken in the realm of e-governance, and at the discursive congruence between corporate and state policies on issues of equity and justice. This present chapter has argued that the push toward an info-nation is equally present within the domain of civil society. The grassroots movement that resulted in the passage of the Right to Information Act demanded that every citizen possess a basic set of informational rights. In other words, it claimed that in the digital age the citizen-subject was first and foremost an informational subject. The sensational impact of the Anna movement and the subsequent electoral successes of the Aam Aadmi Party demonstrated that demands based on informational issues could provide the ground for collective social action. Info-activism in this sense points to the possibility of info-politics. Finally, my discussion of Aamir Khan's *Satyamev Jayate* shows that such new expressions of subjectivity and collectivity can migrate beyond the boundaries of traditional civic action into the realm of commercial entertainment and popular culture. This analysis provides a convenient bridge to the next chapter where I look at how an informational perspective informs a range of programming on Indian television. There I provide an information-theoretic account of the history of Indian television that identifies and describes three major eras each characterized by a different stance toward information and communication. I go on to focus on one specific genre—reality television—to argue that it is an example, par excellence, of how information can become the basis of aesthetic production.

Notes

1. Several scholars have discussed the impact of the information revolution on specific aspects of human life. See Boutang (2011), Castells (2009), Lessig (2006), Hansen (2006), Manovich (2001), MacKinnon (2013), and Turkle (2012) for rich accounts of its effects on economics, social organization, law, aesthetics, media, social movements, and self-identity.
2. See Biswas (2011) and Pokharel (2011) for accounts of these movements as embodying civil society's struggle against the state.
3. My project here is strongly indebted to the work of several scholars of Indian media who have explored the complex relationship between media, identity, and nationalism. Purnima Mankekar (1999), in a groundbreaking study, showed how television programming profoundly shaped how women would be situated

as both domestic and national subjects. Arvind Rajagopal's (2001) seminal work demonstrated how Doordarshan's airing of serials based on religious epics enabled a resurgent Hindu nationalism. Shanti Kumar (2006) provided a rich overview of how television contributed to the construction of national identity from its early days to the present. I extend this mode of analysis to examine the relationship between information and nationhood. My thinking on how information constructs communities is influenced by the research on electronic mediation and the formation of virtual communities in the works of Aswin Punathambekar (2008), Radhika Gajjala (2014), and Madhavi Mallapragada (2014). I pursue the place of my research in relation to these and other scholarly works more fully in the Introduction to this book.

4. See Shah (2004) for a comprehensive review of the literature on social movements, and Ray and Katzensein (2005) for an analysis of movements in India that were based on factors such as gender, lower castes, environment, the Hindu Right, labor, farmers, and biotechnology.

5. It needs to be pointed out that activism has always had an informational dimension. The "traditional" activist movements I have listed have received great worldwide publicity and have been the object of many scholarly works. For example, on the Chipko movement, see Weber (1990) and Gandhi (2000); for the Narmada Bachao movement, see Shiva (2002) and Wood (2007). What is different in the case of info-activism is the shift from activism as information to activism over and about information.

6. I use the term "informationalism" in the sense proposed by Manuel Castells (2004) connoting the belief that "information and communication are the most fundamental dimension of human activity."

7. See Gupta (2012) and Hull (2012) for a rich account of information management and knowledge production in postcolonial bureaucracies in India and Pakistan, respectively.

8. The many shifts involving the Indian state's stance toward information, broadcasting, and entertainment has been superbly analyzed by Daya Thussu (1998, 2008).

9. For more on how online technologies enable the formation of the contemporary subaltern, see Gajjala (2014).

10. For my commentary on the history of the Right to Information Act, I am largely indebted to the following three accounts written by activists in the field: Roy and Dey (undated), Mishra (2003), and Mander and Joshi (1999). Aruna Roy and Nikhil Dey founded the Mazdoor Kisan Shakti Sangathana, the organization that spearheaded the demand for the RTI. Harsh Mander was a founding member of the National Campaign for the People's Right to Information. Neelabh Mishra is a journalist who writes on social issues. For an informative discussion of the larger context within which the RTI movement took shape, see Sharma (2014).

11. The RITA enjoined that "Every public authority shall, within one hundred days of the enactment of this Act, designate as many officers as the Central Public Information Officers, or State Public Information Officers, as the case may be, in all administrative units of offices under it as may be necessary to provide information to persons requesting for the information under this Act" (http://rti.gov.in/rti-act.pdf). As should be evident, the number of extant PIOs is woefully short to deal with the huge number of requests for information; moreover, more often

than not such officers are part of the bureaucratic machinery they are supposed to be disclosing.

12. For more on the idea of such an "info-politics," see Koopman (2014).

13. After winning the December 2013 Delhi Assembly elections, the Aam Aadmi Party abruptly quit office after only 49 days in power. Delhi was without a local government until the elections of February 2015 when the AAP won an even more spectacular victory.

14. For an account of the transnational aspects of identity formation in the networked world, see Hedge (2011).

15. The 2G scam involved massive kickbacks paid to a Cabinet minister to obtain electromagnetic spectrum licenses that resulted in losses over $35 billion to the national exchequer; the 3G scam that followed almost immediately afterward had to do with licensees bidding among themselves in direct contravention of governmental rules; the Commonwealth Games scam resulted in costs over $4.1 billion (against an initial estimate of $270 million) and revenues of only $38 million; while the Adarsh Housing Society Scam resulted in major politicians, bureaucrats, and military personnel being awarded prime property in violation of governmental rules. For a detailed analysis of these and other scams, see Maske (2007) and Vittal (2012).

16. *Tehelka* (Sensational) magazine, founded by Tarun Tejpal and Aniruddha Bahal in 2000, was the first and most notorious exponent of this new brand of journalism. Its first major sting, Operation West End, revealed footage of government officials taking bribes in a fake arms deal. For more academic discussions on the politics of information and technology, see Rajadhyaksaha (2011) and Sundaram (2011).

17. Kiran Bedi was the first woman officer in the Indian Police Service. Upon retirement, she became well known as a reformer and activist. She was a key figure in the India Against Corruption movement but later split with Kejriwal when the latter founded the Aam Aadmi Party. In early 2015 she joined the BJP and was their chief ministerial candidate for the Delhi Assembly elections in which she lost her race in the face of the sweep by the AAP.

18. Acharya Vinoba Bhave (1895–1982) was a noted social reformer and a leading disciple of Mahatma Gandhi.

19. These two readings are not irreconcilable; it is possible to combine them into one formulation that would argue that the anti-corruption movement is a specific articulation of middle-class ideology within the larger frame of neoliberalism. Though framed as a fight against corruption and injustice, the apolitical politics of the middle classes implicitly facilitate the domination of private capital over the elected government and the state.

20. In the Indian electoral system a candidate for office loses deposit money if he or she receives less than one-sixth of the total votes that were cast in that race.

21. While the BJP and Congress do this at the national level, regional parties like the BJD or AIADMK follow the same model at the level of the state.

22. I use "actant" in the sense that Bruno Latour has proposed – any entity, human or non-human that enters into relationships that result in action. See Latour (1987).

23. In other words, the AAP's manifesto presents both the technical aspects of info-activism and also tries to project its affective powers through the use of a notion like Swaraj. For an illuminating account of the role of affect in contemporary Indian modernity, see Mankekar (2015).

24. For informative accounts of the early history of Indian television and its transition from state broadcasting organ to a privatized medium and for contextualizing the medium's role in cultural politics, see Kumar (2006), Mankekar (1999), Mehta (2008), Ninan (1995), Punathambekar and Kumar (2014), and Sen and Roy (2014).
25. Nasir Hussain is perhaps best known as the director of the Hindi film classic *Yaadon Ki Baaraat*.
26. The last three titles were three of the highest-grossing films in Bollywood history.
27. Advocacy on Indian television goes back to the serials that ran on Doordarshan in the 1980s, the most notable of these being *Rajni* that featured a housewife whose mission was to combat social ills.
28. It could be convincingly argued that much of Khan's filmic oeuvre is strongly marked by his activist beliefs.

References

AAP. 2014. AAP Manifesto. Retrieved February 9, 2015, from https://app.box.com/s/q9k6f7e21265olkpxrzq.

Anand, P. 2012. The More They Change. *OutlookIndia*. Retrieved February 9, 2015, from http://www.outlookindia.com/article/The-More-They-Change/281825.

Baisakh, P. K. 2006. Right to Information: Principles, Practice and Prospects. *Orissa Review*, February-March 2006. Retrieved February 8, 2015, from http://orissa.gov.in/e-magazine/Orissareview/Feb-March2006/engpdf/right_to%20information_-%20principles.pdf.

Bannerjee, S. 2011. Anna Hazare, Civil Society and the State. *Economic & Political Weekly*, 46(36), 12–14. Retrieved April 12, 2015, from http://www.epw.in/commentary/anna-hazare-civil-society-and-state.html.

Bhatnagar, S. 2006. India's Software Industry. In V. Chandra (Ed.), *Technology, Adaptation and Exports: How Some Developing Countries Got It Right* (pp. 95–124). Washington, DC: World Bank.

Baviskar, A. 2006. Is Knowledge Power?: The Right to Information Campaign in India. Institute of Development Studies. Retrieved January 25, 2015, from http://rtiworkshop.pbworks.com/f/2006-00-IN-Is-Knowledge-Power-The-Right-to-Information-Campaign-in-India-Amita-Baviskar.pdf.

Biswas, S. 2011. Can Civil Society Win India's Corruption Battle? *BBC News South Asia*. Retrieved January 24, 2015, from http://www.bbc.com/news/world-south-asia-13745643.

Boutang, Yann Moulier. 2011. *Cognitive Capitalism*. Ed Emery (Trans.), Cambridge, UK: Polity.

Bratich, Jack Z. 2007. Programming Reality: Control Societies, New Subjects and the Powers of Transformation. In Dana Heller (Ed.), *Makeover Television: Realities Remodelled* (pp. 6–22). London: I.B. Taurus.

Castells, Manuel. 2004. Informationalism, Networks and the Networked Society: A Theoretical Blueprint. In Manuel Castells (Ed.), *The Network Society: A Cross-Cultural Perspective* (pp. 3–45). Northampton, MA: Edward Elgar.

Castells, Manuel. 2009. *The Rise of Network Society: The Information Age: Economy, Society and Culture*. Hoboken, NJ: Wiley-Blackwell.

Chandhoke, N. 2012. Whatever Has Happened to Civil Society? *Economic & Political Weekly*, 47(23), 39–45. Retrieved January 24, 2015, from http://www.epw.in/perspectives/whatever-has-happened-civil-society.html.

Chatterjee, P. 2012. The Movement against Politics. *Cultural Critique*, 81(1), 117–22.

Ciol Bureau. 2012. Satyamev Jayate under a New Lens Now. Retrieved February 5, 2015, from http://www.ciol.com/satyamev-jayate-lens/.

Cohn, B. 1996. *Colonialism and Its Forms of Knowledge*. Princeton, NJ: Princeton University Press.

Colachal, D. A. 2013. Delhi Poll Result: Common Man's Party to Form Government. Retieved August 17, 2014, from http://www.epw.in/perspectives/whatever-has-happened-civil-society.html.

Denyer, Simon. 2011. India's Anti-Corruption Movement Aims to Galvanize Democracy. *Washington Post*, August 12, 2011. Retrieved February 8, 2015, from http://www.washingtonpost.com/world/asia-pacific/indias-anti-corruption-movement-aims-to-re-energize-democracy/2011/08/09/gIQAWMVWAJ_story.html.

Deshmuskh, V. 2006. RTI: An Enormous Power with the People. Retrieved January 27, 2015, from http://indiatogether.org/arvind-interviews.

Dnaindia. 2012. After 'Satyamev Jayate', 1 Lakh People Dial in to Speak to Aamir Khan. Retrieved January 12, 2015, from http://www.dnaindia.com/entertainment/report-after-satyamev-jayate-1-lakh-people-dial-in-to-speak-to-aamir-khan-1686133.

Gajjala, R. (Ed.). 2014. *Cyberculture and the Subaltern: Weavings of the Virtual and Real*. Lanham, MD: Lexington Books.

Gandhi, R. 2000. *The Unquiet Woods: Ecological Change and Peasant Resistance in the Himalayas*. Berkeley: University of California Press.

Government of India (n.d.). Official Secrets Act, 1923. Retrieved January 24, 2015, from http://www.archive.india.gov.in/allimpfrms/allacts/3314.pdf.

Government of India. 2011. Right to Information Act, 2005. Retrieved January 27, 2015, from http://rti.gov.in/rti-act.pdf.

Government of India. 2015. A Programme to Transform India into a Digitally Empowered Society and Knowledge Economy. Department of Electronics and Information Technology, Government of India. Retrieved January 23, 2015, from http://pib.nic.in/newsite/PrintRelease.aspx?relid=108926.

Goyal, N. 2013. *The Summer of Discontent: How the 'India Against Corruption' Movement Unfolded*. Singapore: National University of Singapore.

Gupta, A. 2012. *Red Tape: Bureaucracy, Structural Violence and Poverty in India*. Durham, NC: Duke University Press.

Gupta, R. 2014. *Criminalization of Politics*. Retrieved August 13, 2014, from http://www.satyamevjayate.in/Criminalization-Of-Politics/EPISODE-5Watchvideo.aspx?uid=E5-EV-V2&lang=hindi.

Hansen, Mark B. N. 2006. *Bodies in Code: Interfaces with Digital Media*. New York: Routledge.

Harris, D. 2012. How India's Favorite TV Show Uses Data to Change the World. Retrieved January 15, 2015, from https://gigaom.com/2012/08/11/how-indias-favorite-tv-show-uses-data-to-change-the-world/.

Hegde, R. (Ed.). 2011. *Circuits of Visibility: Gender and Transnational Media Cultures*. New York: New York University Press.

Hull, M. S. 2012. *Government of Paper: The Materiality of Bureaucracy in Urban Pakistan*. Berkeley: University of California Press.

India Against Corruption. 2012. About IAC. Retrieved January 28, 2015, from http://www.iacahmedabad.org/about/about-iac.

Jain, B. 2013. Home Ministry Opposes Changes in Official Secrets Act. *Times of India*, July 25, 2013. Retrieved November 15, 2014, from http://timesofindia.

indiatimes.com/india/Home-ministry-opposes-changes-in-Official-Secrets-Act/articleshow/21321623.cms.

Jamkhandikar, S. 2012. Bollywood Chat: Aamir Khan on 'Satyamev Jayate'. *Reuters*. Retrieved from http://in.reuters.com/article/2012/08/02/bollywood-amir-khan-satyamev-jayate-idINDEE8710FA20120802.

Jeelani, M. 2011. The Insurgent. *The Caravan: A Journal of Politics & Culture*. Retrieved August 8, 2014, from http://www.caravanmagazine.in/reportage/insurgent.

Kirpal, R. 2011. Anna Was an Afterthought in Anti-Corruption Crusade. Retrieved November 22, 2014 from http://www.firstpost.com/politics/anna-was-an-after-thought-in-anti-corruption-crusade-62635.html.

Koopman, C. 2014. The Age of 'Infopolitics'. *New York Times*, January 26, 2014. Retrieved January 27, 2015, from http://opinionator.blogs.nytimes.com/2014/01/26/the-age-of-infopolitics/?_r=1.

Kumar, S. 2006. *Gandhi Meets Primetime: Globalization and Nationalism in Indian Television*. Urbana-Champaign, IL: University of Illinois Press.

Latour, B. 1987. *Science in Action: How to Follow Scientists and Engineers through Society*. Berkshire: Open University Press.

Lessig, Lawrence. 2006. *Code 2.0*. New York: Basic Books.

MacKinnon, Rebecca. 2013. *Consent of the Networked: The Worldwide Struggle for Internet Freedom*. New York: Basic Books.

Mallapragada, Madhavi. 2014. *Virtual Homelands: Indian Immigrants and Online Cultures in the United States*. Urbana, IL: University of Illinois Press.

Mander, H., and Joshi, A. 1999. The Movement for Right to Information in India: People's Power for the Control of Corruption. Commonwealth Human Rights Initiative. Retrieved January 26, 2015, from http://www.humanrightsinitiative.org/programs/ai/rti/articles/india_articles.htm.

Mankekar, P. 1999. *Screening Culture, Viewing Politics: An Ethnography of Television, Nation, and Womanhood in Postcolonial India*. Durham, NC: Duke University Press.

Mankekar, P. 2015. *Unsettling India: Affect, Temporality, Transnationality*. Durham, NC: Duke University Press.

Manovich, Lev. 2001. *The Language of New Media*. Boston: Massachusetts Institute of Technology Press.

Maske, V. *2G Scam ... The Biggest Corruption Scam in India: Highlighting Corruption Scams since 1947*. Saarbrücken, Germany: Lambert Academic Publishing.

Mehta, K. 2012. Satyamev Jayate Twitter Journey—A Film Made by Ketan Mehta. Retrieved January 24, 2015, from https://www.youtube.com/watch?v=eU3OOpVa6zE.

Mehta, N. 2008. *India on Television: How Satellite News Channels Have Changed the Way We Think and Act*. New York: HarperCollins.

Metcalf, T. 1997. *Ideologies of the Raj: The New Cambridge History of India* (Vol. 3). Cambridge: Cambridge University Press.

Mishra, N. 2003. People's Right to Information: Lessons from Rajasthan. Human Development Resource Centre, UNDP, New Delhi. Retrieved January 26, 2015, from http://www.undp.org/content/dam/india/docs/people_right_information_movement_lessons_from_rajasthan.pdf.

Murphy, I. B. 2012. Indian TV Show Uses Social Media Analytics to Rally Viewers around Social Change. *DataInformed*. Retrieved January 5, 2015, from http://data-informed.com/indian-tv-show-uses-social-media-analytics-to-rally-viewers-around-social-change/.

NDTV. 2011. Anna Hazare Makes It to Time Magazine's Top 10 List. Retrieved August 9, 2014, from http://www.ndtv.com/india-news/anna-hazare-makes-it-to-time-magazines-top-10-list-570556.

Ninan, S. 1995. *Through the Magic Window: Television and Change in India.* New Delhi: Penguin Books India.

Oneindia. 2014. Moved by Arvind Kejriwal, Bollywood Actor Aamir Khan to Join AAP?.*Oneindia.* Retrieved January 26, 2015, from http://www.oneindia.com/india/arvind-kejriwal-swaraj-in-india-will-bollywood-aamir-khan-join-aap-1369864.html.

Persistent Systems. 2012. The Persistent Journey of Satyamev Jayate. Retrieved January 18, 2015, from http://content.persistent.com/Satyamev_Jayate/Case_study.html#.

PNS. 2015. Aamir, Hazare, Kejriwal Bat for Kiran Bedi as New CIC. Retrieved February 2, 2015, from http://www.vigilonline.com/index.php?option=com_content&task=view&id=1253&Itemid=1.

Pokharel, K. 2011. Politics Journal: Who Makes Up India's Civil Society. *Wall Street Journal India*, June 20, 2011. Retrieved January 24, 2015, from http://blogs.wsj.com/indiarealtime/2011/06/20/politics-journal-who-makes-up-india's-civil-society/.

PTI. 2013. India's Ranking on Global Corruption Index Improves. *Times of India*, December 3, 2014. Retrieved January 28, 2015, from http://timesofindia.indiatimes.com/india/Indias-ranking-on-global-corruption-index-improves/articleshow/45358144.cms.

Public Cause Research Foundation. 2006. Retrieved January 28, 2015, from http://www.pcrf.in/aboutus.html.

Punathambekar A. 2008. We're Online, Not on the Streets: Indian Cinema, New Media and Participatory Culture. In Anandam P. Kavoori and Aswin Punathambekar (Eds.), *Global Bollywood* (pp. 282–99). New York: New York University Press.

Punathambekar, A., and S. Kumar (Eds.). 2014. *Television at Large in South Asia.* London: Routledge.

Rajadhyaksaha, A. 2011. *The Last Cultural Mile: An Inquiry into Technology and Governance in India.* Online book. Centre for Internet and Society, India. Retrieved January 21, 2015, from http://cis-india.org/raw/histories-of-the-internet/last-cultural-mile.pdf.

Rajagopal, A. 2011. Notes on Postcolonial Visual Culture. *BioScope: South Asian Screen Studies, 2,* 11–12.

Rajagopal, A. 2001. *Politics after Television: Hindu Nationalism and the Reshaping of the Public in India.* Cambridge, UK: Cambridge University Press.

Ramon Magsaysay Award Foundation. Kejriwal, Arvind Citation. 2015. Retrieved February 8, 2015, from http://www.rmaf.org.ph/newrmaf/main/awardees/awardee/profile/141.

Rao, S. L. 2013. A New Dispensation. *The Telegraph, 32*(165), 8.

Ray, R., and Katzenstein, M. F. 2005. *Social Movements in India: Poverty, Power, and Politics.* Lanham, MD: Rowman & Littlefield.

Roberts, A. 2010. A Great and Revolutionary Law? The First Four Years of India's Right to Information Act. *Public Administration Review, 70*(6), 925–33.

Roy, A. 2011. I'd Rather Not Be Anna. *The Hindu*, August 22, 2011. Retrieved February 8, 2014, from http://www.thehindu.com/todays, paper/tp-opinion/id-rather-not-be-anna/article2380789.ece.

Roy, A., and Dey, N. 2001. The Right to Information: Facilitating People's Participation and State Accountability. Retrieved January 27, 2015, from http://www.undp.org/governance/docsaccess/right_to_information.pdf.

Roy, S. Being the Change: The Aam Aadmi Party and the Politics of the Extraordinary in Indian Democracy. *Economic & Political Weekly*, 49(15), 45–54.

Sangvai, S. 2007. The New People's Movements in India. *Economic and Political Weekly*, 42(50), 111–17. Retrieved August 14, 2015, from http://www.epw.in/authors/sanjay-sangvai.

Sarangi, P. 2012. Can the Right to Information Help? *Journal of Democracy*, 23(1), 149–54.

Satyamev Jayate. 2012. *Satyamev Jayate* [profile]. Retrieved October 22, 2014, from https://www.facebook.com/SatyamevJayate/timeline.

Satyamev Jayate. 2015. *Satyamevjayate Don't Waste Your Garbage*. Retrieved from http://www.satyamevjayate.in/dont-waste-your-garbage.aspx.

Sen, B. 2014. A New Kind of Radio: FM Broadcasting in India. *Media, Culture and Society*, 36(8), 1084–99.

Sen, B., and A. Roy (Eds.). 2014. *Channeling Cultures: Television Studies from India*. New Delhi: Oxford University Press.

Sengupta, S. 2011. Hazare, Khwahishein Aisi: Desiring a New Politics, after Anna Hazare and beyond Corruption. *Kafila*. Retrieved August 15, 2014, from http://kafila.org/2011/08/27/hazare-khwahishein-aur-bhi-hain-hazare-there-are-things-still-left-wanting-what-is-to-the-left-of-anna-hazare-and-india-against-corruption/.

Shah, G. 2004. *Social Movements in India: A Review of Literature*. Wassenaar, Netherlands: SAGE.

Sharma, A. 2013. State Transparency after the Neoliberal Turn: The Politics, Limits, and Paradoxes of India's Right to Information Law. *Political and Legal Anthropology Review*, 36(2), 308–25.

Sharma, G. 2006. Aamir Khan Lends His Support for the Narmada Bachao Andolan. *Bollywoodmantra*. Retrieved September 11, 2014, from http://www.bollywoodmantra.com/news/aamir-khan-lends-his-support-for-the-narmada-bachao-andolan/1135/.

Sharma, P. 2014. *Democracy and Transparency in the Indian State: The Making of the Right to Information Act*. Edinburgh: Routledge.

Sharma, R., and Shrivastava, A. 2012. Jan Lokpal Bill: Combating Against Corruption. *International Journal of Social Sciences*, 1(6), 1–8.

Shiva, V. 2002. *Water Wars: Privatization, Pollution and Profit*. Boston: South End Press.

Shreyaskar, P. K. 2014. Known Unknowns of RTO: Legitimate Exemptions or Conscious Secrecy? *Economic & Political Weekly*, 49(24), 32–38. Retrieved August 13, 2014, from http://www.epw.in/perspectives/known-unknowns-rti.html.

Shukla, S.P. 2013. Myopia, Distortions and Blind Spots in the Vision Document of AAP. *Economic & Political Weekly*, 48(7), 16–18.

Sitapati, V. 2011. What Anna Hazare's Movement and India's New Middle Classes Say about Each Other. *Economic & Political Weekly*, 46(30), 39–44. Retrieved from http://www.epw.in/perspectives/what-anna-hazares-movement-and-indias-new-middle-classes-say-about-each-other.html.

Sridharan, E., and deSouza, P. 2006. Introduction: The Evolution of Political Parties in India. In Peter Ronald DeSouza and E.Sridharan (Eds.), *India's Political Parties* (pp. 15–36). New Delhi: Sage.

Sundaram, R. 2011. *Pirate Modernity: Delhi's Media Urbanism*. New York: Routledge.

Thussu, D. K. 1998. *Electronic Empires: Global Media and Local Resistance*. London: Arnold.

Thussu, D. K. 2008. *News as Entertainment: The Rise of Global Infotainment*. London: Sage.

Times of India. 2011. India's Income Inequality Has Doubled in 20 Years. *Times of India*, December 7, 2011. Retrieved January 24, 2015, from http://timesofindia. indiatimes.com/india/Indias-income-inequality-has-doubled-in-20-years/article-show/11012855.cms.

Times of India. 2013. Researchers Want Satyamev Jayate Data. *Times of India*, March 18, 2013. Retrieved January 12, 2015, from http://timesofindia.indiatimes.com/ city/nagpur/Researchers-want-Satyamev-Jayate-data/articleshow/19027175.cms.

Times of India. 2014. Satyamev Jayate 2 Opens with Phenomenal Reach. *Times of India*, March 13, 2014. Retrieved December 14, 2014, from http://timesofindia. indiatimes.com/tv/news/hindi/Satyamev-Jayate-2-opens-with-phenomenal-reacharticleshow/31953978.cms?.

Tolan, C. 2014. Cities of the Future? Indian PM Pushes Plan for 100 'Smart Cities.' *CNN*. Retrieved from http://www.cnn.com/2014/07/18/world/asia/india-modi-smart-cities/.

Turkle, Sherry 2012. *Alone Together: Why We Expect More from Technology and Less from Each Other*. New York: Basic Books.

Varshney, A. 2011. State of Civil Society. *Indian Express*, June 14, 2011. Retrieved August 14, 2014, from http://archive.indianexpress.com/news/state-of-civil-society/803327/.

Vigilonline. 2015. Aamir, Hazare, Kejriwal Bat for Kiran Bedi as New CIC. Retrieved February 12, 2015, from http://www.vigilonline.com/index.php? option=com_content&task=view&id=1253&Itemid=1.

Visvanathan, S. 2012. Anna Hazare and the Battle against Corruption. *Cultural Critique*, *81*, 103–11.

Vittal, N. 2012. *The End of Corruption: How to Clean Up India*. New York: Viking.

Webb, M. 2012. Activating Citizens, Remaking Brokerage: Transparency Activism, Ethical Scenes, and the Urban Poor in Delhi. *Political and Legal Anthropology Review*, *35*(2), 206–22.

Weber, T. 1990. *Hugging the Trees: The Story of the Chipko Movement*. New Delhi: Penguin.

Wheatley, M. 2012. The Indian TV Show That's Making Waves with Big Data. Retrieved January 25, 2015, from http://siliconangle.com/blog/2012/08/14/ the-indian-tv-show-thats-making-waves-with-big-data/.

Wood, J. R. 2007. *The Politics of Water Resource Development in India*. New Delhi: SAGE.

World Bank. 2013. What Is Governance? Retrieved July 25, 2014, from http:// go.worldbank.org/G2CHLXX0Q0.

YouTube. 2015. Retrieved February 8, 2015, from https://www.youtube.com/ playlist?list=PL3wCAbnO7JKlnlAJL0WL9MlxGRfFZEiGb.

4 Reality Television as Informational Culture

In the Oscar award-winning film *Slumdog Millionaire* (2008) the protagonist Jamal Malik, who grew up in the desperate slums of Juhu beach, enters as a contestant in the Indian equivalent of *Who Wants to Be a Millionaire*. Almost miraculously Jamal manages to answer every question and is on the threshold of winning the grand prize of 20 million rupees in the final round.[1] The show's host is unwilling to believe that a slum-child could possess so much "information" and reports him to the police who then charge him with "cheating." As is common with mainstream films, especially Oscar winners, the story ends on a happy note. Jamal is released from custody and allowed to participate in the final round and is asked to name the third of the Three Musketeers. This time Jamal doesn't know the answer but guesses (rightly) that it is Aramis and so he wins the big prize. *Slumdog Millionaire* had several selling points—a vivid depiction of Mumbai's famous slums, a glimpse into the ways of the underworld, a standard Hollywood/Bollywood love story involving Jamal and Latika, a girl who grew up with him in the slums, and a scintillating soundtrack by A. R. Rehman, India's most distinguished music director of the past three decades—but perhaps its greatest achievement lay in the way it foregrounded the importance of information in contemporary Indian popular culture. Not only did it reference the hugely popular quiz show *Kaun Banega Crorepati*, but also by inserting Jamal's quiz odyssey as the central hook for the story it presented in fictional form the main argument of this book. The slum-kid Jamal, like all other Indians, aspires to be a citizen of the info-nation.

In the previous chapter I demonstrated how the highly popular television show *Satyamev Jayate* functions within an informational matrix: the show's creator Aamir Khan had strong ideological connections with info-activists like Aruna Roy and Arvind Kejriwal; its broadcast content is heavily dependent on the use of social statistics; its operational structure is based on data analytics; and its strong web presence inserts it within the context of today's participatory culture. It is my argument in this concluding chapter that *Satyamev* is representative of a larger trend, that of the increasing informatization of popular culture. While much attention has been paid to the fact that Indian popular culture today is much more commercial and globalized than it used to be, it is equally true that it is increasingly being shaped by the parameters, protocols, and practices that derive from the informational milieu at large. I demonstrate my claim by focusing on one medium—television. Such a narrow focus can be justified on the grounds that television is the largest presence in the current Indian media environment, occupying nearly 50% of the media and entertainment industry. India is today the world's third largest television market with approximately 146 million TV households, and there are more than 650 channels in operation at the current moment. As one noted commentator puts it, "it is impossible to imagine, or explain, modern India without reference to television" (Mehta, 2014). Indeed, as I have suggested elsewhere, television is the medium that most adequately represents the various territorial levels that make up the totality of modern Indian society and thus constitutes a privileged object of inquiry for media scholars. Staging a complex interplay of various geopolitical levels (local, regional, national, transnational, and global), it enables an analysis of the complex ways these societal layers are constituted and related and thus affords us a unique understanding of contemporary Indian modernity (Sen and Roy, 2014).

This chapter makes the case for an informational approach to television studies. I begin by offering an "information-theoretic" account of the history of Indian television that complements existing accounts that offer a narrative in terms of the transition from state-run to privately funded broadcasting. My own telling plots the development of television as a progression from one informational paradigm to another. In the early years of its existence, roughly the period 1959–82, television was regulated through the prism of an informational philosophy that held the belief that only the state ought to have access to all the facts surrounding governance and that it should disseminate only that information to the general public that would be conducive to the good of the nation. The main purpose of broadcast media, from this perspective, was to impart information that could further national growth and development.

The second era of television broadcasting begins in the 1980s with the emergence of what has been referred to as "communicative modernity" (Rajagopal, 2011). As I have described in the second chapter, in this period the state took a series of measures that altered the communications landscape as it pertained to hardware, policy, and content. Along with telephony and computer technology, television too began to change. The introduction of color television on the occasion of the 1982 Asian Games may be said to have marked the death of the proprietary model and signaled the dawn of what may be called a "populist" model. There was, first of all, a new focus on entertainment. The televising of sports was followed by the introduction of genres that increased television's audience in an exponential manner: soap operas, privately produced news shows, and religious epics. At the same time commercials began to be aired on Indian television for the very first time. There was thus an effective withdrawal of the state's information apparatus in favor of a system where information from non-governmental sources—in the form of news, entertainment, and commercials—was allowed increasing access to the airwaves. Along with the press and a newly transformed Bollywood, television was, by the end of the last century, an integral part of an emerging communicative landscape.

A second iteration of the information revolution occurs, I argue, in the first decade of the new millennium, with the emergence of reality television. The reality form is a radically new mode of storytelling that fuses traditional storytelling with a documentary aspect that presents "real" people and their "real" lives. Reality television is perhaps the single biggest phenomenon on Indian television of the past two decades. Many consider *Sa Re Ga Ma*, a singing contest show that debuted on Zee TV in 1995, to be the first reality show in India. However, it is only in the first decade of the new millennium that reality television has attained the status of the most "happening" genre. Between 2005 and 2011 the number of reality shows on air rose from 3 to 35. As one executive working for TAM, India's premier ratings agency, commented, "The genre share of reality shows on Hindi television channels is equivalent to the entire news genre" (Ohja, 2011). Most crucially, the reality genre has very strong appeal for future markets. According to a survey conducted by the Associated Chambers of Commerce and Industry of India, 76% of children in the 12–18 age group who were surveyed said that they preferred to watch reality shows when they are in charge of the television set. As one industry executive explains, "What appeals to the youth is essentially reality programming ... It is difficult for them to watch a show that is fictionalized" (Timmons, 2011).

In the second section of this chapter, I try to account for reality television by locating it within the context an evolving informational culture. I begin the section by examining current "theories" of reality television to suggest that these accounts need to be supplemented with an analysis that recognizes and gives due weight to reality television's informational aspect. At the basis of this discussion is the claim that the informational aspect of reality television is substantive and cannot be totally reduced to social or political "causes" that are supposed to lie underneath it. In other words, information (whether in reality television or elsewhere) is not simply an effect of capital or neoliberal governmentality or something else but also a cause. That is, the informational matrix structures social life as a whole. One of its effects, I suggest is to generate the genre of reality television. To put it differently, the domain of fiction—normally associated with literary forms like drama, romance, and comedy—is modulated by the imperatives of informational society to give rise to informational culture.

I conclude the second section by examining three key Indian reality shows of the past decade—*Kaun Banega Crorepati*, *Indian Idol*, and *Bigg Boss*—to demonstrate how they embody three different notions of information and communication. The quiz show *Kaun Banega* reflects the Nehruvian conception of information as a valuable resource for both the state and the individual; *Indian Idol* represents television's power to create an informational space for the masses, while *Bigg Boss* illuminates how personal life and emotions can get informatized by the mechanics of a global format. The enormous success of reality television—especially among youth audiences—implies that information has begun to acquire an aesthetic aspect and can be seen as constitutive of pleasure. An examination of popular reality shows in India demonstrates how information in contemporary India extends beyond commerce, governance, and politics into the realm of culture as well.

An Informational History of Indian Television

The story of Indian television is standardly narrated as a passage from a state-controlled organ to a privatized medium.[2] The "nationalist" era that lasted roughly from 1959 (the year Indian television was born) to the mid-1980s envisioned television as a medium whose main role was to promote economic growth and social justice and that therefore had to be placed under governmental supervision. All programming in this period was created and distributed by Doordarshan, a governmental entity that was housed in the Ministry of Information and Broadcasting and was governed by an austere mindset that saw television in a very serious and high-minded fashion.[3] Entertainment, from this viewpoint, was at best a necessary evil. The dismaying properties of state broadcasting that contemporary observers complained about—its drab style, its imperial imperviousness to audience demand, and its frequent lapses into propaganda—were a direct function of this guiding philosophy. Though the suffering public may have feared that this state of affairs would go on forever, the nationalist paradigm began to erode during the course of the 1980s and collapsed soon afterward. The first step in this direction was the introduction of color television on the occasion of the 1982 Asian Games held in New Delhi. This attempt to make television visually more attractive to its audience was followed by a major shift in programming policy. The immense popularity of *Hum Log*, a soap opera created at the behest of a US-based NGO as a means to promote family planning, pushed the government squarely into the entertainment business. Buoyed by *Hum Log*'s success, Doordarshan aired a spate of shows that suddenly turned television into a truly popular medium. Commercials were introduced into television at the same time; it was perhaps no coincidence that *Hum Log* was the first commercially sponsored show on Indian television.[4]

The commercialization of television was accompanied by a privatization of the distribution system. The eighties saw a huge boom in cable television, and literally thousands of small-scale cable operators sprang up all around the country becoming the "last mile" service providers. Cable TV has its roots in the late seventies. Indian television viewers were looking for entertainment options other than what the government provided, and they got a break with a change in policy permitting the manufacture and import of videocassette recorders (VCR). This led to the rapid growth of an informal broadcasting sector that saw enterprising individuals use satellite dishes to receive programming and then distribute it at minimal cost to neighboring households.

In spite of these developments, Doordarshan's monopoly over television broadcasting would continue relatively unchallenged. Indeed, its most glorious moment came in the late eighties with the airing of two Hindu religious epics, *Ramayana* and *Mahabharat*. Both these shows earned unprecedented ratings, and their reception defined the cultural moment characterized by a revival of Hindu fundamentalism.[5] But this was destined to be state broadcasting's last hurrah. It may have been more than a coincidence that foreign programming entered the Indian airwaves the very year the Indian economy was drastically "liberalized," ending four decades of Nehruvian socialism. The government's decision to allow the broadcasting of CNN's coverage of the first Gulf War led to the birth of the satellite age and the introduction of dozens of private channels of which Star TV and Zee TV were the most prominent. In merely the space of two decades Indian television would change from a state-owned, single-channel operation to a highly capitalized and highly competitive private market reaching 168 million households and generating revenues of 475 billion INR ($74 billion) in 2014 (IndianTelevision.com, 2015).

In short then, the trajectory of Indian television has paralleled that of Indian political economy as a whole, moving from a "socialistic" order characterized by bureaucratic control to a highly "open" system that is almost exclusively determined by market considerations. Such a transition has its share of both champions and detractors. Addressing the question as to whether private news channels have benefitted the public sphere, one observer asserts, "Despite all their shortcomings and sensationalism, the emergence of satellite television news networks has enhanced and strengthened deliberative Indian democracy" (Mehta, 2014, 151). On the other hand, another commentator points out that "the all-news channels in India are just over a decade in existence but even in their early formative years, their pro-business agenda was well formed ... the almost total absence of development news on commercial channels, who perceive their viewers little more than as consumers of infotainment, is deeply ironic in a country which was the first in the world to use satellite television for educational and developmental purposes" (Thussu, 2014, 133, 141). It is not my intention here to enter the debate surrounding the liberalization of the Indian media. My purpose instead is to retell the story of Indian television through an informational lens. I do this in order to demonstrate that information was an operative category that partly determined the nature of media policy, media institutions, and media content in postcolonial India. By showing information's substantive role in modulating the contours of mass communication, I hope to demonstrate how the increasing informatization of culture is part of the general move toward the building of an info-nation.

As I indicated in the introduction to this chapter, such a narrative consists of three arcs: an initial stage when television was considered to be the purveyor of useful information on behalf of the state; a second stage—denoted by the term "communicative modernity"—during which the exclusive focus on proprietorial information is supplanted by an opening up of televisual speech to the "public" as it were; and finally a period— still in progress—where television responds to the ambient informational culture by developing new modes of programming that are congruent with the discursive universe set up by the Internet, the Web, mobile telephony, and other digital platforms. A very rough timeline for these three periods would be 1959–82, 1982–2000, and 2000–present. In what follows I spell out the crucial elements of each phase of television in support of the thesis that the history of Indian television can be reconceptualized in informational terms.

Indian television had a quiet beginning when some broadcasting equipment left behind by the Dutch electronics company Philips after a trade fair was used to set up a venture called AIR Experimental Service (Television). Such a modest start—in contrast to the grand ribbon ceremonies for the unveiling of dams and factories and even the first computer—needs to be understood in the context of the Indian state's philosophy of media. Television was by then a dominant form of entertainment in the advanced nations but had little appeal for a government whose main goal was economic development. India's first prime minister, Jawaharlal Nehru, was loath to spend government money on what he saw as frivolous entertainment. As his minister for information and broadcasting put it, "Though television might appear to be a useful thing in the country, the expenses involved installing it are very high" (Kumar, 2006, 24). Prodded by UNESCO to use television for educational purposes, the Indian government inaugurated its experimental television service in September 1959. The initial broadcasts were restricted to the capital city of Delhi and were highly pedagogical in nature. They were aimed at audiences located in adult education centers as well as at high school students. Most crucially, this launching saw the new technology as a conduit for the sort of information that was thought to be necessary for economic growth and social justice. Thus this first broadcast focused on five subjects, each of which was pertinent for social health: traffic and road sense, adulteration of food, community health, public property, and citizen manners! (Rao, 1992, 63).

While such a programming list may seem almost cartoonish from today's vantage, it made sense in the context of a broadcasting philosophy that highly valued civic knowledge while being impervious to the mission of entertainment. As Bhaskar Ghose, a director-general of Doordarshan, recalls:

> I once watched a song being telecast; throughout the song, only one image occupied the screen: a record playing on the turntable of a gramophone. I could only suppose that the person who made the programme thought he was reproducing what happened in real life when someone put a record on a player, which was daft, because no one spends his time watching a turntable with intense concentration.
>
> (Ghose, 2005, 22)

"Road sense" and the static image of the gramophone record stem from the same ground: the equation of television with informational governmentality. Television, in the eyes of the Indian state, was quite literally a "channel" that transmitted information from source to receiver, much as Shannon's famous model of communication had diagrammed it.[6] Such a notion would govern broadcasting philosophy in the years that followed. In 1965, general television services were launched with daily one-hour transmissions from the Delhi station.[7] These early broadcasts were heavily informational, containing a 10-minute "News Round Up" as well as segments on adult literacy and rural development. Perhaps the most enduring symbol of television's first informational era was the show *Krishi Darshan* (loosely, "Agricultural Vision") that began airing on January 26, 1967, and still continues to be broadcast on Doordarshan today. Aimed at India's large peasantry, the show dispensed agricultural advice to farmers and was originally cosponsored by agencies as disparate as the Indian Agricultural Research Institute and the Department of Atomic Energy. It needs to be remembered that between 1965 and 1967 India faced severe food shortages with food imports rising from a modest 1 million tonnes in 1950 to 10 million tonnes in 1966 (Business & Economy, 2015). *Krishi Darshan* can therefore be seen as a direct intervention by the government, intent on a "Green Revolution," and typified the state's resolve to use television to address issues of vital national importance.

The purest expression of informational television occurred not on national television but within the framework of one of the most remarkable experiments in all of broadcast history. Satellite Instructional Television Experiment (SITE) had its origins in the vision of Vikram Sarabhai, a physicist who founded and headed India's space program between 1962 and 1971. While at the helm of the Indian Space Research Organization (ISRO), he began to feel that a satellite-based television system could play a big role in promoting economic and social development. In a talk entitled "Television and Development" delivered in 1969 he argued that:

> We should consciously reach the most difficult and least developed areas of the country and, because they are in this state, we should reach them in a hurry … .TV can provide a qualitative improvement in the richness of rural life and thereby reduce the overwhelming attraction of migration to cities and metropolitan areas through education and entertainment of a high standard.
>
> (Harvey et al., 2010, 148–49)

Sarabhai's initiatives led to the signing of the Television for Development agreement between NASA and the Atomic Energy Commission of India. It was decided that a NASA satellite, ATS-6, would be made available to Indian broadcasters in order to transmit programs to approximately 2,400 villages in five backward regions of the country. The SITE program was put into effect in August 1975 (sadly, Sarabhai had passed away in 1971) and was operational till July 1976. Programs were uplinked from India's first ground station in Ahmedabad to ATS and then retransmitted for about four hours a day. The transmissions reached a target audience of approximately 5 million people living in over 2,400 villages in six Indian states. According to the original memorandum of understanding between India and the United States, the objective of the mission was to demonstrate the practical value of satellite technology in creating effective mass communications for developing countries. The content of SITE programming adequately reflected this goal: of the three hours of transmission every day, half an hour was reserved for science education for children, while the rest covered such topics as agriculture, health, hygiene, family planning, rural development, and literacy. SITE was evaluated by hundreds of social scientists who conducted field studies in several villages covered by its programming and, as one set of authors put it, "was called 'the largest sociological experiment in history'" (Harvey et al., 2010, 157).

When SITE officially ended in July 1976, the AST-6 satellite was returned to NASA. Satellite television would be revived with the launching of India's own INSAT series. Thus in 1987 INSAT-IB was transmitting educational programs to over 10,000 community-viewing television sets provided for by the national government. But it would never assume the importance that SITE enjoyed (Contractor et al., 1988, 134). The reason behind this decline is not difficult to identify. As I have argued earlier, starting in 1982 Indian television shifted to a new broadcasting paradigm—one that prioritized communication and entertainment over the transmission of privileged information. In this new dispensation, the emphasis on entertaining programming and informational television as epitomized by SITE lost whatever little appeal it had even for the rural masses. In a piece criticizing the SITE model for an inadequate understanding of its audience, William Mazarella asks, "Why was it so hard to make informative shows for the underprivileged that were also fun to watch?" (2012, 224) and goes on to blame the Sarabhai doctrine. He quotes Sarabhai as saying, "The process of education is basically related to an information dissemination/transfer process ... Mass media are clearly the main components in this system of information transfer" and argues that the continued reliance on an information-transfer model (as opposed to a truly interactive model exemplified by the short-lived Kheda Project) is to be blamed for the underdevelopment of developmental television. What needs to be noted, however, is that the information-transfer model was not an accidental or contingent strategy but rather a doctrine that lay at the very core of the postcolonial state. If planning was the action that allowed the state to realize itself, then information was the substance with which such action could be put into motion. In other words, the information-transfer model could be jettisoned only when the state decided to rethink its relationship with private capital. This renegotiation occurred, as I have pointed out in the second chapter, under the stewardship of Rajiv Gandhi from the early 1980s onward. The liberalization of the telecommunications sector was a sign that the state no longer adhered to the notion of information as privileged that had driven all media policy since Independence.

Mazarella's question opens a second line of inquiry: Why would information transfer result in an absence of "fun?" There is perhaps an inevitable process at play here as well, as Bhaskar Ghose notes:

> As the years passed it [Doordarshan] degenerated into nothing but more than a propaganda machine for the government, carrying boring programmes on different development schemes, on what was happening abroad and in the country as given to them by the Ministry of External Affairs and the Ministry of Home Affairs, and broadcasting "cultural" programmes that someone influential wanted shown, irrespective of how disgracefully shoddy and cheap they were. (2005, 213)

During the first three decades of the postcolonial state, the information-transfer model was girded by a bureaucratic system of information management. Information had to be filtered through government gatekeepers and then outputted by means of vendors who were government servants themselves. In such a scenario, information almost invariably tends toward propaganda, a process that may be defined as the subjectivization of objective fact. Information may be data about the state of affairs, but it must also pay fealty to the state that rules. Since the state cannot think beyond its own limits, any "information" is automatically refracted through its own epistemic lens such as to emerge as what a disinterested observer would describe as propaganda. One may consider this tendency to be the natural condition of all pre-modern social formations; every deviation from "normal" capitalism— semi-feudalism, totalitarianism, communism, and the postcolonial socialism that characterized Nehruvian India—has subjectivized information in the manner I have described. The lack of "fun" in early Indian television is then a function of the state's relation to information, which itself is a function of its relation to capital. It is only in advanced capitalism that the state finds it useful to allow for the expression of "unbiased" information. Information and fun are let loose, so to speak, when the state adopts a more congenial stance toward capital.

The first era of Indian television consisted, then, of information transfer mediated by and for the state. In the periodization I am proposing, the second era (roughly 1982 to the end of the millennium) is characterized by the following: first, it allows for the "free flow" of information on the airwaves, especially in the decade of the nineties following the introduction of private channels, both foreign and domestic. Second, starting as early as 1982, Indian television tacitly redefines its mission and sees itself as primarily a purveyor of entertainment. In other words, it is in this second era that television becomes popular culture. As one well-known scholar puts it, "Television became a mass medium in India only during the 1980s" (Mehta, 2008, 37). Three main factors—each of which reinforced the other—led to this development: a concerted push toward entertainment, growing commercialization, and creation of an enhanced infrastructure regarding reception and distribution.[8] The push toward entertainment began, as we have noted above, in 1982 with the introduction of color television on the occasion of the New Delhi Asian Games. Though the decision to host the Games was in keeping with the grandiose ambitions of the state, the shift from black and white to color—made against stout opposition by many bureaucrats—was a sign that Doordarshan was finally paying attention to aesthetic issues. Such a move would have important ripple effects in the economics of the medium. The introduction of color television led to a take-off in the cable industry, since the ability to transmit in color meant that there was now a market for films that cable operators could provide by merely hooking up a VCR to their small-scale networks. "The local operator in most areas would show a couple of Hindi films daily. The tapes were of poor quality and there were too many ads, but it was manna from heaven for an entertainment-starved country" (Kohli-Khandekar, 2010, 69).[9]

Almost simultaneously, Doordarshan took a number of programming initiatives that would rapidly move television to the forefront of popular culture. Prodded by an American NGO, the government decided to introduce a soap opera based on a Mexican original that would promote the values of family planning to a conservative audience. The legendary Bollywood actor Ashok Kumar was chosen to appear on the show as messenger on behalf of the nation. As it turned out, entertainment trumped information transfer: *Hum Log* proved so popular—more than 80% of India's 3.6 million TV households were tuned in to the show every week—that it started a wave of similar shows that Doordarshan would air in the next few years. These included *Buniyaad, Katha Sagar, Khandaan, Nukkad,* and several others. The decade culminated with the airing of two religious epics—*Ramayana* and *Mahabharat*—that galvanized the Indian viewing audience. As Shanti Kumar has noted, "*Mahabharat* was reportedly watched with ritual regularity in over 90 per cent of all Indian television homes, transcending boundaries of religion, caste, class, language, region and political allegiance" (2006, 38). In short, from a stodgy medium that people turned to only because of a lack of alternatives, within the space of a decade television became a magnetic force that held the entire nation in thrall.

The turn to entertainment was accompanied by two other trends: the growing commercialization of Doordarshan and the gradual formation of nationwide television. As we saw, *Hum Log* carried India's first commercials and was underwritten by its sponsoring company, Maggi Noodles. In the next few years, advertising on television would grow at an exponential rate: whereas advertising accounted for only 1% of Doordarshan's annual budget, the corresponding figure in 1990 was 70% (Mehta, 2008, 41). The commercializing of Doordarshan would undoubtedly be responsible for the privatizing of television that was to occur in the next decade. At the same time, television would increase in scope. The launching of the INSAT satellite meant that programming could be broadcast all over the country and thus allowed for the creation of a national network that would be immensely attractive to advertisers. This expansion also served another function. As Purnima Mankekar has observed, "Television played a crucial role in the state's project of constructing a pan-Indian culture" (1999, 18) by promoting "the ideological construction of nation, womanhood, identity and citizenship." Doordarshan "unleashed sweeping and far-reaching cultural changers in a relatively short time" (ibid., 4–5). The popularity of *Ramayana* and *Mahabharat* in particular cannot be, as Arvind Rajagopal (2001) has pointed out in his authoritative study of "politics after television," dissociated from the rise of religious fundamentalism and Hindu nationalism in this period.

Communicative modernity would, in turn, lead to the last informational stage of Indian television. The crucial factor at play here was the introduction of satellite broadcasting. The new technology had two very significant consequences. First, by allowing foreign companies like Star TV to beam content to the domestic audience, it created a demand for a globalized style of content creation and delivery. Audiences were now able to access programming from transnational giants like CNN, ESPN, and MTV, which meant that Indian companies like Zee, Sun, and others were forced to adapt to international norms of television broadcasting in order to capture and retain market share. Second, satellite technology also led to what may be termed a second "cable revolution" by dramatically increasing the scope of cable transmission. Not only was the quality of transmission far superior to that of the previous cable era, but also the technology now allowed hundreds of channels to become accessible for any cable-owning household.

This numerical explosion would contribute directly to ushering in the current informational era. First, there was the sheer increase in the number of news channels and, therefore, of "data." Although the news held a sanctified position in the Doordarshan era (at least in the eyes of producers), it was doled out in small doses. With privatization of the medium, news became a commodity in its own right. Thus, the first of India's private 24-hour news channels aired in 1998, and by 2009 there were more than 70 such all-day news channels broadcasting in 11 languages (Mehta, 2014, 149).[10] Television thus became quite literally "informational." The fact that news anchors like Arnab Goswami, Barkha Dutt, and Rajdeep Sardesai have become national icons is testament to this change. However, this development is less important than it seems. Given television's belated conversion to a modern mode of broadcasting, the role it plays as newsmonger may only illustrate the fact that it is "catching up" with the press. In other words, television is now informational in the sense that newspapers and magazines were in the first four decades after Independence. What may be different in this case, however, is that in the post-liberalization period news is far more commoditized than it was in the Nehruvian period.

There is another deeper sense in which the current era of Indian television can be thought of as an informational medium. My analysis of *Satyamev Jayate* in the previous chapter showed how this new form of talk show was informational at several levels: content, interface, and operational logic. It is therefore an exemplar of what I call television's third stage, one in which the structure and content of television shows begin to reflect the impera- tives of our digitally constructed informational age. Reality television as a genre, I claim, represents this latest moment in the evolution of television in India as well as globally. I attempt to substantiate this claim in the second and concluding section of this chapter. I begin my discussion by looking at current theories of reality television and evaluating their usefulness in expli- cating the Indian reality television market. I then offer a detailed analysis of three major reality shows to demonstrate how they embody the characteris- tics of the emergent informational culture.

Reality Television and the Birth of Informational Culture

While reality television is too complex a phenomenon to be explained by a single "theory," it is possible to identify the major interpretive approaches with which any analysis of the genre must contend. I will, at the cost of gross simplification, group these approaches under three rubrics: economic, political, and formal. Such a tripartite division is not meant to be a definitive one; my motive here is to merely disentangle these different lines of inquiry for the heuristic purposes of relating them to my own informational account of reality television.

By an "economic" approach, I mean those accounts that seek to explicate reality television in terms of the logic of contemporary capitalism. Thus Chad Raphael has pointed out, "As a fiscal strategy, Reali-TV emerged in the late 1980s in response to the economic restructuring of the U.S. television" (Murray and Ouellette, 2008, 125). By the mid-1980s rising costs and lower network license fees meant that most producers could no longer get a decent return on investments through first-run network showings. As a response to this situation, production companies and networks initiated cost-cutting measures that involved a sustained attack on unionized labor and the "invention" of a new mode of programming that was substantially cheaper to produce. For example, while the average dramatic show in the 1990s cost over a million dollars per episode, reality TV (RTV) programming based on low-paid non-actors and poor production values could be much more cost-effective. Moreover, RTV was also a viable product in the low-fee, first- run syndication and made-for-cable fields. As Ted Madgar observes, "The emergence of reality television is most certainly part of the general effort to reduce production costs and financial risk" (Murray and Ouelette, 2008, 149). Madgar, however, extends Raphael's analysis by pointing out that RTV is a reaction to four other significant changes to the production side of television: the enthusiasm for pre-packaged formats as a basis for program production, the emergence of product placement as a source of revenue, the use of television as a springboard for multimedia exploitation of creative property, and finally the impact of global program suppliers like Endemol and FreMantle Media in the international market.

It needs to be noted that this argument does not fit the Indian case very well. Unlike in the West, reality shows often cost much more to make than their fictional counterparts. Thus, while a typical reality show costs between 50 lakhs and 1 Crore rupees to produce, a fiction serial costs only 8–10 lakhs per episode. The reason for this is that while fiction shows do not have the same production values that top shows (*Mad Men* or *Game of Thrones*) in the United States have, reality shows feature celebrities and thus cost much more. As a result, hit shows don't necessarily make money. For example, as Yashvini Yardi, the programming head of the Colors channel observes, the popular reality show *Fear Factor* "is a loss maker for us because there are fewer episodes and we do not have the necessary long window for advertisers" (Chakraborty, 2010). Or, as another television executive put it, "Reality shows are just the icing on the cake and fiction serials are the cake" (ibid.). Reality shows still make some economic sense because they help to draw in new audiences: thus, as Yardi explains, *Fear Factor* "drew a large number of first-time viewers to the channel. It is like a 'burst programming vehicle' that gets us additional eyeballs" (ibid.).

A traditional political economy approach that looks at the macroeconomics of television production and distribution needs to complemented by one which takes into account reality television's specific characteristics—its deployment of "real" people, its use of surveillance as a mode of storytelling, its emphasis on confessional self-displays, and its use of antagonism as a way to depict social relations—so that we may better understand how the genre serves the needs of contemporary capitalism. In doing so, it turns out the emergence of reality television is intimately connected with the rise of an informational economy. The work of Mark Andrejevic is exemplary in this regard. In an essay on the classic show *The Real World*, Andrejevic argues that texts ostensibly seeking to foreground individual personalities in fact "help to define a particular form of subjectivity consonant with an online economy: one which equates submission to comprehensive surveillance with self-expression and self-knowledge" (2002, 253). The reasoning behind this claim can be summarized in the following manner: changes in the technologies of production and distribution have led to an ever-increasing reliance upon the rapid accumulation, management, and commodification of information. As many sectors of the economy go online, there is an increasing need for highly specific sets of information regarding individual customers. However, producers cannot reap the benefits of the online economy if there is a mistrust of the forms of surveillance on which it is based; that is, the development of e-commerce is predicated on the development of a "new person" who is accepting of online surveillance. It is thus to the interest of new capitalism that consumers see self-disclosure as an empowering practice that guarantees one's own authenticity. In short, a show like *The Real World* may implicitly promise a more democratic mode of entertainment but actually "serves as a form of acclimatization to an emerging economic regime predicated on increasingly unequal access to, and control over, *information* ... . As with labor power before it, personal information can be extracted from consumers only to be sold back to them in a congealed commodity form" (ibid., 267, italics mine).

There is little doubt that contemporary capital is increasingly going online and is informational.[11] The dominance of online retailers like Amazon and Netflix goes hand in hand with the centrality of social media sites like Facebook and Twitter. While developing countries may be a little behind in terms of e-commerce, all trends suggest that markets in emerging economies will increasingly go online just as in advanced nations. Thus, while India's online retail industry may only account for less than 1% of its $500 billion retail market, it has grown at a swift pace in the last five years from around Rs 15 billion revenues in 2007–08 to Rs 139 billion in 2012–13, translating into a compounded annual growth rate (CAGR) of over 56%, and the expectations are that it will be worth Rs 504 billion by 2015–16. This amazing growth comes on the back of increasing Internet penetration and changing lifestyles and has primarily been driven by the sale of books, electronics, travel, and apparel on online sites like Flipkart, Myntra, makemytrip, and Jabong. There is also a growing trend of traditional retailers with Shopper's Stop, Crossword Bookstores, Estee Lauder, and Airport Business opening online counterparts to cash in on this growing market (CRiSiL Research, 2014). Online retailing is clearly the way of the future if capital investment is any guide. A fledgling company like Snapdeal recently raised $233 million, while India's online giant Flipkart managed to raise an astounding $1 billion from investors matching Facebook's fund-raising round in 2011 (Bearak, 2014). An analysis of the political economy of reality television therefore brings out its informational aspect by showing how the genre creates an aesthetic of self-disclosure that is an essential component of the digital economy. The burgeoning popularity of reality television in India is in tandem with the exponential increase in online retail, as information about self becomes imbricated with the commercial and financial information.

Reality television has also been analyzed from a perspective that sees it not so much as an instrument of capital as one of capitalist governmentality. According to one well-known discussion that "situates the surge of popular nonfiction on television within strategies of liberal governance," reality television is a product of a contemporary neoliberalism, a mode of social organization characterized by the increasing introduction of the *economic* into the spheres of civil society and government (Ouellette and Hay, 2008, 3). Such a tendency leads to the devolution of the welfare state and an outsourcing of the state's responsibilities to the media and other private sectors of the society. Thus, "The management and care of the self becomes an imperative .... not only in the sense of replacing public services, but in terms of obliging citizens to actualize and 'maximize' themselves not through 'society' or collectively, but through their choices in the privatized spheres of lifestyle, domesticity, and consumption" (ibid., 11). The world of entertainment becomes the ideal sphere within which such an actualization can take place. As Ouellette and Hay ably document, the various types of reality programming that are on the air at any given moment together comprise a vast educational mission: how to succeed at work, how to win a desirable mate, how to be stylish, how to nourish our health and psyche, how to manage our families and domestic lives, and so on and so forth, such that hardly any aspect of human endeavor is left unattended.[12]

This impressive analysis needs to be complemented with an analysis of the important role that information plays in governmental projects.[13] In the first chapter I showed how crucial information was to colonial governmentality—in fact it could be argued that the colonial project was inconceivable without an "information revolution" of its own. A similar argument can be made for neoliberal governmentality whether in India or elsewhere.[14] The data explosion of the last two decades is, I suggest, an integral part of the neoliberal order that dominates the globe today. The connection I am proposing is not difficult to establish: if neoliberalism is fundamentally based on an economic calculation of all the events and processes that comprise social life, then information is the basic operator of this calculus. That is, neoliberalism is not possible without information being continuously recorded, measured, calibrated, extrapolated, and manipulated. Information is neoliberalism's raw material. Should this observation be true, then an art form that processes information in the manner described would be the perfect aesthetic correlate for the current mode of governance.

I would like to extend Ouelette and Hay's analysis by demonstrating how governmentality within reality television works not only to delegate responsibility to individuals but also to *create* the sort of hyper-individuated subject who can function as a citizen of the emergent neoliberal order. That is, what the state does by means of a project like the Aadhaar card, a reality show does by means of its format and rules. In both cases we witness a highly refined process of individuation whose end goal is the neoliberal citizen-subject. A fundamental characteristic of reality television is its reliance on the production of difference. Such a process occurs at two levels—externally at the level of the format, and internally at the level of the show. All reality shows consist of a few simple rules and operations that are implemented in a range of settings in order to produce a series of outputs. The format is the variable that is initially empty and gets a value only when plugged into specific game situations. Thus, the *Big Brother* format yields *Big Brother Africa* in one instance and *Bigg Boss* (India) in another. The study of formats, then, amounts to an investigation of multiple differences between a series of contexts. Difference operates not only between versions of the same format (the many instantiations of *Big Brother*) but within a particular show as well. A consideration of *any* reality show alerts us to the fact that *every* reality show alludes to, creates, and exacerbates the differences between individual participants. This process of differentiation announces itself at the beginning, middle, and end of every reality episode. Contestants in a reality show are chosen such that they are complete strangers to each other. This is in marked contrast to the way standard literary texts function: every novel or film begins with a set of interconnected characters. Furthermore, according to a well-established formula, contestants are chosen by type such that individual difference is enhanced by sociological distance. In other words, at the very beginning there is a disavowal of relationality that helps inaugurate the "social contract" upon which reality game-space is constructed. The "middle" of any reality show consists of a series of contests and confrontations that place every individual participant in mutual antagonism with other players. Finally, the end of every episode is marked by elimination—a radical act that removes the individual from the temporary society erected by the game and hurls him or her outside of all sociality. In short, reality television functions as a *difference engine* that processes the ephemera of games and contests in order to produce the individual as both separated and sovereign. I will later examine how *Indian Idol*—one of the most popular reality shows in India—makes use of this formal feature in order to insert regional politics into a show that is ostensibly about singing. In India, as elsewhere, the highly differentiated individual that reality television projects for the audience serves as the perfect template for the neoliberal order to which writers like Ouelette and Hay have drawn our attention.

The two sets of analyses that I have described above—reality television as an example of late informational capitalism and reality television as an instance of neoliberal governmentality—provide strong accounts of the specificity of the genre. As Andrejevic has persuasively argued, the self-disclosure involved in reality programming aids and abets the needs of informational capital for more and more data about our intimate lives. Similarly, the techniques of self-management that the genre imposes on participants serve as a model for the citizen-subject that the current neoliberal configuration demands. As I just argued, both these functions are crucially dependent on information processing. That suggests that there is room to develop a more information-theoretic account that analyzes reality television not so much as an instrumental instantiation of these global macro-level processes but rather as an example of the way the information society extends into the domain of popular culture with an autonomous logic of its own.

My approach here is based on the premise that reality television embodies a new kind of informational aesthetics that seeks to create art not so much with the use of traditional literary devices, like character, plot, conflict, and resolution, but by creating an assemblage of data-generating participants, situations, and outcomes. In other words, a reality show can be seen as an informational machine that creates, processes, and outputs large datasets of information concerning a large array of variables: personalities, affects, conflicts, sociality, alliances, strategy, winners and losers, background sociology, and so on. It could be argued that such an entity is nothing but an agent of informational capitalism or of neoliberal governmentality. My own inclination is to suggest that while information culture may very well promote such interests, information also exists in a substantial mode, as an agential object that creates effects not reducible to the calculus of market or political logic. Thus, while a giant informational system like Facebook may be imbricated in a vast network of digital capitalism, it is at the same time a repository of information that cannot be easily commoditized and an initiator of informational vectors that are autonomous of the flow of capital. At the most general level, reality television can be conceptualized as an apparatus that generates (and stores) a large dataset. The production of an incessant stream of data about show "participants" mirrors what happens in the "real" world and is at one with what "really real" people habitually do with Facebook, Twitter, and Instagram. The overwhelming presence of data in both life and art suggests that information now lies at the basis of our subjectivity. In the next section of this chapter I look at three seminal Indian reality shows—*Kaun Banega Crorepati*, *Indian Idol*, and *Bigg Boss*—to demonstrate how information begins to shape the contours of Indian popular culture.

Reality and Information

In this section I examine three recent hit shows in order to flesh out my argument that reality television represents a novel aesthetic form that is crucially structured around the category of information. My exposition parallels that provided in the first section of this chapter: *Crorepati*, I argue, reflects the statist view of information as both a valuable commodity, access to which has to be earned; *Idol* exemplifies the era of communicative modernity where information begins to be exchanged among the citizenry, while *Bigg Boss* reflects both the global dimensions of the information age as well as reality television's strong links to the informational milieu of our contemporary age. I look first at *Kaun Banega Crorepati* (henceforth *KBC*), a hugely successful game show that first aired in 2000 and is currently on its eighth season. *KBC* is the Indian version of the *Who Wants to Be a Millionaire* format that was developed in the United Kingdom and had its debut in 1998. Hosted by the Bollywood superstar Amitabh Bachchan, the show initially ran on the Star TV in the 2000–01 season, went on a four-year hiatus, and then resumed in 2005–06. Due to Bachchan's ill health, it had to be hosted by another movie idol, Shah Rukh Khan, for the 2007 season. The show was then canceled by Star TV and picked up by Sony TV in 2010. By then, Bachchan had recovered and could resume his duties as host once again. It has since had an uninterrupted run on that channel and completed its eighth season at the time of writing.

KBC's format conforms to that of any successful quiz show: a host who is perhaps the greatest Indian celebrity of all time, a parade of hopeful aspirants often hailing from the country's hinterland, a format involving an exciting progression such that each successive question is worth double the previous one, a set of gimmicks like the Lifeline to keep monotony at bay, and an outlandish final prize, currently worth 70 million INR ($1.1 million), for those fortunate and talented enough to answer all the questions in the pyramid and thus achieve the exalted status of a Mahacrorepati (Multi-Millionaire).[15] The formula seems to work very well. In 2011, for example, *KBC* emerged as the most watched game show of the year, beating out *Big Boss* (the Indian version of *Big Brother*) and *Khatron Ke Khilari* (*Fear Factor*) (Raghavendra and Chumbale, 2011).

The show's ratings owe a lot to its programming strategy that goes beyond merely capitalizing on Bachchan's immense charisma. Thus, in a departure from the typical strategy of trying to capture the urban middle-class market, it consciously reaches out to the vast hinterland of India's demographic geography. As the show's producer Siddarth Basu observes, "It was very much a programming decision to reach out to contestants and from further afield, from interiors, to have video windows on each one of them, their lives and milieus, their hopes and disappointments" (Saxena, 2011). This demographic strategy was closely linked to the economics of selling eyeballs—*KBC*'s decision to expand its target audience was strongly conditioned by the fact that between 2000 (when the show first aired) and 2010 the number of cable homes has grown from 25 to 100 million households. This marketing move has in turn affected the show's rhetorical pitch. By featuring contestants drawn, in Basu's words, from "the base of the social pyramid," *KBC* is constructed around a humanitarian discourse that seeks the redress of social injustice. As in *Satyamev*, each contestant is represented as part victim of an unjust social order. To take a contemporary example, the October 21, 2014, episode featured a contestant who had aspired to appear on the show in order pay for his brother's kidney condition, while another contestant was an unsuccessful farmer who was struggling with rising costs and falling profits.

That said, the essence of *KBC* is information. After Sushil Kumar, the son of a landless farm laborer in Motihari, Bihar, won a 50 million INR jackpot in Season 5, a large number of general knowledge groups started mushrooming in the village (Saxena, 2011). This curious little fact alerts us to the genealogy that constitutes the show. *KBC* is a quiz show, and at its very basis it is simply a sequence of questions that have a "right answer." In other words, *KBC* is an "examination" of the contestant's knowledge. Examinations—or "exams"—are typically administered by organizations far less entertaining than a quiz show: schools, colleges, and most notoriously "entrance boards." Whereas examinations in schools, colleges, and universities are part of the regular process of education in modern societies, those held by entrance boards are of far more climacteric nature, for they can often decide the trajectory of an individual's life. In underdeveloped and developing countries, success or failure in one of these examinations is equivalent to success or failure in life.

The most famous set of examinations in the history of the nation was that for the Indian Civil Service (ICS). Set up in 1858, after the Mutiny, it was designed to annually select approximately a thousand officers who comprised the elite administrative level of the British Raj.[16] Though the ICS was dissolved at the time of Independence, it was reincarnated as the IAS (Indian Administrative Service) that retained the form of the ICS down to the last letter. The IAS continues to be the most prestigious government cadre in the country. Not surprisingly, the examination it holds to select its recruits is a national event. Over 200,000 applicants sit for a rigorous set of examinations—administered by an august body known as the Union Public Service Commission (UPSC)—that finally selects only 900 candidates. The UPSC civil services exams (including not just IAS but also allied services like Income Tax and Customs) consist of two papers, the second of which is almost completely devoted to "General Studies," a rubric that encompasses a wide range of disciplines and topics ranging from history and geography to biodiversity and disaster management. In other words, these examinations presume a "general knowledge" of a vast set of phenomena that is assumed to be indispensable to the art of governance. It needs to be pointed out the civil service exam is the most prestigious examination out of many. The UPSC also sets and conducts examinations for the Forest Services, Defence Services, Medical Services, and the Central Police Force, among others. Further, there are many other governmental bodies that conduct their own independent examinations in order to recruit staff. For example, in the period 2010–13, the nationalized banking sector administered exams to hire 34,000 employees at the officer level and 51,000 employees at the clerical level (Prokerala, 2015). In short, India is the land of many examinations.

The above discussion suggests that the entire machinery of both colonial and postcolonial India has rested on a corpus of "knowledges" that was thought to be of essential importance to the process of governing. Insofar as the bureaucratic servants selected on the basis of their mandarin-like mastery of these knowledges enjoyed unparalleled benefits as a consequence of their appointment, it is not surprising that the trove of knowledge the selecting examinations were based on became a kind of Brahminical object that was venerated and elevated above all other forms. This bureaucratic epistemology explains the role of trivia and quizzes in contemporary Indian culture. Quizzes, in the Indian context, are contests based upon knowledge of trivia. The caveat here is that in such a paradigm "trivial knowledge" is always more than just that, for it is an indication of, a salutation to, and a preparation for its big brother—governmental knowledge. The enormous popularity of quizzing in post-Independence India is therefore a consequence of this fundamental relation of trivia to its more serious counterpart.

The very first quiz event in India was reputedly held in Calcutta in 1967 under the stewardship of Neil O'Brien. Quizzing became a national phenomenon with the introduction of the Bournvita Quiz Contest that was first broadcast on radio (compered by Hamid and then Ameen Sayani) and then on television. This was followed by the North Star Quiz in 1978 (with Neil's son, Derek O'Brien, as quizmaster) and then by Quiz Time and India Quiz (both compered by Siddharta Basu, perhaps India's best-known host) in the eighties and finally by the BBC's Mastermind India in 1998 (Jayakumar, 2001). *KBC* then can be seen as a natural culmination of this history. As Wing Commandeer G. R. Mulky, the founder of the Karnataka Quiz Association observes, there are three high points to the quizzing movement in the country: "The first of these was Quiz Time. Then came the BBC Mastermind series, and more recently, *Kaun Banega Crorepati*" (Balaji, 2013).

   KBC constitutes a particular version of reality television, one that banks on a specific conception of information as objective, practical, and useful knowledge. Given the chronology that I have been establishing in this chapter and elsewhere in this book, such a perspective is anachronistic insofar as it harkens back to the statist informational philosophy that had its heyday in the first three decades after Independence. However, what *KBC* does is to turn "statist information" into entertainment following a precedent set up by the quiz movement earlier on. Quizzing itself needs to be located in the more general move toward entertainment that began in the 1980s with the commercializing of Indian television. What quizzing does is to acknowledge the necessity of statist information and then sugarcoat it with the trivial by testing contestants with questions concerning Bollywood, cricket, and other "light" topics. The half-trivial, half-serious composition of quizzing means that the figure of the quiz champion is always one that elicits respect rather than the amused condescension that is earned by trivia champions in the West.[17] In the Indian mind, then, the quiz champion is not far removed from the individual who "tops" the civil service or engineering exams.[18] Clearly, *KBC* capitalizes on both paradigms. It treats information as a valuable commodity and, concomitantly, the possessor of accurate information as a figure to be venerated, and at the same time it treats the process of testing as an entertaining one. It then adds one more layer to this process— that of individuation. In the statist examination, there is no room for individuation; the questions are objective and the one who answers is merely mirroring that objectivity. In this model only those who fail or those who are over-successful (the topper) emerge as individuals.[19] Quizzing is also constructed around this template, so even though the questions may be trivial (who sang a particular song as opposed to what to do in the case of a disaster), the process remains that of an examination, the "real" actor in the scenario being the "right answer." What happens on *KBC* is what happens in/on reality television in general: each contestant is publicized in order to emerge as an "individual." Hence, the intimate video-bios of each participant, the equally intimate conversation that Bachchan initiates with every player, the introduction to visiting family members, the elicitation of emotions that go beyond game logic, and finally the four lifelines that are available to each contestant help to "subjectivize" the answer and push it toward performance. In the episode of *KBC* that aired on October 27, 2014, for example (Season 8), Priti Kumari emerged as a winner with a prize of 2.5 million INR. Although her objective knowledge won her an objective amount of money, the logic of ratings demanded that Bachchan "subjectivize" her, harping at length on the fact that she was a tea-seller's daughter and that she had been the victim of polio.

KBC thus represents utilization of statist information by the entertainment machinery of commercial television. It is an example of what may be termed the "first stage of information" in that it involves the use of an external pool of valuable, objective knowledge for the purposes of commercial broadcasting. Yet as I have argued throughout the book, the needs of the current age are not met by such statist information, which has to be supplemented by other modes of information that are both more informal and less obviously connected with the affairs of the state. It is evident that for the past two decades or so the emergence of digital technologies, processes, and platforms has led to a vast outpouring of informal or non-statist information. This secondary mode of information—circulated primarily through the social media—consists of advertisements from the quotidian: likes, dislikes, sharing, posting, emotions, affects. The new social media are explicitly driven by information—thus Facebook, Twitter, Tumblr, Instagram, Snapchat, WhatsApp, and Kik are at bottom differently inflected applications with the same end goal: dissemination of information about the self and its immediate others.

Given the magnitude and reach of these new information devices, it would seem odd that there would be any need for another platform—especially an old-fashioned medium like television—to serve the same sort of informational purpose. It is my claim that television cannot be analyzed only in terms of itself or even in relation to other televisual forms like cinema. Rather it needs to be seen as both continuous and congruent with the forms and functions of the new media. It is more than a coincidence that the Web was born in 1991 and that *The Real World*, the first reality television show of the modern era, went on air in 1992.[20] Reality television possesses two features that make it both different from social media and therefore of crucial value to an informational economy. First, reality television is part of the public sphere in the literal sense that it is consumed and shared by a large mass of viewers. This throwback feature is a strength; reality television is not dependent on stochastic phenomena like "going viral" in order to be widely viewed. By contrast Facebook and Twitter only guarantee that friends or followers will be the audience for a particular message. Second, and more crucially, reality shows offer a kind of space—a relational space—that is unique in its ability to give information of a kind of home that most of new media do not. Information on its own is not a negligible entity, but when a dataset is placed against another dataset, it engenders a deeper perception of what is at stake in the constitution of the world that we inhabit.[21] Reality television is thus a sort of "relational database," not in a formal but in an ontological sense, by means of which information about one person co-exists and interfaces with information about others. To that extent, the game space of reality television is an informational society whose "citizens" are the datasets that accompany each contestant of every show.

Before I flesh out this set of claims, it would be helpful to look at the logical structure of the prototypical reality show that allows it to function in such a manner. At its most basic level any reality show consists of a few simple rules and operations that are implemented in a particular setting (faraway island, isolated house) in order to produce a series of outputs that constitutes the show's substance. In terms of its narrative structure reality television does not—unlike venerable cultural forms like the novel or popular cinema—have any protagonists; rather it is peopled by a set of antagonists. Insofar as the object of the show is to induce individuals into constant competition with each other, its basic logic is to generate meaningful difference between them over the course of its duration. Contestants in a reality show do not know each other; they form temporary connections over the course of the episodes that disappear as the show progresses through rounds in order to determine a winner. This is in marked contrast to the way standard literary texts—whether in novels, movies, or dramatic television—function. In these cases characters contend with each other, fight, fall in love, or break up. In all cases the "ending" in these traditional forms of storytelling draws all the protagonists onto a relational map. The typical plots of the Bollywood movie or the television serial illustrate this truth. Reality television operates by means of a totally different logic. The main purpose of every reality show is to distinguish and isolate each contestant from the other. This is achieved partly by the genre's format: contestants meet as strangers, are pitted against one another through a variety of devices, and are progressively eliminated with every round of play. As I argued earlier in this chapter, reality television functions as a *difference engine* that processes the ephemera of games and contests in order to produce the individual as both separated and sovereign. Though this is not the place to elaborate at any length on this topic, I would like to suggest that the mode of subjectivity that reality television produces is a perfect template of the neoliberal subject. Neoliberalism postulates precisely the sort of hyper-individualism for which reality television offers a blueprint.

Information plays a crucial role in the production of difference. That is, difference—between individuals—is established not merely by the formal rules of the reality format but also by the steady advertisement and compilation of data concerning every single contestant in every show. The accrual of information makes each contestant more distinct and distinguishable from others. There are three layers of information: first is purely visual information about the contestant's sex, age, and ethnicity. This is not trivial given that all reality shows, as I discuss below, use these sociological categories to generate game dynamics. Second is a layer of personal background information: place of origin, occupation, hobbies, family, and unique experiences. Finally, a third layer of information is added by the mechanics of the reality show: self-disclosures, confessionals, politicking, outbursts, and tantrums. Each of these layers of information defines the contestant and helps to situate him or her in a grid of differences.

In what follows I analyze another hit reality show – *Indian Idol* – to demonstrate how the information coded into a reality show can function as a tool to generate audience involvement and participation. *Indian Idol*, a show based on the original British show *Pop Idol* (also the model for the more famous *American Idol*), first aired in 2004 and has had six success-ful seasons, the last one being in 2012. *Idol* was not the first reality show based on musical talent competition. It was preceded by *Sa Re Ga Ma*, and while it is on hiatus its place is being filled by new entries like *The Voice India* (Bhushan, 2015). The show employs the standard *Idol* format used all over the globe. An initial pool of candidates is chosen from thousands (approximately 3,000 to 5,000) who show up at different "city auditions" held in various parts of the country. The selected group (about 100 to 160 nationally out of a total of 50,000 or more who audition) is invited for a "second audition" held in Mumbai. This audition narrows the pool down even further and approximately 30 contestants are selected for the next "rounds" on the show—Theatre, Piano, and finally the Gala Round. The "final ten" competing on the Gala Round are then narrowed down to the "final three" who compete for the big prize on the Grand Finale. Enlisting contestants from all over the country, the list of winners reflects the show's national scope: Abhijit Sawan (Maharashtra), Sandeep Acharya (Rajasthan), Prashant Tamang (West Bengal), Sourabhee Debbarma (Tripura), Agartall, Sreeramachandra Mynampati (Andhra Pradesh), and Vipul Mehta (Punjab). The judges have included prominent names from the Bollywood music scene: Anu Malik, Sonu Nigam, Farah Khan, Javed Akhtar, Alisha Chinai, Kailash Kher, Salim Merchant, and Sunidhi Chauhan as well as the legend-ary Asha Bhosle.

Though the show is based on musical performance, it is my suggestion that it also functions as an informational hub that introduces viewers to the mosaic of cultures, customs, and conventions that make up the "nation." This is true in general of a range of reality-based shows. Thus, as Sujata Moorti (2004) has shown, game shows on Tamil television serve to foreground an intriguing mix of vernacular nationalism and cosmopolitan sensibility. By allowing for extra-textual forces to operate inside the text—in this case, real people who vote for contestants not only determine who wins and who loses but also, more importantly, the real issues that frame the contestants—*Idol* allows for the broadcast of far more than the rendition of hit songs. The third season of *Indian Idol* (2007) was a perfect illustration of the manner in which such forces get mobilized as a category of difference within the frame of reality programming.[22] As noted earlier, song contests shows are very popular with Indian audiences. While it is true that almost all contestants on *Idol*-type shows gain massive exposure, the fanfare that surrounded *Idol 3* was of a different magnitude. When Prashant Tamang, an Indian citizen of

Nepalese origin, made it to the finals, the entire diasporic community in his hometown of Darjeeling celebrated the rise of this "ethnic hero":

> The hills of Darjeeling are burning again. But this time with mobile phones and landlines instead of guns and kukris. And all because of one boy, Prashant Tamang, a resident of Darjeeling and the finalist on the third *Indian Idol* contest on Sony Entertainment Television. Prashant seems to have succeeded where the politicians have failed— and that is to successfully unite the Nepalis, not only in Darjeeling but across the country. Just recently, a ban on liquor was enforced in Darjeeling to curb trouble during voting. Talk about star power!
>
> (rediff.com, 2007)

And when Tamang was selected as the winner of *Idol 3*, the impact went beyond the local and the cultural:

> Nepal and the Nepali-speaking diaspora worldwide erupted in joy after their newest icon, Indian policeman Prashant Tamang, vanquished his closest competitor Amit Paul to lift the third *Indian Idol* title in Sony Television channel's hugely popular reality show.
>
> (IPS Community, 2007)

It was inevitable that an event of such large scope would at some point be inserted into the realm of political discord:

> Several people were injured after fans of newly-crowned Indian Idol Prashant Tamang clashed with locals in India's eastern state of West Bengal on Friday, media reports said. An estimated 2,000 ethnic Nepalese were marching to the district administration office in the Siliguri town to protest a radio jockey's comment against Tamang, a Nepalese-born star of the TV show that is India's version of *American Idol*.
>
> (rediff.com, 2007)

Fortunately, the story has a happy ending: the ethnic furor subsided without causing too much violence, while Tamang himself was able to obtain extended leave from his job as a policeman and embark on a multi-city tour to the United States!

Indian Idol 3 exemplifies how global formats function as conduits for the politics of difference. What the show enabled in this instance was the expression of local pride and regional identity; more significantly, it brought to public notice the complicated and fraught politics that characterizes India's northeastern provinces. Prashant Tamang's victory was celebrated so fervently in Darjeeling because he was local and because he was Gurkha. For many years now the Gurkhas—Nepalese immigrants living in India— have been agitating for a separate homeland, and Tamang's victory in *Idol* quickly turned into a symbol for this cause. Coincidentally, his fellow finalist Amit Paul hailed from Meghalaya, another of the country's "troubled" spots. It is perhaps fitting that both finalists represented a "tribal" population that has traditionally been described as simple, happy, and *musical*. The reaction to *Idol 3* went beyond this benign stereotyping: Tamang and Paul, it was alleged, became finalists only because the minority communities they came from were better able to mobilize phone voters. We can begin to see how global formats acquire relevance and ratings by incorporating ethnic differences into game logic. While the contestant-to-contestant relation in any reality program is formally antagonistic—there exists an imperative to vanquish one's opponent—a show acquires far more significance when that contradiction gets imbued with a set of social and historical parameters. In the case of *Idol 3* the empty antagonism between crooners gets filled with the specific history of ethnic conflict in modern India and thus creates a countrywide controversy. Thus, by disseminating data about specific regions of the country, *Idol* contributes to an informational account of the nation. Thus it is information, more and more of it, which comes to be seen as the glue that holds the fabled "diversity" of India into a composite whole.

I conclude my discussion of the informational basis of reality television by analyzing *Bigg Boss*, the Indian version of *Big Brother*, a hugely popular format that originated in the Netherlands and has since been implemented in over 50 countries. The show follows the standard *Big Brother* format: a number of contestants (known as "housemates") live in a custom-built house and are isolated from the rest of the world. The activities of the house are controlled by a mysterious person known as "Bigg Boss," a person who issues voice commands to contestants but remains unseen. Each week, housemates nominate two of their peers for eviction; housemates who receive the most nominations face a public vote and one of that nominated group is then "evicted" from the house. In the final week, with three housemates remaining, only the public votes for the contestant they want to win. *Bigg Boss* debuted in 2006 and has been running for eight seasons with a ninth season scheduled for late 2015. Aired on the Colors channel and hosted by a succession of Bollywood celebrities including Sanjay Dutt, Amitabh Bachchan, and most recently Salman Khan, the show has had strong ratings for most of its run.[23] More importantly, it has played a big part in creating the reality television wave that has come to dominate Indian broadcasting in the past decade. Like *Idol*, *Bigg Boss* too creates a substantial amount of "fanfare." It has its official website and Facebook and Twitter pages, as well as a game-app for Android (Googleplay, 2015). The show gets constant coverage from the national press; thus the Mumbai-based daily dna tells readers "Bigg Boss News—Check out the latest News on Bigg Boss. Get breaking news updates on Bigg Boss published at Daily News & Analysis" (dna, 2015).

My analysis of *Crorepati* argued that it is informational in the sense that it, quite literally, cashes in on what I termed "statist information." *Idol* is an example of reality television's use of information to generate difference and identity. *Bigg Boss*, I want to argue, provides us with an informational matrix within which we can plot variations in global media culture, while at the same time generating a stream of data concerning modes of individuality and subjectivity in the current era. Let me first expand on the claim that *Bigg Boss* "informs" us about the cultural processes that accompany globalization.[24] To understand why this is so, we must begin by clarifying the very notion of a format. In one sense, formats are the very shows they inhabit—thus *American Idol*, *Big Brother*, and *Survivor* can all be considered to exemplify a particular type of format. But as Albert Moran (2005) has perceptively pointed out:

> In a real sense, to ask the question "What is a format?" is to ask the wrong kind of question. Such a question implies that a format has some core or essence. As our discussion suggested "format" is a loose term that covers a range of items that may be included in a format licensing agreement. The term has meaning not so much of because of what it is, but because of what it permits or facilitates. The format is a technology of exchange in the television industry that has meaning not because of a principle but because of a function or effect. (2005, 17–18)

In other words, formats are relatively content-free; they are "forms" plus a set of economic parameters that enable them to be easily franchised. This structure can be seen as yet another instance of the devaluation suffered by works of art in a commercial age; I would, however, like to suggest that the format's skeletal constitution comes with considerable advantage. It is precisely because formats have so little "essence" or meaning that they acquire the potential to be the most global of all cultural productions. As an industry professional puts it, "[It] is a recipe which allows television concepts and ideas to travel without being stopped by either geographical or linguistic boundaries. To achieve this, the recipe comes with a whole range of ingredients making it possible for producers throughout the world, to locally produce a television program based on a foreign format, and to present it as a local television show perfectly adapted to their respective countries and cultures" (Moran, 2006, 27).

As we have seen, reality shows consist of a few simple rules and operations that are implemented in a range of settings in order to produce a series of outputs; the format then is a variable that is initially empty and gets a value only when plugged into specific game situations. Thus the *Big Brother* format yields *Big Brother Africa* in one instance and *Bigg Boss* (India) in another. And although reality formats are mainly developed in the West (with some exceptions like *Iron Chef* that was developed in Japan), they are not "western" insofar as their implementation necessarily involves the intervention of local conventions and practices. What you get after you implement a format in a specific country is a compromised product unique to that media environment. Consider the wide range of outcomes in the case of *Big Brother*:

- The first British series of *Big Brother* included contestants stripping off their clothes, and in Holland the contestants were even more uninhibited than in Britain. By contrast, the American *Big Brother* contestants talked a lot about sex and relationships, but remained modestly clothed and no sexual liaisons took place. (Bignell, 2006, 49)
- Instead of presenting a summary of daily events in the house as is done elsewhere, the Brazilian producers of *Big Brother* started to develop a hybrid language that mixed reality television with soap opera, a move that created record-breaking profits for Brazil's largest broadcaster Globo. (Campanella, 2009)
- *Big Brother* Australia performed its "Australian-ness" in a variety of ways. According to the network executive in charge of the show the house that was used for the show was very different from those in overseas versions because "we wanted this to be a real Aussie house; that means relaxed lifestyle, sunshine, backyard pool, backyard BBQ, a real Aussie *Big Brother*." Again, there was a far greater emphasis on fitness and outdoor activities in the Australian version.
- Finally, unlike the American *Big Brother*, contestants remained indifferent to the outcome of challenges. Whereas in many countries challenges have played an important role in generating some of the emotional drama and conflict, in Australia "it's a cultural thing... They don't seem to give a bugger whether they win or lose." (Roscoe, 2004, 312–13)
- The original Dutch version had situated participants in a "wealthy" house and sent losers to a stable as the "poor house." This was not considered funny but rather as offensive in the Argentine context given the country's dismal economic condition at the turn of the millennium. Moreover, local producers frowned upon the use of house that featured a swimming pool, gourmet kitchen etc. on the grounds that it was typical of wealthy rather than average people. (Waisbord, 2009, 67)
- *Al –Ra'is*, the Arabic version of *Big Brother*, was shut down after a week following a huge controversy that was started by an on-screen kiss. For Islamists, the show (which interestingly only featured women who were divorced) violated Muslim values by putting unmarried men and women in a confined physical space. Another Endemol format *Star Academy* was described as "Satan Academy" and had a *fatwa* issued against it. (Kraidy, 2009, 33)

Even a cursory look at *Bigg Boss* would yield a number of ways in which it is hybridized or glocalized:

- The introduction of Bollywood figures as hosts and guests. Thus *Bigg Boss 3* was hosted by the superstar Amitabh Bachchan and *Bigg Boss*

4 by Salman Khan. *Bigg Boss 4* also featured a long list of Bollywood notables—Ajay Devgan, Kareena Kapoor, Farah Khan, Rani Mukherjee, Katrina Kaif, Vidya Balan, Dharmendra, and Bobby Deol—who appeared on the show to promote their current work. This "invasion" reflects a peculiar Indian tendency whereby every form of media and entertainment is inflected by Bollywood's influence.

- India's obsession with its political Other is reflected in the inclusion of *two* Pakistani artists—the actress Veena Malik and the crossdressing performer Ali Saleem—in the cast of fourteen.
- While some of the tasks assigned to the inmates are culturally unspecific—thus one episode involved wrestling matches between male inmates while females functioned as cheerleaders—some others are quite unmistakably Indian in form and content. Relevant examples from *Bigg Boss 4* are *Shakti De Bhakti De Mukti De* (Week Two: contestants wear a white gown and chant to a particular tune); *Gaon Gaon Shahar Shahar* (Week Seven: some inmates have to live like villagers while others live like city folk); *Jee Lay Jee Jaan Se* (Week Thirteen: Each housemate is given a specific song every day and each has to dance to it).
- As mentioned before, in keeping with India's newfound celebrity culture, all the contestants are well-known media figures. Thus Season 4 of *Bigg Boss* featured Abbas Kazmi, a famous criminal lawyer, Seema Parihar, a former woman bandit, Dalip Singh Rana, a professional wrestler, and the model Sara Khan. This is in contrast with, say, the American version where housemates are unknown and presented as "average" people.

Bigg Boss provides us with an informative picture of how reality television works with global formats in order to produce glocal versions that resonate with local cultures. We can think of reality shows like *Bigg Boss* as a large database that illuminates the macro process of globalization. But I want to very briefly point to another informational level at which reality television functions. Shows like *Big Boss* generate a stream of micro-data concerning personhood and everyday life: modes of displaying emotions and affects like anger, love, jealousy, frustration, and the like; the art of building alliances, the equally useful art of betrayal, the art of working in a team, and that of going solo; and finally the skills of becoming a part of celebrity culture. In other words, the "real reality" to be found on reality television is the stream of emotions, affects, calculations, and strategies that every contestant must generate in pursuit of the winner's purse.

Reality television can thus be thought of as an informational device that transmits data concerning two variables that impinge continuously on the state of the nation: the globe and the individual subject. In the age of globalization the nation is more susceptible than ever to the slightest perturbations in the world system; at the same time, neoliberal governmental logic implies that the shape of subjectivity is of paramount importance in determining the contours of the social. As a small experiment in globalization, reality formats allow the nation to be interactively informed about its outside; as an affective laboratory it relays news of subjective interiority to the national sphere that must increasingly accommodate the minutest of individual variation. Reality television therefore pushes the realm of popular culture from entertainment to a new kind of reportage whose dispatches feed the very substance of the info-nation.

Notes

1. Jamal manages to connect the questions put to him with incidents in his life and thus succeeds in deducing the right answer.
2. There are many excellent accounts that analyze this transformation. See particularly Gupta (1998), Kumar (2006), Mehta (2008), and Thussu (2008). I am indebted to these and other authors in my reconstruction of this standard historiographical approach.
3. Television broadcasting in India began in September 1959 with short half-hour programming consisting of educational material. The broadcasting was done under the auspices of All India Radio. Doordarshan—a separate entity that would be responsible for television broadcasting—came into existence in 1976.
4. *Hum Log* was sponsored by Maggi Noodles who paid for the telecast and production costs for the show and received about five minutes of commercial time in exchange (Kohli-Khandekar, 2010, 67).
5. For a masterful analysis of the political implications of epic television, see Rajagopal (2001).
6. See Shannon and Weaver (1971).
7. Mumbai would get its first station in 1972, Chennai and Kolkata in 1975.
8. These factors overlap with the threefold approach that Mehta himself proposes: the creation of a national network, commercialization, and a focus on entertainment and economic reforms that made TV sets cheaper (2008).
9. The delay in the introduction of color television is especially telling given that the first color movie, *Kisan Kanya*, was released as early as 1937. However, color would become the default mode of filmmaking only after the releases of classics like *Mother India* (1957) and *Mughal-e-Azam* (1961).
10. As a response to these developments, Doordarshan launched DD-3, an all-news channel in 2003 but by then the momentum for news broadcasting had shifted decisively to the private sector.
11. For comprehensive accounts of this process, see McChesney (2014), Mosco (2005), and Schiller (2000).
12. For an impressive extension of this kind of analysis using Deleuze's notion of a control society, see Bratich (2007).
13. I need to stress that such an analysis is not necessarily at odds with the more economic ones discussed earlier. For one, neoliberal governmentality is clearly a function of this particular moment in the history of capitalism. If capital "decides" to abandon the public sphere and manifest itself entirely through privatized micro-enterprises, then there needs to be a corresponding shift in the modality of governmentality in order for such a turn to be sustainable. The unit of governmentality changes from "population" to "self." In such a scenario, works of art (fictional or non-fictional) need to perform their political functions

not by depictions of collectivities and identities but by burrowing into the vicissitudes of self. And reality television is the perfect vehicle for such a microscopic investigation and reconstruction of what neoliberal selfhood means.

14. For a comprehensive analysis of how neoliberalism structures the form and content of global cinema, see Kapur and Wagner (2013).
15. Contestants who don't know the answer to a particular question can turn to one of several "Lifelines" call a friend, ask a trio of experts (*triguni*) for advice, poll the audience, or do a "double dip" that is, take two guesses at the same question.
16. Members of the Indian civil service were often alluded to as the "heaven born service" because of the power and prestige they enjoyed.
17. For example, in the United States the winners of the popular *Jeopardy!* quiz show are rarely given any respect.
18. The JEE (Joint Entrance Examinations) that chooses candidates for the prestigious IIT and other engineering and technical institutes is as revered as the ones administered by the UPSC.
19. Thus, in the examination for the Mathematical Tripos administered by Cambridge University, students awarded a booby prize known as the "wooden spoon" to the individual who finished last. On the other hand, the student with the highest marks (grades) earned the title of Senior Wrangler (University of Cambridge, 2015).
20. On August 6, 1991, Tim Berners-Lee posted a short summary of the World Wide Web project on the alt.hypertext newsgroup, marking the debut of the Web as a publicly available service on the Internet.
21. It is useful to know that Holland—the birthplace of many reality formats—has a per capita GDP of $40,000, but a lot more illuminating to realize that the comparable figure for Indonesia—a former Dutch colony—is $18,000 (trading economics, 2015).
22. My analysis of *Idol* is drawn from an earlier work that discussed the show in greater detail. See Sen (2012).
23. The show had its highest ratings during Seasons 4–6. Its most recent season has been a disappointment, causing commentators to observe that it has run out of ideas (Abraham, 2014).
24. In what follows I develop my arguments from an earlier piece on the topic. See Sen (2014).

References

Abraham, Letty. 2014. "Bigg Boss 8" Does Not Live Up to the Mark. *Dna* October 13, 2014. Retrieved June 29, 2015, from http://www.dnaindia.com/entertainment/report-trp-report-bigg-boss-8-does-not-live-up-to-the-mark-2025485.

Andrejevic, Mark. 2002. The kinder, gentler gaze of Big Brother. *New Media & Society*, 4(2), 251–270.

Balaji, G. Nalini. 2013. When Curiosity Pays. *The Hindu*, March 10, 2013. Retrieved June 28, 2015, from http://www.thehindu.com/thehindu/mp/2003/03/10/stories/2003031001440100.htm.

Bearak, Max. 2014. The New Bazaar: In India, Online Stores Catch on with Buyers. *New York Times*, July 29, 2014. Retrieved September 9, 2014, from http://dealbook.nytimes.com/2014/07/29/the-new-bazaar-online-shopping-catches-on-in-india-with-buyers-and-global-investors/.

Bhushan, Nyay. 2015. "The Voice" Gets Indian Version. Billboard.com. Retrieved June 29, 2015, from http://www.billboard.com/articles/columns/reality-check/6553527/the-voice-gets-indian-version.

Bignell, Jonathan. 2006. *Big Brother: Reality TV in the Twenty-first Century*. London: Palgrave Macmillan.

Business & Economy. 2015. The Famine That India Did Not Waste! Retrieved June 24, 2015, from http://www.businessandeconomy.org/30092012/storyd.asp?sid=7042&pageno=1.

Campanella, Bruno. 2009. *Big Brother* in Brazil. *Global Media and Communication*, 5(1), 137–40.

Chakraborty, Swarup. 2010. Reality Shows Get More Eyeballs Than Money. *Business Standard*, June 2, 2010. Retrieved June 25, 2015, from http://www.business-standard.com/article/beyond-business/reality-shows-get-more-eyeballs-than-money-110060200010_1.htmlp.

Contractor, Noshir S., Arvind Singhal, and Everett Rogers. 1988. Metatheoretical Perspectives on Satellite Television and Development in India. *Journal of Broadcasting & Electronic Media*, 32(2), 129–48.

CRisiL Research. 2014. E-tail Eats into Retail. Retrieved June 26, 2015, from http://www.crisil.com/pdf/research/CRISIL-Research-Article-Online-Retail-Feb14.pdf.

dna (2015). Bigg Boss 8. Retrieved October 13, 2015, from http://www.dnaindia.com/topic/bigg-boss-8.

Ghose, Bhaskar. 2005. *Doordarshan Days*. Penguin: New Delhi.

Googleplay. 2015. Retrieved October 13, 2015, from https://play.google.com/store/search?q=bigg%20boss&c=apps&hl=en.

Gupta, Nilanjana. 1998. *Switching Channels: Ideologies of Television in India*. New Delhi: Oxford University Press.

Harvey, Brian, Henrik H. F. Smid, and Theo Pirard. 2010. "India: The Vision of Vikram Sarabhai." In Harvey et al. (Eds.), *Emerging Space Powers: The New Space Programs of Asia, the Middle-East, and South America* (pp. 141–72). London: Praxis.

Indiantelevision.com. 2015. TV Industry to Touch Rs. 97 Billion in 2019: Ficci-KMGP Report. Retrieved June 24, 2015, from http://www.indiantelevision.com/specials/event-coverage/ficci-frames/tv-industry-to-touch-rs-975-billion-in-2019-ficci-kpmg-report-150325.

IPS Community. 2007. Darjeeling Boy in *Indian Idol* Becomes New Nepali Icon. June 15, 2007. Retrieved July 23, 2015, from http://www.chautari.wnso.org/forums/index.php?showtopic=10326&page=17.

Jayakumar, Saranaya. 2001. It's a Quizzer's World. *The Hindu*, August 4, 2001. Retrieved October 28, 2013, from http://www.thehindu.com/2001/08/04/stories/1304110j.htm.

Kapur, Jyotsna, and Keith B. Wagner (Eds.). 2013. *Neoliberalism and Global Cinema: Capital, Culture, and Marxist Critique*. Routledge: New York.

Kohli-Khandekar, Vanita. 2010. *Indian Media Business*. New Delhi: Sage.

Kraidy, Marwan M. 2009. Rethinking the Local-Global Nexus Through Multiple Modernities: The Case of Arab Reality Television. In Albert Moran (Ed.), *TV Formats Worldwide: Localizing Global Programs* (pp. 29–38). Chicago: University of Chicago Press.

Kumar, Shanti. 2006. *Gandhi Meets Primetime: Globalization and Nationalism in Indian Television*. Urbana-Champaign: University of Illinois Press.

Mehta, Nalin. 2008. *India on Television: How Satellite News Channels Have Changed the Way We Think and Act*. New Delhi: HarperCollins.

Mehta, Nalin. 2014. When Live News Was Too Dangerous: The Early History of Satellite TV in India. In Biswarup Sen and Abhijit Roy (Eds.), *Channeling Cultures: Television Studies from India* (pp. 148–76). New Delhi: Oxford University Press.

Mankekar, Purnima. 1999. *Screening Culture, Viewing Politics: An Ethnography of Television, Womanhood and Nation in Postcolonial India*. Durham, NC: Duke University Press.

Mazarella, William. 2012. "Reality Must Improve": The Perversity of Expertise and the Belatedness of Development Television. *Global Media and Communication*, 8(3), 215–41.

McChesney, Robert W. *Digital Disconnect*. 2014. New York: The New Press.

Moorti, Sujata. 2004. Fashioning a Cosmopolitan Tamil Identity: Game Shows, Commodities and Cultural Identity. *Media, Culture & Society*, 26(4), 549–67.

Moran, Albert. 2005. *Copycat TV: Globalisation, Program Formats, and Cultural Identity*. Luton: University of Luton Press.

Moran, Albert. 2006. *Understanding the Global TV Format*. Bristol, UK and Portland, OR: Intellect Books.

Mosco, Vincent. 2005. *The Digital Sublime: Myth, Power and Cyberspace*. Boston: The MIT Press.

Murray, Susan and Laurie Ouellette. Eds. Reality TV: Remaking Television Culture. 2nd Edition. New York: NYU Press.

Ninan, Sevanti. 1995. *Through the Magic Window: Television and Change in India*. New Delhi: Penguin Books.

Ohja, Abhilasha. 2011. Reality shows take centre stage on TV. Retrieved October 13, 2015, from http://www.livemint.com/Consumer/djLGAqnyt1697YihkNUktO/Reality-shows-take-centre-stage-on-TV.html.

Ouellette, Laurie and James Hay. 2008. *Better Living Through Reality TV: Television and Post-Welfare Citizenship*. Hoboken, NJ: Wiley-Blackwell.

Prokerala. 2015. Common Entrance Exams for Bank Jobs. Retrieved June 26, 2015, from http://www.prokerala.com/education/common-entrance-exam-for-bank-jobs.php.

Raghavendra, Nandini, and Amaya Chumbale. 2011. *Kaun Banega Crorepati*: The Secret Behind Making Millions. *Economic Times*, November 19, 2011. Retrieved July 15, 2015, from http://articles.economictimes.indiatimes.com/2011-11-19/news/30419540_1_game-show-kbc-kaun-banega-crorepati.

Rajagopal, Arvind. 2001. *Politics after Television: Religious Nationalism and the Reshaping of the Indian Public*. Cambridge: Cambridge University Press.

Rajagopal, Arvind. 2011. Notes on Postcolonial Visual Culture. *Bioscope*, 2(1), 11–22.

Rao, B. S. S. 1992. *Television for Rural Development*. New Delhi: Concept Publishing.

Rediff.com. 2007. Prashant Tamang, Already an Idol. Retrieved August 28, 2014, from http://specials.rediff.com/movies/2007/sep/20sld1.htm.

Roscoe, Jane. 2004. *BIG BROTHER AUSTRALIA*: Performing the "Real" Twenty-Four-Seven. In Robert C. Allen and Annette Hill (Eds.), *The Television Studies Reader* (pp. 311–21). London and New York: Routledge.

Saxena, Poonam. 2011. Five Crore Question: What Makes KBC Work? *Hindustan Times*, November 19, 2011. Retrieved October 23, 2014, from http://articles.economictimes.indiatimes.com/2011-11-19/news/30419540_1_game-show-kbc-kaun-banega-crorepati.

Sen, Biswarup. 2012. *Idol* Worship: Ethnicity and Difference in Global Television. In Tasha Oren and Sharon Shahaf (Eds.), *Global Formats: Understanding Television Across Borders* (pp. 203–22). New York: Routledge.

Sen, Biswarup. 2014. *Big Brother, Bigg Boss*: Reality Television as Global Form. In Biswarup Sen and Abhijit Roy (Eds.), *Channeling Cultures: Television Studies from India* (pp.152–187). New Delhi: Oxford University Press.

Sen Biswarup and Roy Abhijit. 2014. Eds. *Channeling Cultures: Television Studies from India*. New Delhi: Oxford University Press.

Shannon, Claude, and Warren Weaver. 1971. *The Mathematical Theory of Communication*. Urbana: The University of Illinois Press.

Schiller, Dan. 2000. *Digital Capitalism: Networking the Global Market System*. Boston: The MIT Press.

Thussu, Daya K. 2008. *News as Entertainment: The Rise of Global Infotainment*. London: Sage.

Thussu, Daya K. 2014. Television News and an Indian Infotainment Sphere. In Biswarup Sen and Abhijit Roy (Eds.), *Channeling Cultures: Television Studies from India* (pp. 129–47). New Delhi: Oxford University Press.

Timmons, Heather. 2011. In India, Reality TV Catches On, With Some Qualms. Retrieved October 13, 2015, from http://www.nytimes.com/2011/01/10/business/media/10reality.html?_r=0.

Trading economics. 2015. Retrieved June 28, 2015, from http://www.tradingeconomics.com/indonesia/gdp-per-capita-ppp.

University of Cambridge. 2015. The History of Mathematics in Cambridge. Retrieved June 28, 201, from http://www.maths.cam.ac.uk/about/history/.

Waisbord, Silvio, and Sonai Jaslin. 2009. Imagining the National: Television Gatekeepers and the Adaptation of Global Franchises in Argentina. In Albert Moran (Ed.), *TV Formats Worldwide: Localizing Global Programs* (pp. 57–74). Bristol, UK and Chicago, IL: Intellect.

Conclusion

The processes of informatization that this book describes continue to be in play in India at the present time. In the realm of science and technology, the state's commitment to planned scientific enterprise that, I argued, resulted in the computer revolution was strikingly showcased by the success of the Mangalayan mission to Mars. This launch gathered a lot of international coverage because it was the least expensive space probe into that planet. As India's prime minister boasted, India spent less to reach Mars than Hollywood producers spent on the movie *Gravity* (Choudhury and Sugden, 2014). This "cheap" launch recapitulated the Indian software industry's earlier success in providing services at prices that other competitors could not match. In other words, India's skilled workforce and cheap labor costs will continue to provide the country with a comparative advantage in the globalized informational economy.

In politics, the elections of 2014 were characterized by the extensive use of social media—and even digitally constructed holograms—by Narendra Modi, the winning candidate. Moreover, many of his party's platforms echoed the issues and policies first articulated by the info-activists that I have discussed in this book. Since coming to power, the BJP government has pursued informational issues with almost missionary zeal. I have already mentioned the Digital India initiative and the grand plan to build a hundred smart cities. The government's keen interest in building the informational society is personified by its prime minister. Alarmed at the abysmally slow speeds of Internet connectivity in India—the country is currently ranked 115th in the world with an average speed of only 2 Mbps, the lowest in the entire Asia-Pacific region—Modi has personally intervened in order to start the building of a national fiber optic network that will redress this embarrassing problem (tech2, 2015). In other words, at the time of writing, the Indian state continues to be intensely involved in planning and constructing the info-nation.

The informational economy in India has also been growing at a fairly rapid pace. Compared to countries like the United States and China, the industry is still in its infancy, but it has been growing steadily in the last few years with revenues having risen from $3.8 billion in 2009 to $12.6 billion in 2013. Although online travel dominates the e-retail industry, online markets in areas such as electronics, clothing, books, and home products have shown sharp growth, increasing their market share from 10% to 18% over the course of four years (Assocham India, 2015). The spectacular rise of online retailers like Flipkart, Snapdeal, and MyGrahak is testament to the growing importance of e-commerce in the Indian marketplace. While these retailers mostly target India's new urban consumer class, the information economy is also making inroads into rural areas. For example, the start-up Inthree (and its sister company Boonbox) is targeting customers in rural Tamil Nadu, Karnataka, and Andhra Pradesh selling such items as solar lamps and water purifiers as well as more traditional household products (Vardhan, 2015). Even though there are many obstacles that could impede its growth—India's per capita income is only $1,500 compared to $6,800 for China—the prospects for e-commerce are rosy given that the number of Internet users is steadily increasing and that two-thirds of the country's population is under 35 (Nayyar, 2015). Thus the commercial infrastructure of the nation is being digitally redesigned in order to bring it in congruence with emerging trends in the global marketplace.

The Indian populace at large, or at least a substantial fraction of it, is also immersed in the emergent informational milieu. According to the latest State of the Internet report presented by the noted cyber guru Mary Meeker, India adds the highest number of new cyber users annually (63 million in 2014), is the second largest market for Facebook and LinkedIn, and is highly mobile in the sense that 65% of the country's Internet traffic is through the medium of cell phones (Amberber, 2015). The mobile market too is extremely vibrant. There are currently almost 900 million mobile subscribers and the average mobile device is only 10 months old (Soni, 2015). While mobile users typically employ their devices to access globally popular social sites like WhatsApp Messenger and Facebook, they also use cell phones for a variety of unique purposes: as copiers and scanners, as radios, to listen to audio versions of videos, and even as flashlights (Banerjee, 2014). In short, with nearly 250 million Internet users, 106 million active social media users, and 92 million active mobile social media users, the Indian population is increasingly an informational public. Thus the state, the polity, the economy, and the public in contemporary India contribute in equal share to the forming of the info-nation.

This book has been concerned with outlining the processes—both material and ideational—that have contributed to the project of building an info-nation. However, a responsible overview of the info-nation must place these discussions against the sobering backdrop of contemporary reality in India. If we consider digital access alone, the big data tells a story of a very sharp and substantial digital divide: as of mid-2014, Internet penetration was only 19%, social media penetration only 8%, and broadband Internet access penetration only 4.8% (Srivastava, 2014). Given that 70% of the population is still rural, the task of wiring and connecting the entire nation is a formidable one. Some of the most obvious obstacles toward realizing this goal are poor infrastructure, low literacy, diversity of languages, and general economic backwardness (Paloti and Naikal, 2004).

The contrast between the actual state of the nation and the projected info-nation is succinctly captured by the popular binary that pits India against Bharat. "India" in this formulation belongs to the urban middle classes that sustain the country's current consumer boom and are deeply plugged into the informational universe that has flourished in the wake of this age of the market. "Bharat," on the other hand, signifies a very different space. According to the World Bank, 23.6% of India's population live below the poverty line, defined as an income of $1.25 a day (World Bank, 2015a). Figures for child nutrition are even more shocking. Another World Bank study found that rates of malnutrition among India's children are almost five times more than in China and twice those in Sub-Saharan Africa. Nearly half of all India's children—approximately 60 million—are underweight, about 45% are stunted (too short for their age), 20% are wasted (too thin for their height, indicating acute malnutrition), 75% are anemic, and 57% are vitamin A deficient (World Bank, 2015b). And according to the 2010 census, half of Indian households don't own a toilet; almost paradoxically more people own mobile phones than have access to a toilet (BBC News, 2012).

The inchoate info-nation, then, stares into an abyss that is right beside it. It would be tempting to speak of this abyss as an informational black hole that exists in the shape of a vast inertial mass. In such a topology the info-nation is but a sliver that may be "shining" but whose import is of very slight consequence, but information—as content, as technology, and as practice—may yet create openings and enable maneuvers within the darkest and densest of spaces. As Ravi Sunderam's exciting study of "pirate modernity" in Delhi demonstrates, poorer urban populations occupying non-legal spheres are capable of creating their own networks and circuits of commodity exchange to create a parallel informational order that cannot be folded into dominant practice (2011). Only when the generative power of information releases the thwarted energies of the social whole can the info-nation truly come into its own.

References

Amberber, Emmanuel. 2015. India, Not China, Adding Most Internet Users: Highlights of Mary Meeker's State of Internet Report. *Your Story*, May 28, 2015. Retrieved July 23, 2015, from http://yourstory.com/2015/05/state-of-internet-2015-report-mary-meeker/.

Assocham India. 2015. Evolution of E-Commerce in India: Creating the Bricks behind the Clicks. Retrieved July 22, 2015, from http://www.pwc.in/assets/pdfs/publications/2014/evolution-of-e-commerce-in-india.pdf.

Banerjee, Tushar. 2014. Five Unusual Ways in Which Indians Use Mobile Phones. *BBC News*. February 12, 2014. Retrieved July 23, 2015, from http://www.bbc.com/news/world-asia-india-26028381.

BBC News. 2012. India Census: Half of Homes Have Phones but No Toilets. March 14, 2012. Retrieved July 23, 2025, from http://www.bbc.com/news/world-asia-india-17362837.

Choudhury, Santanu, and Joanna Sugden. 2014. How India Mounted the World's Cheapest Mission to Mars. *Wall Street Journal India*, September 23, 2014. Retrieved July 22, 2015, from http://blogs.wsj.com/indiarealtime/2014/09/23/how-india-mounted-the-worlds-cheapest-mission-to-mars/.

Nayyar, Dhiraj. 2015. Beware India's E-Commerce Bubble. *BloombergView*, May 7, 2015. Retrieved July 23, 2015, from http://www.bloombergview.com/articles/2015-05-08/india-s-e-commerce-boom-may-turn-to-bust.

Paloti, Ramesh, and Appasaheb Naikal. 2004. Bridging Digital Divide in India: An Emphasis on Rural Libraries. IASLIC National Seminar. Retrieved July 23, 2015, from https://www.academia.edu/3308322/Bridging_Digital_Divide_in_India_an_Emphasis_on_Rural_Libraries.

Soni, Alok. 2015. "Average Device in India is Only 10 Months Old!" What Does the Data of 8M Mobile App Users in India Indicate. *Your Story*, July 22, 2015. Retrieved July 23, 2015, from http://yourstory.com/2015/07/mobile-app-india-2015/.

Srivastava, Bhavya. 2014. Mobile and Internet in India 2014: 349 Million Unique Mobile Phone Users, 70% Traffic From Mobile [INFOGRAPHIC]. *Dazeinfo*, July 11, 2014. Retrieved July 23, 2015, from http://dazeinfo.com/2014/07/11/mobile-internet-india-2014-349-million-unique-mobile-phone-users-70-traffic-mobile-india-shining-infographic/.

Sunderam, Ravi. 2011. *Pirate Modernity: Delhi's Media Urbanism*. New York and Oxford: Routledge.

tech2. 2015. PM Modi Wants to Know the Reason behind Slow Internet Speed in India. February 3, 2015. Retrieved July 22, 2015, from http://tech.firstpost.com/news-analysis/pm-modi-wants-to-know-the-reason-behind-slow-internet-speed-in-india-252828.html.

Vardhan, Jai. 2015. This Startup Is Bringing E-Commerce to Rural India. *Your Story*, July 23, 2015. Retrieved July 22,2 015, from http://yourstory.com/2015/07/inthree-boonbox/.

World Bank. 2015a. Poverty and Equity. Retrieved July 23, 2015, from http://povertydata.worldbank.org/poverty/country/IND.

World Bank. 2015b. Helping India Combat Persistently High Rates of Malnutrition. Retrieved July 23, 2015, from http://www.worldbank.org/en/news/feature/2013/05/13/helping-india-combat-persistently-high-rates-of-malnutrition.

Index